First Presbyterian Church

Rev. Don Meekhof
Associate Pastor of Care and Healing
(509) 747-1058 - office
448-5144 - home
(509) 747-1171 (fax)

318 South Cedar Street ▪ Spokane, Washington ▪ 99204

By the same author:

A FORETASTE OF HEAVEN (Autobiography)
   (I FOUND THE KEY TO THE HEART OF GOD — American edition)
BEHOLD HIS LOVE
COUNTDOWN TO WORLD DISASTER — HOPE AND
   PROTECTION FOR THE FUTURE
FATHER OF COMFORT (Daily Readings)
IF I ONLY LOVE JESUS
IN OUR MIDST — JESUS LOVES AND SUFFERS TODAY
MIRROR OF CONSCIENCE
MY ALL FOR HIM
POLLUTION — BUT THERE IS AN ANSWER
   (A MATTER OF LIFE AND DEATH — American edition)
PRAYING OUR WAY THROUGH LIFE
REALITIES — THE MIRACLES OF GOD EXPERIENCED TODAY
REPENTANCE — THE JOY-FILLED LIFE
RULED BY THE SPIRIT
THE BLESSINGS OF ILLNESS
THE EVE OF PERSECUTION
THOSE WHO LOVE HIM
YOU WILL NEVER BE THE SAME

British publishers
Marshall, Morgan & Scott, Ltd.
London, Great Britain

American publishers
Bethany Fellowship, Inc.
Minneapolis, Minnesota, USA
and
Zondervan Publishing House
Grand Rapids, Michigan, USA

THE HOLY LAND TODAY

M. BASILEA SCHLINK

1975
EVANGELICAL SISTERHOOD OF MARY
DARMSTADT-EBERSTADT, WEST GERMANY

THE HOLY LAND TODAY revised edition
© Evangelical Sisterhood of Mary, 1975
ISBN 3 87209 610 9

Original Title:
HEILIGES LAND – HEUTE,
STÄTTEN DES LEBENS UND LEIDENS JESU
First German Edition 1962
First English Edition 1963/64
Revised English Edition 1975
Third English Edition 1982

Printed in West Germany

TABLE OF CONTENTS

INTRODUCTION

In a sense this book is both a guidebook and the account of a pilgrimage, although it does not follow the usual style of either. It is the outcome of a number of visits to the Holy Land, to the places where Jesus lived and suffered. The privilege of such an experience awakened in me the desire to paint for others the picture of Jesus Christ — in His words and actions, in His love and suffering — as it comes to life again today against the historical background of many places mentioned in the Gospels. This is what this book seeks to provide for those who take it as their companion on a journey to the Holy Land. It is also written for those who have no opportunity for such a journey but who are seeking to follow the footsteps of Jesus in spirit. Passages from the Gospels remind us of the Scriptural facts of each site. A word about the spiritual significance of the place seeks to bridge the gap from the past to the present as a challenge for us today. Prayers and hymns, many of them written at these very places, as well as devotional readings, provide various ways of responding to this challenge and draw us into the Gospel events.

The historical and geographical descriptions, compiled with the help of Sisters of Mary who have visited the places, are only meant as a further means to this end. History of art and purely historical aspects have not been considered here, although a brief history of the place is given in each new chapter to inform the reader of the essential facts of the historical development. For this purpose reliable scholarly works have been consulted.* Different points of view have been taken into consideration in regard to the authenticity of particular traditions.

* See bibliography

The descriptions of routes are not very detailed, but are designed to enable pilgrims to find their way about on their own. The visiting hours listed are subject to change and unfortunately there is no uniformity in the spelling of place names. Old Testament sites are only mentioned when they are directly connected with Gospel events at the particular place.

The Sisters of Mary on the Mount of Olives are happy to welcome guests, either alone or in groups, for short visits. (They regret that they cannot provide overnight accommodation.) Please write or telephone in advance.
Evangelical Sisterhood of Mary
P.O. Box 19518, Jerusalem 91194, Tel. 284719

AND THE WORD WAS MADE FLESH,

AND DWELT AMONG US,

AND WE BEHELD HIS GLORY,

THE GLORY AS OF THE

ONLY BEGOTTEN OF THE FATHER,

FULL OF GRACE AND TRUTH.

JOHN 1:14 A V

Holy Land! The Lord Once Lived Here

8. 8. 7. 7. 7.

Holy Land! The Lord once lived here,/
He who reigned above in splendour./ I would greet
each sacred place/Where God's footsteps I can
trace./ Blessèd land! O blessèd land!

Holy Land, your places tell me
How God left His throne of glory,
Brother of us all to be.
Son of man, yet God was He.
Blessèd land! O blessèd land!

Holy Land, here I sing praises,
Honouring Christ at the places
Where He dwelt in mortal frame,
As the Saviour to us came.
Blessèd land! O blessèd land!

Holy Land, with joy I'm singing,
All my worship to Him bringing.
Here He wrought such wondrous deeds,
Healed the blind, supplied all needs.
Blessèd land! O blessèd land!

Holy Land, my voice lamenting
Here proclaims the grievous suff'ring
That my Saviour bore for me,
From sin's pow'r to set me free.
Blessèd land! O blessèd land!

Holy Land, I yearn to love Him
And with sin no more to grieve Him.
For my guilt such pain He bore;
I would thank Him evermore.
Blessèd land! O blessèd land!

Holy Land, that I may walk here!
Step by step my Lord and Saviour
Tells me of His life and way,
Draws me with Him every day.
Blessèd land! O blessèd land!

Holy Land, beside my Saviour
I would stand in grief and sorrow,
Live for Him who for me died,
That He may be glorified
At these sites when He returns.

WHY DO WE VISIT
THE HOLY PLACES?

"Put off your shoes from your feet, for the place on which
you are standing is holy ground." This is the Lord's summons
to us when we have the privilege of visiting the Holy Land.
It was God's summons to Moses when He appeared to him
in His holiness in the burning bush (Exodus 3 : 5); likewise
it was the command of the angel of the Lord to Joshua as
the Israelites were about to enter the Land of Canaan
(Joshua 5 : 15). How much more then do these words, "Put
off your shoes from your feet" apply to us as we visit the
holy places! Here it was not only an angel that appeared,
nor a mere sign through which God revealed Himself. The
almighty God, the second Person of the Holy Trinity, set
foot on this very ground — the Son of God as the Son of
man. Therefore, this land with its sites truly deserves its
name, the Holy Land.

God became flesh. This is what we worship Him for, in
contrast to those who merely consider Jesus to be a prophet
or acknowledge Him as a noble figure, great among His
people. Jesus, though God, became man so completely that
His feet actually trod the earth. Here in the Holy Land He
walked on the same roads as sinful men did. He journeyed
through Galilee, seeking shelter with others in the inns,
drinking from the same wells as other wayfarers. Here in
this land He mingled with the crowd, preached to the people
and healed the sick. He walked along the streets of Jerusalem
carrying His Cross. As the Son of man Jesus knew fear in
Gethsemane, and beholding His city from the slopes of the
Mount of Olives, He wept.

Jesus, who as the Son of God became man and entered
history, born as a member of a particular nation, in a particular country, is acknowledged as Lord only by Christians.
The Incarnation of the Son of God is not a tenet included in
the creed of other religions. Yet at the places where Jesus

lived people from other religions often come and listen to narrations of past events with a reverence that is lacking in us Christians. Is that not unnatural? Our reverence and adoration at the holy places of Jesus should be a testimony to all the world, especially to the non-Christian world, that the Word became flesh, that God did indeed take upon Himself our flesh and blood and become man for the salvation of mankind. Our adoration at the holy places would testify to everyone that Jesus truly became man, that here He lived, suffered, died and rose again, and is thus worthy of all honour, glory and love.

Only if we come to this land and the holy places with such an attitude of profound reverence, shall we have a personal encounter with Jesus here today. How else can we expect a blessing? God only draws close to humble, contrite hearts. There He can make His dwelling as we read in Isaiah 57 : 15. Nowhere is humility so befitting as in this land, for here we are treading where God's feet also trod, where He deigned to walk among sinners upon this earth.

To set foot on the Holy Land where Jesus' feet had trod! To visit the holy places, which heard His powerful words, saw His mighty deeds and miracles, and witnessed His suffering, death and resurrection! Who can comprehend how great a privilege it is to visit these places today? And who would not long to make such a journey? If we wish to learn more about great men, we readily travel to their countries, heeding neither difficulties nor expenses, and study everything there with interest so as to gain a better understanding of them. How much more readily then should we invest time and money and bear all the inconveniences of travelling in order to visit the land of our Lord Jesus where He was born and raised — where He not only ministered, but suffered and died for us!

At every turn we meet traces of Jesus in this land. Everything speaks of Him as nothing in our own land can. Surely no one can claim that he is so close to Jesus in spirit elsewhere that he has no need to visit the land of our Lord Jesus for himself. Who can say that the life and suffering of Jesus and His words are so vivid and comprehensible to him that a visit to the Holy Land would not deepen his understanding? Often we give the Word of God too abstract a meaning. But to seek out the holy places would make the Bible come alive for us. It would help us to draw closer to Jesus in His sufferings and give us deeper insight into His life and ministry. Surely all of us would benefit from a visit to the Holy Land. By following the footsteps of Jesus, we could comprehend in a new and deeper way that which took place for us here.

Whoever loves Jesus and longs to understand Him better in His ministry and suffering will naturally be drawn to this land. He will especially yearn to thank the Lord here that He became man and suffered death for our sakes. He will want to kneel at the place where the Cross was once erected. He yearns to seek out the place where our Lord Jesus offered up prayers and supplications with tears and sweat of blood for our sakes — Gethsemane. Here, probably more than anywhere else, the suffering of our Lord Jesus and His wrestling in prayer will become vivid for us.

He who loves Jesus will also long to stand upon the Mount of Olives where Jesus ascended to heaven. Here he will yearn to worship and rejoice in our Lord, who triumphantly returned home to His Father as Victor and is now seated at the right hand of God. On the Mount of Olives who would not be filled with new expectation of the Lord's return as he recalls the prophecy that when Jesus comes again His feet will stand on the same mount from which He ascended on high (Zechariah 14 : 4)? All the words of Scripture, including those about the end-time events, will come alive for us here.

However, we may sometimes be disappointed by the holy places, especially if it was love that drew us here. We may be sad to find that the sites have been completely built over. Their appearance may not suit our taste or meet our expectations. We may be distressed at the way certain holy places are being administered. And we may question the historical authenticity of some of the sites. Such doubts and disappointments are inevitable, but it is best to face them beforehand so as to approach the holy places in the right attitude.

Many of the places, such as the Sea of Galilee, the Mount of Olives, the Valley of Kidron, the Temple Site and Jacob's Well are easily identified as the ancient Biblical sites. In some of the holy places the historical authenticity is fairly well established, whereas in other places it is less certain. Since excavations on many of the sites have not yet been completed and new finds are constantly to be expected, no absolute assertion can be made. But even if the historical accuracy of a site is not quite certain, the churches built here, for example, give us an opportunity to contemplate a particular Biblical event prayerfully, although it might have actually taken place a few miles away.

And if we are disturbed by the outward appearance of some of the holy places, let us remember that the almighty God did not disdain to become man and to enter our imperfect world. He let Himself be laid in a manger and veiled His holiness. Likewise today Jesus is obscured at the holy places by the "veils" man has laid upon Him. But whoever lovingly seeks Jesus Himself will find Him even under these "veils", which stem from our wretched, sinful human nature.

When we come to the holy places associated with the earthly life of Jesus, who came to us sinners in overwhelming love and mercy, should we not look with eyes of love upon the work of those who sought to preserve these sites for us? Though their ways may seem strange to us, let us remember the great sacrifices they made to guard the sites. Often we do not realize how much we owe to the guardians of the holy places, mostly Franciscans. Through the centuries they have even risked their lives to preserve these sites and many of them have become martyrs.

Jesus surely expects us to approach the holy places and their guardians with thoughts of blessing and gratitude, and not with feelings of superiority. Then it will be easier for us to dispel any objections we may have. Here and there we may find a holy place that is not kept holy. We may hear of disunity and strife, or even witness it. In such instances Jesus expects all the more that we humble ourselves in view of these conditions and admit that as Christians, without exception, we obscure and dishonour Jesus ever anew with our unholy ways. Such places need our special prayers.

Indeed we are called to support all the sites of Jesus' earthly life with our prayers and love, that they may be truly holy places. They will not necessarily bear testimony to God if their message is not backed by people's lives there. It is a fact that a place where God once revealed Himself does not automatically remain sacred. This would justify the argument of those who ask, "Are there really any holy places left today?" According to Scripture holy places certainly do exist; for example, God calls one city "the holy city"

15

(Isaiah 52 : 1) and the Temple His sanctuary (Ezekiel 23 : 38). Yet we know the history of Jerusalem and the Temple. Men desecrated the Temple and did not give God the glory. They did not keep His commandments there; instead they did business, turning the House of God into a den of thieves. For this reason the judgment of God later descended upon this site and it was devastated. A similar fate befell a number of other holy places. How deeply this must have grieved God! And ever anew we inflict sorrow upon God when the places where He chose to reveal Himself are dishonoured through our quarrelsomeness, jealousy, irreverence or indifference.

The holy places present a challenge to us. We are being summoned to revive them through our repentance, love for Jesus and heartfelt adoration, which will testify to our Lord and let His image shine brightly before many. But this we cannot do if we visit the holy places like museums, seeking to pack as much as possible into our programme, only to gain but a fleeting impression of them. Rather the holy places expect us to linger in prayer, so that we may have an encounter with Jesus. Consequently, whether we go alone or with a group to the holy places, we must prepare ourselves inwardly a long time beforehand in order to visit them in the right spirit.

A visit to the Holy Land is a God-given opportunity. It is not merely an interesting study, let alone a pleasure excursion. And it is more than a spiritually enriching gift, for by giving us the possibility to visit the holy places, God has entrusted us with a task, a commission. So may our hearts yearn not only to receive a spiritual blessing wherever we go, but to give thanks to God. Because Jesus lived at these places as God incarnate and suffered there for the sake of us sinners, the holy places wait for us to bring Jesus gifts of our love. But what gifts can we bring Him?

May our gifts be many prayers of thanksgiving and love for Jesus! Everywhere we go let us give Him a response for what He has done. Let us respond to His message with an act of dedication. Let us respond to His suffering with contrition and follow Him by taking up our cross in daily life. Let us often sing together so that the holy places may resound with anthems of praise and thanksgiving. And as we lament our sins, let us worship Jesus, who took them upon Himself.

Then when others hear our songs of lamentation and adoration, they will ask, "Who is it that you are praising? Who is it that you love so much?"

Jesus is waiting for people who come to the holy places in love for Him, for love makes the Belovèd come alive for others, so that they may be inspired to love Him. Love also helps to revive the places where He tarried, so that they may be filled with His presence today. Love will help to manifest our Lord Jesus at the holy places before all the world. Love yearns for Him to be revealed as the Lord of yesterday, who once lived in this land, suffered, died on the Cross, rose from the dead and ascended to heaven. And love also yearns that He will be manifested as the Lord of today, who is alive and present in our midst and to whom all love and dedication, glory, praise and honour is due for ever and ever.

What a privilege to be able to visit His land, to follow in His footsteps here and to express our loving gratitude! And here we may praise and acclaim Him in song as we look forward to the day when He returns to this earth, to His city, where He will be greeted with the joyful shout, "Blessed be he who comes in the name of the Lord!" (Matthew 23 : 39). But our rejoicing will resound even more at the thought of the day when the heavenly Jerusalem comes down and the dwelling of God will be with men (Revelation 21).

A PRAYER AT THE OUTSET OF A JOURNEY
TO THE HOLY LAND

Lord Jesus,

We thank You from the depths of our hearts for this gift, this amazing privilege of visiting the land where You lived and suffered. We pray, let us always be deeply conscious that we are treading on holy ground and that we must therefore in spirit remove our shoes. In deep shame and grief we remember how our forefathers came here under the sign of the Cross and massacred Jews and Moslems. Grant us heartfelt contrition that as Christians we have brought such dishonour and disgrace upon You and continue to do so ever anew, even at Your holy places. In view of all our guilt, let us now visit Your land and its inhabitants with a humble heart. During this journey grant us the grace to make amends wherever possible for our serious guilt.

May we enter Your land with God-fearing hearts. Keep us from coming with any uncleansed sin. During our pilgrimage help us not to tolerate the slightest sin or any discord, which would imperil the unity of love in our travelling group. Prepare us to approach with penitent hearts the places where You suffered, so that these sites will be sanctified and others too will regard them as holy.

Rekindle our love for You there, so that we may bring joy to You when we visit the places associated with Your earthly life. Impart to us Your Spirit, that we may fill these sites with our prayers, with lamentation over Your suffering, and with adoration and rejoicing. O Jesus, let us have an encounter with You in Your land at the holy places as we sing to You, give thanks to You and seek to bring joy to Your heart. Grant that we may also be able to make You known to others there. Let us encounter You in spirit and in truth in Your country, that we may return home richly blessed and share the blessings with many others.

May Your angels protect us on our journey, and may the loving hands of the Father guide us and guard us from all dangers and difficulties en route and bring us safely back home.

Amen.

Sacred Places, Softly Whisp'ring

8. 7. 8. 7.

Sacred plac-es, softly whisp'ring/

That our King will soon be here, /

Making read-y for His coming, /

Long that He will soon ap-pear.

And His ransomed ones who love Him
Sense the King is drawing nigh.
How their hearts go out to meet Him
With a yearning, joyful cry!

Wide the Father's arms are open
For His people to come home.
Then His longing through the ages
Will be stilled by joy unknown.

On the Mount of Olives weeping,
Jesus bade His people come.
By His love their hearts are melted
And His sorrow draws them home.

O Jerusalem, fair city
Of our mighty Lord and King,
Open wide your gates to greet Him,
Highest honours to Him bring.

O ye chosen people hasten,
For the King is on His way.
Haste, that you may stand beside Him
When the night brings forth His day.

THE TEMPLE SITE

Let us visit the Temple Site, Mount Moriah. From the very first sight of Jerusalem our attention is caught by the glittering "golden dome" of the huge Dome of the Rock in the middle of the Temple premises. The large expanse of the Temple Site occupies about one sixth of the Old City. Nine gates lead to the Temple Site, six of which are on the western side and three on the northern side.

But first of all let us go to the Western Wall (also known as the Wailing Wall), which is on the outer western side of the Temple Site. The most popular route to the Western Wall and Mount Moriah is the street Al Wad (King Solomon's Street), which begins at the Damascus Gate and passes through the Old City. At the end of this street there are a number of narrow, winding lanes. Signposts indicate the way and soon we find ourselves standing in a wide, open square before the Western Wall.

We can also take the road outside the eastern city wall, passing by the Golden Gate and the Temple Pinnacle and continuing until we reach the Dung Gate in the southern wall. It is the nearest city gate to the Western Wall and Mount Moriah. After taking a few steps inside the gate, we reach the square in front of the Western Wall, which towers high above our heads. With its massive hewn stone blocks dating from the day of Herod the Great this wall is the most imposing remains of the Temple Jesus knew. The foundations and first few layers of stone above the bedrock of the Tyropoeon Valley date from the time of Solomon's Temple.

Whenever we come to the Western Wall, we shall find people praying here. During Israel's high holidays in spring and autumn, many thousands of people flock here in surging crowds. According to tradition, when the Temple was destroyed, the presence of God withdrew into this wall. For centuries Jews have come here to weep over the destroyed Temple and their bitter fate. However, ever since the reunification of Jerusalem in 1967 prayers of thanksgiving and joy have been raised here.

An upward sloping path leads away from the Western Wall and brings us to the Mograbi Gate, the entrance to the Temple area. Here we can buy our entrance ticket for the El Aqsa Mosque and the Dome of the Rock.

Our gaze falls on the magnificent octagonal Dome of the Rock, which is built approximately in the middle of the Temple area on a raised, terrace-like platform. Stairways lead up to it from every side with graceful arcades at the head of each. The surrounding area is dotted with various structures of interest. These small domes, prayer alcoves, fountains and basins for ritual washing remind us that this place, once the spiritual centre of the Old Testament people of God, bears the impress of centuries of Islamic history. With the exception of a Byzantine church that once stood where the El Aqsa Mosque now stands at the southern end of the Temple premises and the brief occupation by the Crusaders, the entire Temple Site is untouched by Christian history.

The Temple area will be familiar to us from many Biblical events and therefore we are drawn to the place that preserves these memories the most. It is the former site of Solomon's Portico on the eastern side of the Temple area. Here, looking over the city wall, we have a view of the Mount of Olives, and in this wall we find the Golden Gate, whose bricked-up exterior has most likely caught our attention before. On the inside is a gateway dating from Byzantine times. A flight of steps leads down about 10 m. This is probably the only place where we can see the approximate level of the Temple area in Jesus' time, since the rest of the original Temple premises lies buried beneath the debris accumulated over the centuries. Here we contemplate the events of Jesus' earthly life that took place in the Temple area. The first time Jesus walked here He was twelve years old. On His last entry, He came seated upon an ass — perhaps passing through this very gate.

The next site of interest is the Dome of the Rock, standing on almost the same site as the Temple once did. Beneath the dome of this magnificent building is the rock on which the altar of burnt offering probably stood. The Rock of Moriah is much larger than one would expect. It is roughly 15 m. long and 12 m. wide and up to 2 m. high. Visitors are not asked to keep silence here, but before this rock the Christian pilgrim, deeply moved, naturally falls silent as he considers its history from the sacrifice of Isaac to the symbolic offering of the infant Jesus at His Presentation in the Temple.

To this day there is a cave below the rock, probably that of Ornan the Jebusite, whose threshing floor David bought in order to erect an altar. Perhaps the opening visible in the surface of the rock served to drain away the sacrificial blood into the cave at the time when the altar of burnt offering stood here.

Solomon's Stables will also be of interest to us, since they are structures dating from the time of Jesus. They lie in the south-east corner of the Temple area below the paved open space, which is bordered on two sides by the wall and on the third side by the basilica-like El Aqsa Mosque. The entrance is at the southeast corner of the wall, close to the Temple Pinnacle, which rises above the Valley of Kidron. A wide staircase leads down to the large expanse formed by the huge substructures that Herod built to support the Temple premises. (At present Solomon's Stables are not open to the public.)

Main visiting hours for the Temple Site:
9 a.m. — 11:30 a.m., 2 p.m. — 5 p.m. every day except Friday.

THE HISTORICAL ASPECT

The history of the Temple is closely interwoven with that of the city, for ever since the time of Solomon, the Temple played a major role in both the spiritual and external development of the city. The earliest settlement of Jerusalem was on the southern spur of the hill whose northern extension was later to contain the Temple area. This hill is bordered on the west by the Tyropoeon Valley and on the east by the Kidron Valley. The origin of this ancient settlement was probably at the Gihon Spring at the eastern foot of the hill in the Kidron Valley. Ex-cavations have shown that this settlement was inhabited from 3000 B.C. onwards. Today on this hill called Ophel, which slopes down to the Kidron Valley, is a village bearing the same name. It lies beyond the southern wall of the Old City.

In the Bible Jerusalem is first mentioned when Abraham en-countered Melchizedek, King of Salem (Genesis 14 : 18), about 2000 B.C. Likewise one can assume that the beginning of the Biblical history of the Temple dates from Abraham. According to Jewish tradition, Mount Moriah, which Abraham ascended to sacrifice Isaac, was the same mount on which the Temple was later built (Genesis 22 : 1-19).

When the Israelites under Joshua took the land, they did not capture Jerusalem, which continued as a Canaanite city-state under the Jebusites. They reigned there throughout the period of the Judges (1300—1050 B.C.). It was David who first con-quered the city about 1000 B.C. and built it up to be the capital of his kingdom. The City of David occupied the site of the earliest settlement, Ophel, on the southern spur of the Temple Mount. But more important than the establishment of his royal residence was the fact that David made the city the centre of religious life by bringing the Ark of the Covenant here (2 Samuel 6). He also planned to build a temple for it, but instead he received the divine summons to erect an altar for the Lord on "the threshing floor of Araunah [Ornan] the Jebusite" (2 Samuel 24 : 18), which lay to the north of his royal palace. David erected this altar as a sign of repentance for his sin of census-taking, which he had committed in disobedience to God, who had answered by smiting His people with pestilence. In the centre of Ornan's threshing floor on the Rock of Moriah, the altar to the Lord was erected. Here David intended to build the Temple, but the Lord restrained him from undertaking this project himself (1 Chronicles 22 : 1, 8-10).

David's son, Solomon, however, was able to build the Temple to the glory of the name of God (2 Chronicles 3 : 1) in about 960 B.C.; he also walled in the Temple premises and his palace buildings to form an enclosure. The first Temple, Solomon's Temple, conformed to the pattern of the Tabernacle given to Moses in the Law. The subsequent temples followed its pattern in most respects. The rectangular building — viewed from east to west — consisted of the Sanctuary and the Holy of Holies with the Ark of the Covenant. Directly before the Temple, in the Priests' Court, stood the altar of burnt offering upon the rock where David had probably erected his altar.

The Babylonian conquest under Nebuchadnezzar in 587 B.C. brought about the destruction of the Temple. When Cyrus allowed the captive Jews to return in 538, they erected under Zerubbabel's leadership the second Temple on the ground plan of the first, and the work was finished in 515. But the Holy of Holies no longer housed the Ark, which has been irretrievably lost since the captivity. And although the second Temple was not as magnificent as Solomon's, it became more and more the "heart" of Jerusalem.

In 168 B.C. the Temple was sacked and desecrated by the Greek king, Antiochus Epiphanes, and Jewish worship was forbidden. In 165 B.C. Judas Maccabaeus cleansed the Temple after his victory. When the Roman general, Pompey, assumed control of the country in 63 B.C., he left the Temple and its services unmolested. In 20 B.C. Herod the Great, whom the Romans appointed as king, began the rebuilding, and a third and very magnificent Temple was erected.

Meanwhile the original Jerusalem had spread from the eastern hill, Ophel, towards the west and northwest. Beyond the Tyropoeon Valley, with the Valley of Hinnom as the southern boundary, the upper city had come into being on a second hill, with a "suburb" to the north. Thus the Temple area was completely bounded on the west by the city. Herod extended the Temple premises southwards, doubling their size, and in order to do so he raised the downward slope of the Temple Mount with substructures. These substructures form the subterranean Stables of

24

Solomon on the south side of the Temple premises, on the former site of Solomon's royal palace. To the northwest of the Temple on a rocky elevation Herod erected the Fortress of Antonia, from where one could survey the entire district. Steps led down from the Fortress to the Temple area.

The Temple grounds were enclosed by walls, which in those days contained eight gates. The Shushan (Susa) Gate, although bricked up now, can still be seen in the northern part of the eastern wall. Since Byzantine times it has been called the Golden Gate. One tradition says that Jesus entered here on Palm Sunday, and therefore since the time of the Crusaders a procession passed through this gate on every Palm Sunday till it was bricked up in the sixteenth century.

On the inner side of all four walls there were pillared porches. The best known is Solomon's Portico on the eastern side above the Kidron Valley. This is probably where the scribes gathered for their discussions in Jesus' times. Thus as a twelve-year-old Jesus may well have sat here (Luke 2 : 46). And according to John 10 : 22 f., He walked here at the Feast of the Dedication and spoke of the Good Shepherd. Acts 3 : 11 ff. relates how Peter preached here to the people. In these same porches the first Christians met together. The southern porch, the Royal Portico, was probably the scene of the cleansing of the Temple when Jesus drove out the moneychangers and the vendors who were selling animals for sacrifice (Matthew 21 : 12 f.).

In the space enclosed by the porches lay the wide Court of the Gentiles. The Temple proper was in the centre of the area on a raised platform and entrance was highly restricted. It was immediately surrounded by the Priests' Court. To the east of this lay the Court of Israelites. And in the same direction, several steps below lay the Women's Court. This was reached from the Court of the Gentiles through the Beautiful Gate, where according to Acts 3 : 2 the lame man was healed. Mary must have brought her Child to the Women's Court for the Presentation. And it was here that the widow gave her two copper coins (Mark 12 : 41-44). The woman taken in adultery was brought here to Jesus, for the Jewish law court was also situated in the Temple premises (John 8 : 2-11). During the Feast of Tabernacles huge candlesticks were lighted in the Women's Court and these most probably occasioned Jesus' testimony, "I am the light of the world" (John 8 : 12, 20).

In the Priests' Court stood the altar of burnt offering and the laver. During the Feast of Tabernacles water from the Pool of Siloam was brought to the Temple and daily poured out at the foot of this altar before the morning sacrifice as a libation. This was the only time when men who were not priests could enter this part of the Temple area. It must have been here that

Jesus proclaimed on the last day of the feast, "If any one thirst, let him come to me and drink" (John 7 : 37). The actual Temple was a comparatively small building standing within the Priests' Court and elevated by several steps. In the front part was the Sanctuary, where the angel appeared to Zechariah and announced the birth of John the Baptist. Behind it was the Holy of Holies, separated by the veil, which was rent in two at the death of Jesus.

Early Christian tradition regarded the Temple Pinnacle, the southeast corner of the Temple wall, as a significant Scriptural site also, since it is mentioned in the Bible as the scene of Jesus' second temptation. From this same pinnacle James, the Lord's brother and the first Bishop of Jerusalem, is said to have been cast down.

This Herodian Temple was totally destroyed only a few years after its final completion. On August 10, A.D. 70 Jerusalem was captured by the Roman general, Titus. The Emperor Hadrian, who rebuilt Jerusalem as the Roman city Aelia Capitolina, erected a temple to Jupiter in A.D. 135 on the Temple ruins and also a statue of himself. At the time of Constantine (A.D. 335) this Roman temple vanished. Later the Roman Emperor Julian the Apostate wished to revive the ritual sacrifices of the Jews and thus in A.D. 363 he encouraged the Jews to attempt a reconstruction of their Temple, but an earthquake prevented the plan from being enacted. The Temple premises remained desolate, apart from a sixth-century church, which probably stood at the southern end where the El Aqsa Mosque now stands. This church was destroyed together with all the other churches in Jerusalem in 614.

When the Arabs conquered Jerusalem in 637, Caliph Omar built a mosque on the former site of the Temple, but the magnificent mosque, which now covers the Rock of Moriah, dates from fifty years later, during the rule of Caliph Abd al-Malik. The octagonal building was modelled on the Church of Ascension, now the Mosque of Ascension, on the Mount of Olives. The Dome of the Rock has become the most important shrine of Islam after Mecca and Medina. At the time of the Crusaders (1099—1187), when the Latin Kingdom of Jerusalem was proclaimed by Godfrey of Bouillon, the Dome of the Rock temporarily became a Christian church, the Templum Domini, and the centre of the Order of the Knights Templars, but afterwards it reverted to being a place of prayer for Moslems. In 1517 the Turks conquered Jerusalem and reigned there till the British Mandate of 1917, which lasted till 1948. An extensive restoration of the Dome was begun in 1959 and completed in August 1964.

FROM THE HOLY BIBLE

God said to Abraham, "Take your son, your only son Isaac, whom you love, and go to the land of Moriah, and offer him there as a burnt offering upon one of the mountains of which I shall tell you."   cf. Genesis 22 : 2

Then Solomon began to build the house of the Lord in Jerusalem on Mount Moriah, where the Lord had appeared to David his father, at the place that David had appointed, on the threshing floor of Ornan the Jebusite.   2 Chronicles 3 : 1

Now Jesus' parents went to Jerusalem every year at the feast of the Passover. And when he was twelve years old, they went up according to custom; and when the feast was ended, as they were returning, the boy Jesus stayed behind in Jerusalem ... After three days they found him in the temple, sitting among the teachers, listening to them and asking them questions ... He said to his parents, "How is it that you sought me? Did you not know that I must be in my Father's house?"   cf. Luke 2 : 41-49

Jesus was walking in the temple, in the portico of Solomon. So the Jews gathered round him and said to him, "How long will you keep us in suspense? If you are the Christ, tell us plainly." Jesus answered them, "My sheep hear my voice, and I know them, and they follow me; and I give them eternal life. My Father, who has given them to me, is greater than all, and no one is able to snatch them out of the Father's hand. I and the Father are one." The Jews took up stones again to stone him ... Again they tried to arrest him, but he escaped from their hands.   cf. John 10 : 23-39

Jesus entered the temple and began to drive out those who sold, saying to them, "It is written, 'My house shall be a house of prayer'; but you have made it a house of trade and a den of robbers!" His disciples remembered that it was written, "Zeal for thy house will consume me." And he was teaching daily in the temple. The chief priests and the scribes and the principal men of the people sought to destroy him; but they did not find anything they could do, for all the people hung upon his words. cf. Luke 19 : 45-48/ John 2 : 16 f.

"O Jerusalem, Jerusalem, killing the prophets and stoning those who are sent to you! How often would I have gathered your children together as a hen gathers her brood under her wings, and you would not! Behold, your house is forsaken and desolate. For I tell you, you will not see me again, until you say, 'Blessed be he who comes in the name of the Lord.'"

Matthew 23 : 37-39

THE TEMPLE SITE –
A MESSAGE FOR US

What memories are awakened as we make our way across the Temple Site in Jerusalem where the Dome of the Rock now stands! The Temple was the sanctuary of God under the Old Covenant, the place He had chosen for Himself as a visible sign that He dwelt in the midst of Israel. Consequently, the Temple was of great significance for Jesus, the Son of God, during His earthly life. We hear how Jesus at the age of twelve was drawn to the Temple where He spoke the moving words, "Did you not know that I must be in my Father's house?" From this we can sense how much Jesus suffered – having to live here on earth separated from the Father and far away from heaven. It shows us how He longed to touch but the hem of His Father's garment in the Temple where God Himself dwelt according to His Word (Exodus 25 : 8).

Yet it was probably here in the Temple area more than anywhere else that Jesus felt the cost of laying aside His glory and of walking the path of humiliation, for according to the revelation under the Old Covenant, the actual place of God's presence was the Holy of Holies in the Temple, where formerly the Ark of the Covenant had stood. Should not the Son of God have had more right than any of the priests to enter here? But as a layman He was not even permitted to enter the Sanctuary with the priests, let alone the Holy of Holies, which only the High Priests could enter. Jesus was obliged to remain outside in the Court of Israelites. This must have been not only a deep grief to Him, but a great humiliation.

Thus Jesus had no other place to minister in His Father's house than the porches bordering the Temple area. Here in

Solomon's Portico Jesus used to walk to and fro with His disciples. Here during the feast days He would sit surrounded by crowds of Jews and speak with great power and authority. So powerful were His words that the officers whom the Pharisees sent to seize Him at the Feast of Tabernacles returned saying that they could not take Him, because "no man ever spoke like this man" (John 7 : 46). Indeed, it was the Temple premises that witnessed the frequent attempts to seize Jesus. When He held His discourse here about the Good Shepherd, which expressed His deep love for His people, His flock, they responded by taking up stones to stone Him (John 10 : 31).

Thus the Temple area, the sanctuary of Jerusalem, as well as the city itself became the site of deepest suffering for Jesus. In this district He experienced rejection by the people and was exposed more than anywhere else to the hatred of the Pharisees, who had their stronghold here. In this most sacred place repeated attempts were made on His life. Here Jesus, the Son of God, was made painfully aware that the sanctuary of His Father, which He had desired for His habitation (Psalm 132 : 13), had become a den of thieves. Therefore, in holy, anguished zeal, Jesus was obliged to drive out the moneychangers and vendors. With a deeply grieved heart He pronounced the woes upon the Pharisees here, since the Pharisees in their pride and hypocrisy desecrated the sanctuary of God even more than the moneychangers did (Matthew 23). When Jesus daily beheld how perfunctorily the sacrifices were offered, profound sorrow must have filled Him, for He knew how halfhearted and insincere they were and that the true sacrifice of the heart was missing. Thus the Rock of Moriah, where the sacrificial beasts were slain, must have been a constant reminder to Jesus that because of all these sins He must bring the one true offering and become the Lamb of God.

Thus the Temple area is a vivid illustration of the distressing fact that God often finds the least room in the very places that should radiate His presence — the sites where He has chosen to reveal Himself. And why? Here dwell the "devout", who are so absorbed by their religiosity that instead of giving God the glory, they idolize their own piety. The ultimate result of such an attitude and the answer of the holy God in judgment can be seen in the subsequent history of the Temple. According to Jesus' words it was destroyed and will remain desolate until the day His people say, "Blessed be he who comes in the name of the Lord" (Matthew 23 : 39). Therefore, the Temple Site has a special message for us. "If you call yourselves devout, if you live at holy sites and serve at consecrated places, at churches and other sacred places, be careful how you treat the holy things of God. Take care that you do not grieve the living Lord, perhaps without even realizing it. Beware that you do not drive Him away from holy places and crucify Him anew, by idolizing your devotion, churchgoing, prayers and service for God, and by growing self-confident and satiated in your religiosity." The Temple Site is a warning for all Christians. "Awake and take care that your sanctuary does not turn into a 'market place' and finally a 'den of thieves', because you have forgotten that God seeks a broken and contrite heart, filled with love for Him and mercy towards men.

Jesus is alive today. And today we can grieve Him and the Holy Spirit just as the Pharisees and the people once did in the Temple area when we, like them, seek our own glory in religious activities, when in our pride we live for ourselves instead of serving God and man in truth by denying ourselves. After the untold suffering of Jesus' earthly life, should we not bring Him joy today? How He would rejoice to find souls who would truly honour Him, by no longer striving for their own honour and recognition! Should we not respond to His sacrifice by giving Him a genuine sacrifice, by dying to self? Only in this way shall we bring Jesus true love and adoration at His holy places and prevent them from becoming a "den of thieves", thus sparing Jesus much anguish of heart. He waits for our love and humility, which will help the sites associated with His life to be truly holy places.

PRAYER ON THE TEMPLE SITE

Lord, at this place where You suffered so much, let me remember my sins. I humbly confess all the times I have treated the holy things of God without due reverence and respect, whether it was prayer, church services or the Lord's Supper. How often have I actually loved and honoured myself and not You, because I had become proud, self-confident and satiated in my devotion, prayers and faithful participation in church life, and idolized them!

Lord, at this place where the Temple was destroyed, You show me how severely You judge such false piety. Place me here in the light of Your truth, so that I can see with Your eyes all that is not genuine in my Christian life and activities. Help me to turn from such ways, so that I no longer grieve You and kindle Your wrath. Grant that I may not merely give the appearance of leading a godly life, but that the power of such a life may dwell within me – the power of love and true authority, which stems from humility. Give me a heart that is ever lowly, for only then can my prayers and actions bear fruit for You.   Amen.

O Jesus, Who Can Comprehend

8. 8. 8. 8. 4.

O Jesus, who can com - prehend:/ Although

You did to earth descend,/ So few___

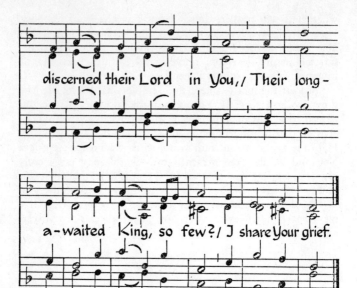

discerned their Lord in You,/ Their long-a-waited King, so few?/ I share Your grief.

O Jesus, who can comprehend:
We shut You out for years on end?
We do not want You as our Lord,
You who should be by all adored.
I share Your grief.

O Jesus, who can comprehend
How much our sin Your heart can rend?
Within Your Church blasphemed today,
Yet still You go the Lamb's meek way.
I share Your grief.

O Jesus, I can understand
The boundless grief Your heart must stand.
O make my heart with love to burn
That more and more I can discern
And share Your grief.

Well-spring of Joy 85

THE POOL OF BETHESDA

Turning off the Jericho Road, we enter the Old City by the Lion's Gate (St. Stephen's Gate). In our quest of the Pool of Bethesda, the miraculous pool of God's mercy, we are directed to a large enclosure on the right. We enter the third door, which brings us to a spacious courtyard belonging to the property of the White Fathers, a Greek Catholic missionary order. A broad path leads past a lovingly tended garden with sub-tropical plants and on to St. Anne's Church on our right, one of the most beautiful Crusader churches in the Holy Land. The crypt of the church commemorates the birthplace of Mary, the mother of Jesus.

Beyond the church, to the left, we arrive at the site of the excavations of the Pool of Bethesda. Looking down, we can determine the level of Jerusalem at the time of Jesus. The debris, some 20 m. deep, is a silent indication of the many times this sorely tried city of God has been destroyed. The main outlines of the former double pool can be defined and the ruins of the side walls of the pool have been partly laid bare, as well as the ruins of the churches that were later erected on the dividing wall. The remains of these ancient walls, brought to light after nearly 1,900 years, help to turn our thoughts to the Pool of Bethesda mentioned in the Gospel of John.

Times of opening: 8 a.m. till noon; 2 p.m. — 6 p.m.

THE HISTORICAL ASPECT

The Pool of Bethesda is mentioned only in the Gospel of John, chapter five. Later sources sometimes refer to it as the Pool of Bethzatha, naming it after the district in which it lay, a suburb north of the Temple. But the name Bethesda, which means "House of Mercy", predominated. According to John, the pool lay near the Sheep Gate, but it is no longer possible to determine the exact location of this gate. It may have been on the north side of the Temple premises or near the present Lion's Gate.

The five porticos described by John were probably built by Herod the Great; four surrounded the pool, the fifth was upon the wall that divided the pool in two. It was in these porches that the sick waited for the troubling of the waters when they could claim the healing properties of the pool.

The memory of the pool and of the miracle wrought there by Jesus persisted. In A.D. 300 the historian Eusebius described the five porches as well as the double pool; likewise the Pilgrim of Bordeaux in 333, his being the earliest pilgrim's description extant. But according to both of these reports, healings no longer occurred here through the troubling of the waters as they had done in Jesus' day. With the passing of time the porches deteriorated and the pool was gradually filled in. About A.D. 450 a Church of the Paralytic built on this site is mentioned for the first time, but in the same century a church built in the vicinity to the memory of Mary, over the grotto regarded as her birthplace came to the fore. After the Persians destroyed the church over the pool in 614, it remained in ruins, whereas the Church of St. Mary was rebuilt.

In 1100 the Crusaders built a chapel on the site of the Pool of Bethesda and enlarged the Church of St. Mary, renaming it in honour of St. Anne. The chapel on the pool was probably destroyed soon after the defeat of the Crusaders in 1187. The pool completely disappeared beneath the ruins and fell into oblivion.

After the Crimean War in 1856 the Turkish sultan gave this site to Napoleon III as an acknowledgment of indebtedness to the French for their assistance. In 1873 traces of the ancient pool were rediscovered. The White Fathers, who now run a Greek Catholic seminary here, acquired the site in 1878. Their excavations, which continually brought new finds to light, witness to the strong probability that this is the site of the miracle described in John 5.

FROM THE HOLY BIBLE

After this there was a feast of the Jews, and Jesus went up to Jerusalem. Now there is in Jerusalem by the Sheep Gate a pool, in Hebrew called Bethesda, which has five porticoes. In these lay a multitude of invalids, blind, lame, paralyzed, waiting for the moving of the water; for an angel of the Lord went down at certain seasons into the pool, and troubled the water: whoever stepped in first after the troubling of the water was healed of whatever disease he had. One man was there, who had been ill for thirty-eight years. When Jesus saw him and knew that he had been lying there a long time, he said to him, "Do you want to be healed?" The sick man answered him, "Sir, I have no man to put me into the pool when the water is troubled, and while I am going another steps down before me." Jesus said to him, "Rise, take up your pallet, and walk." And at once the man was healed, and he took up his pallet and walked.

Now that day was the sabbath. So the Jews said to the man who was cured, "It is the sabbath, it is not lawful for you to carry your pallet." But he answered them, "The man who healed me said to me, 'Take up your pallet, and walk.'" They asked him, "Who is the man who said to you, 'Take up your pallet, and walk'?" Now the man who had been healed did not know who it was, for Jesus had withdrawn, as there was a crowd in the place. Afterward, Jesus found him in the temple, and said to him, "See, you are well! Sin no more, that nothing worse befall you."   cf. John 5 : 1-14

THE POOL OF BETHESDA –
A MESSAGE FOR US

Once again Jesus was in Jerusalem, probably for the Festival of Purim. And where was He drawn? To the place where so many of the sick, the blind, and the crippled lay – to people who lived under the shadow of adversity and severe suffering, having many infirmities to bear. Jesus' heart of love went out to these poorest of the poor, for He is a Saviour and Physician for His children. And therefore He was especially drawn to the cripple who probably had the heaviest burden of all, since he had lain there ailing for thirty-eight years without receiving any help.

Why did this particular sick man have no one to carry him to the water, although others could find people who were willing to perform this service for them? Jesus' words after He had healed the man, "Sin no more", seem to indicate that the man's sickness was connected with his sin. The additional burden of having no one to help him may have been due to his sin as well. And perhaps he had an unpleasant personality. Apparently no one wished to associate with him; he was most likely left to his misery, because people thought, "He deserves it."

But now Jesus singles out this man. His arm reaches down into the depths where a person is sunk in sin and misery. He rejects no one, although He is God and has every right to cast off sinners. Our human love soon reaches its limit. It ceases when others are nasty and act badly, when they appear to be unworthy of our love. But there is no limit to Jesus' love. It never ceases, because He is the very essence of love, which has the divine quality of being boundless and all-embracing. It is this love that moves Jesus, our Saviour and Healer, to minister to this man in his severe physical need, and thus also in his even greater spiritual need, his sin. Approaching him, Jesus speaks the powerful, almost incredible words, "Take up your bed and walk." How can an incurably sick man rise, take up his bed and walk? Yet to everyone's astonishment this is precisely what happens.

The Pharisees scold the sick man, saying, "It is not lawful to carry your bed on the Sabbath." Their reaction is typical of human nature in its limited love. Rules and regulations are given precedence to love. When the cripple, overjoyed that he can move his limbs again after thirty-eight years of illness, carries his bed home, the Pharisees rebuke the man as if he were committing some wrong. Yet despite all their criticism they cannot give him the correction he so needs. They cannot tell him the truth about himself and his sin as Jesus does; they lack the authority of love that can help to bring sinners to repentance through a word of truth.

How different from the Pharisees does Jesus address sinners, the poor and sick! How differently He acts in their lives! Truly, as high as the heavens are above the earth, so different is His judgment from our judgment, His words from ours, His help from that which we show one another. Jesus addresses the healed man with words that have retained their power to this day, piercing the hearts of all who hear them, "Sin no more, that nothing worse befall you."

Jesus' saving, healing love first helps this man, who has been chastened for thirty-eight years, by healing him, for the Saviour's heart suffers with the cripple the untold misery of those long years. But true love does not stop there; it sees even deeper. It perceives that the real misery of this person's life is not his illness and all the hardship and pain involved, but rather his evil, sinful heart, which would bring him torment even in eternity. Accordingly, Jesus deals with the sick man's sin, so that he might be truly healed, having been released from his sin. Then as a new creation he will be able to live in the Kingdom of God for eternity. God's goodness, which brought the man relief from his ailment and misery, is meant to lead him to repentance. Therefore, God's goodness and Jesus' act of loving-kindness to the cripple are accompanied by words of truth. This is what lies behind Jesus' words, "Sin no more, that nothing worse befall you."

Jesus helps this sick man, but after relieving him of his burden, He admonishes him. In His love Jesus does not want to chasten the man even more severely, as He would have to do if the man trampled underfoot the goodness of God and fell into even greater sin after his healing. No, in His love Jesus yearns for this man to lead a new life and to find true health and happiness without having to undergo further severe chastening.

This ministering love of Jesus was meant not only for the sick man long ago; it is also available for us today. When we visit the ruins of the Pool of Bethesda, it is as if Jesus is waiting for us here today as our loving Saviour and Physician, so that we too may experience His goodness in body and soul. When we are sunk in misery and distress with no one to help us, Jesus speaks words of healing to us. He has power to help us. By placing ourselves in His hands, we entrust ourselves to His true love, which seeks not only to heal our bodies, but to minister to our souls. Therefore, Jesus also bids us to take care that we turn from our sins and lead a life of thanksgiving and commitment to Him in response to the goodness and help He has shown us in our troubles. Jesus asks us to make a fresh start today, so that He does not have to chasten us more severely. Truly, in His love He longs to help us, so that we shall be made whole for all eternity.

PRAYER AT THE POOL OF BETHESDA

Dear Lord Jesus,
I thank You that Your name means "Saviour" and that You have come to heal our ailments. I thank You that You are concerned not only about my physical needs, but also

about my other needs, having created me with a body, soul and spirit. In Your love You wish to help me in every sphere, for You see all three – body, soul and spirit – as a whole.

My Saviour, I worship You for Your saving love, which embraces all mankind. And I bring You the needs of my body and soul, that You may help me as You once helped the man at the Pool of Bethesda. I trust You. You are my Saviour and divine Physician, and You will heal all that is sick and sinful in me.

Here I want to give thanks for every time You helped me in physical illness or even restored my life when I was on the verge of death. But I also want to heed Your warning today and ask myself whether I have continued to sin in spite of Your goodness, for then You will have to chasten me even more.

My Lord Jesus, by faith in the power of Your redemption, I now renounce every sin that You have shown me or that others have pointed out to me. In this way, my Saviour, I long to show You gratitude for all that Your love has lavished upon me and for every time Your love has helped me and brought me back to the right path.

Amen.

✝

What love can compare with the saving love of Jesus, which reaches down to the most wretched of all, lifting them out of the deepest depths?

A love that mercifully embraces all who live under the shadow of adversity.

A love so bounteous that it longs to heal the soul as well as the body.

A love that does not gloss over sin, but calls it by its proper name and implores us to turn from it, yearning to mould us into a new creation, so that we may be fit for the kingdom of heaven and dwell there in eternal happiness.

A love that therefore won us redemption from every sin and offers us salvation.

What love can compare with His? None, for no one possesses such love as our Saviour Jesus Christ, who for our sakes endured suffering and death in order to bring healing to all.

Jesus' Name! Our Saviour's Name

7. 8. 7. 8. 7. 7.

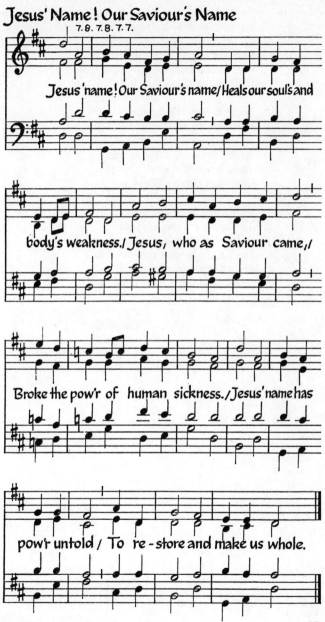

Jesus' name! Our Saviour's name/ Heals our souls and body's weakness./ Jesus, who as Saviour came,/ Broke the pow'r of human sickness./ Jesus' name has pow'r untold / To re-store and make us whole.

Jesus' name glows like a flame,
Radiant with such life and splendour.
He who calls upon this name
Can but saving grace encounter,
For Your name such power wields,
Only triumph, vict'ry yields.

Jesus' name! My Saviour's name,
Breaking all my chains and fetters;
In its strength I freedom claim,
As my prison walls it shatters.
Jesus' name almighty proves,
Conquers Satan's crafty moves.

Praise and laud and honour bring
To the holy name of Jesus.
All ye heavens join to sing!
He alone has won the vict'ry;
His all-conquering love adore.
Jesus, Saviour, Christ our Lord!

Can also be sung to the melody,
"Holy God, Thy Name We Bless"

THE MOUNT OF OLIVES

If we want to go by foot to the Mount of Olives, the shortest route is to leave the Old City by the Lion's Gate (St. Stephen's Gate). But before crossing the Kidron Bridge, let us turn off the Jericho Road to the right and take a short detour. Now we are on the road that leads to the Dung Gate. Between the Golden Gate and the Temple Pinnacle we pause for a few moments of contemplation, for here we have a splendid view of the Mount of Olives, which lies between the city and the Judean Desert like an embankment with its three summits and gentle slopes. Now in February, the Mount of Olives is at its loveliest, a tender green dotted with light-coloured rocks. At our feet lies the deep rift of the Kidron Valley. The slope opposite is strewn with tombstones. This vast cemetery spreads out to the southwest as far as the village Silwan, which is located on the southern hill of the Mount of Olives and reaches down into the Valley of Kidron. On account of its history (see 1 Kings 11 : 7) this hill is also known as the Mount of Offence. On the northern summit of the Mount of Olives lies Viri Galilaei, a compound belonging to the Greek Orthodox Patriarchate. And the middle hill? It is of special interest to us. At the foot of this hill lies the Basilica of the Agony, surrounded by olive trees. It is now separated from the terraced olive gardens by the wide motor road to Jericho, whose traffic sadly enough disturbs the stillness and solitude of Gethsemane. Further up the hill the bulbous spires of the Russian Orthodox Church of St. Mary Magdalene emerge from behind the huge cypress and pine trees. Somewhat higher to the right is the tear-shaped chapel of Dominus Flevit, which commemorates Jesus' weeping over Jerusalem. Almost at the summit we can see the tower of the Pater Noster Church, and to the left rises the Tower of Ascension, the highest in the Holy Land, belonging to the Mount of Olives convent of the Russian Orthodox nuns. Nearby is the minaret beside the Mosque of Ascension.

Whereas the original appearance of most of the places connected with the earthly life of Jesus in Jerusalem is difficult to imagine due to destruction, debris or new buildings, the contour of the Mount of Olives is practically the same as it was 2,000 years ago. Probably there were more olive trees on the western slope in Jesus' day, but because of the ground formation we may well assume that the course of the three main paths is the same as it was when Jesus and His disciples walked along them scores of times. All three paths, which spread out fan-wise from Gethsemane, lead up to the top (see sketch-map).

After having taken in the Mount of Olives from afar on the road to the Dung Gate, we retrace our steps in order to visit the sites. We walk over the Kidron Bridge, which crosses the valley at the same place where a bridge once stood in Jesus' day. Jesus must have gone this way many a time when He approached Jerusalem from Jericho or when He left the city for the Mount of Olives or Bethany. To the left, beyond the bridge, lies the entrance to the Cave of Betrayal (also known as the Grotto of Gethsemane, which is not to be confused with the Basilica of the Agony). It can be reached via the sunken courtyard before Mary's Tomb. Diagonally opposite lies the gate to the Garden of Gethsemane with the Basilica of the Agony, where we shall certainly wish to spend some time *(see chapter on Gethsemane)*.

After lingering there a while, we continue the climb and take the southern path, the first to the right behind the Basilica of the Agony. At first the path is enclosed on either side by high walls, which allow no view of the city. But soon we are rewarded by a view of the Old City as we near the grounds of Dominus Flevit, which lies to the left of the path *(see chapter on Dominus Flevit)*. The view improves as we ascend. On our right we pass the walled-in grounds that contain the Tombs of the Prophets. Now we have almost reached the summit. From here we have a sweeping view of the Kidron Valley and the Temple Site. We can see the whole of the Old City and far beyond. A few steps later our path meets the motor road from Et-Tur, which leads to the Intercontinental Hotel. We follow it to the north, passing a Benedictine convent on the left. Here the middle path, the steepest but shortest path of the Mount of Olives, meets the road to Et-Tur. At the crossroads we see on our right the grounds of the Carmelite nuns with the Pater Noster Church and the ruins of the ancient Eleona Church *(see chapter on the Olivet Discourses and the Ascension)*. From the cloister of the Pater Noster Church a staircase leads down to the crypt and the adjoining grotto, where we shall want to linger, since this place, one of the most significant sites where Jesus stayed, has a special message for us.

Later we return to the motor road. On our way north to the Arab village of Et-Tur we reach the octagonal Mosque of Ascension after about 70 m. Walking through the village, we come to a smaller road on the right about 50 m. beyond the Mount of Olives Hotel. It leads to the premises of the Russian Orthodox convent with its high Tower of Ascension.

Times of opening:

Cave of Betrayal (R.C.)	9:30 a.m. — 11:30 a.m.
	3 p.m. — 6 p.m.
Basilica of the Agony (R.C.)	8:30 a.m. — 11:30 a.m.
	2 p.m. — 6 p.m.
	(in winter till sundown)
Church of St. Mary Magdalene (Russian Orthodox)	Tuesday, Thursday, Saturday
	9 a.m. till noon
	2 p.m. — 5 p.m.
Dominus Flevit (R.C.)	8:30 a.m. — 11:30 a.m.
	3 p.m. — 5 p.m.
Pater Noster Church and the Eleona ruins (R.C.)	8:30 a.m. till noon
	2 p.m. — 5 p.m.

An Arabian guard is in charge of the Mosque of Ascension and a small admission fee is made.

There is a continuous bus service to the Mount of Olives running from the Old City bus station near the Damascus Gate.

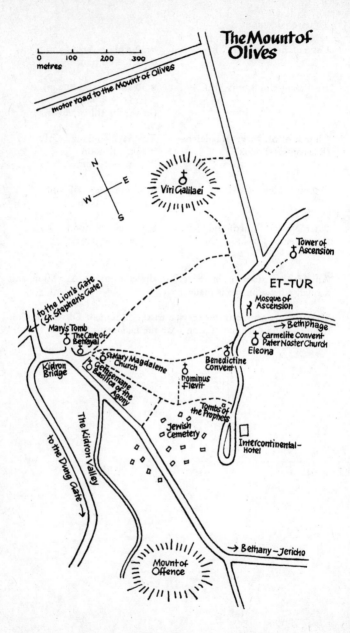

The Mount of Olives

0   100   200   300
metres

motor road to the Mount of Olives

N
W — E
S

Viri Galilaei

Tower of Ascension

ET-TUR

Mosque of Ascension

→ Bethphage

Carmelite Convent
Pater Noster Church
Eleona

to the Lion's Gate
(St. Stephen's Gate)

Mary's Tomb
The Cave of Betrayal

St Mary Magdalene Church

Benedictine Convent

Kidron Bridge

Gethsemane Basilica of the Agony

Dominus Flevit

Tombs of the Prophets

The Kidron Valley

Jewish Cemetery

Intercontinental Hotel

to the Dung Gate →

→ Bethany – Jericho

Mount of Offence

SITE OF THE OLIVET DISCOURSES
AND THE ASCENSION

THE HISTORICAL ASPECT

In ancient times the cave over which the Eleona Church was built was regarded as the site of the Ascension. The historian Eusebius writes in A.D. 330 that the Emperor Constantine chose two "mystic caves", in addition to the Holy Sepulchre, which were to be honoured with magnificent buildings. These were the Grotto of the Nativity at Bethlehem and this cave on the Mount of Olives. At the command of his mother Helena, a "holy church" was built over it to commemorate the Ascension. Eusebius wrote that the feet of our Lord and Saviour stood upon the Mount of Olives by a certain cave, from where He ascended into heaven after having prayed and revealed the mysteries concerning the end of the world to His disciples.

Thus the site recalls yet another event, one that took place before the Ascension. According to Eusebius, in this cave, which Jesus frequented, He taught His disciples about the hidden mysteries. It is said that as Jesus sat here facing the Temple (Mark 13 : 3), He spoke those deeply moving words about the end of time and His second coming (Matthew 24 : 3 ff.). The Early Christians venerated this cave as much as the Grotto of the Nativity and the Holy Sepulchre. Constantine found that it was generally recognized as a holy place and thus caused the Eleona Church to be built over it. But whereas the Church of the Nativity and the Church of the Holy Sepulchre retained their spiritual significance throughout the centuries, the tradition concerning the Eleona Church was lost. A few decades after its erection the memory of Jesus' Ascension here had vanished and only His teaching of the disciples and His eschatological discourses were remembered here.

In the year 614 the Persians destroyed both the Eleona Church and the Basilica of the Agony in Gethsemane, which had also been built in the fourth century. Since the Eleona no longer perpetuated the memory of the Ascension, it was not rebuilt like the Basilica of the Agony, for example. The Crusaders erected merely a modest church over the remains of the Eleona, for by that time the site only bore the tradition that Jesus taught His disciples the Lord's Prayer here and the memory of His apocalyptic utterances had faded.

The exact position of Constantine's church was eventually forgotten. In 1876 the French Carmelite nuns built their convent and church beside the ruins of the Eleona without realizing that the ruins were there. They named the church after the Pater Noster, and in their church and cloister the Lord's Prayer is inscribed on majolica tiles in over sixty different languages. Not until the beginning of this century did excavations reveal the remains of the Eleona Church. Research then revived the ancient tradition that this was the site of the Ascension.

The tradition of the Ascension at the Eleona was lost at such an early date, probably because the built-over cave made it difficult to visualize the Ascension. By the end of the fourth century the memorial of the Ascension had been moved to the central summit of the Mount of Olives about 70 m. north of the Eleona. About 378 a Church of Ascension was built there, also known as "Imbomon", the Greek word for "on the hill". Later a convent was founded nearby. In the octagonal church, which was open to the sky, a stone said to bear the footprint of the ascending Lord, was revered. The church must have been a splendid piece of architecture, for in the seventh century the Arabs used it as their model for the immense Dome of the Rock.

In contrast to the Eleona Church, the Imbomon was rebuilt after the Persian destruction and again after the entry of the Crusaders. However, in the twelfth century it was converted into a mosque, for the Moslems also believe in the ascension of the "prophet" Jesus, whom they call Isa. In its essential features the building has retained its shape through the centuries, but the arcaded porches of the external octagon have vanished. This small octagonal mosque was covered over by the Mohammedans with a cupola. Only on Ascension Day are the various branches of Christianity allowed to hold services there. The actual site of the Ascension, which has been preserved for the Christian world to this day, can still be found in the Eleona ruins.

The Greek Orthodox Church regards the northern summit of the Mount of Olives as the site of the Ascension and has named it "Viri Galilaei" after Acts 1 : 11.

FROM THE HOLY BIBLE

And every day he was teaching in the temple, but at night he went out and lodged on the mount called Olivet.

Luke 21 : 37

As he sat on the Mount of Olives, the disciples came to him privately, saying, "Tell us, when will this be, and what will be the sign of your coming and of the close of the age?"

Matthew 24 : 3

And Jesus answered them, "Then the kingdom of heaven shall be compared to ten maidens who took their lamps and went to meet the bridegroom." Matthew 24 : 4 a; 25 : 1

He was praying in a certain place, and when he ceased, one of his disciples said to him, "Lord, teach us to pray, as John taught his disciples." And he said to them, "When you pray, say: 'Our Father who art in heaven.'"

Luke 11 : 1 f. and Matthew 6 : 9

Then he led them out as far as Bethany ... While he blessed them, he parted from them and was carried up into heaven. Luke 24 : 50 f.

THE MOUNT OF OLIVES –
A MESSAGE FOR US

Why did Jesus choose the Mount of Olives for His significant discourses with His disciples about the last times? Why did He choose this very mount after His Resurrection to be the site of His Ascension and triumphant return to the Father? The Mount of Olives was Jesus' mountain in a special sense. When He could no longer stay in "His city" owing to the plots of His adversaries, He would withdraw to the Mount of Olives at night (Luke 21 : 37). When He was continually rejected in His Father's house, the Temple, which had become a den of thieves, He would go to the Mount of Olives to His prayer cave, to converse with His Father.

On the slope of the Mount of Olives Jesus paused before His entry into Jerusalem and wept over His city, which had rejected Him. At the foot of this mount, in Gethsemane, Jesus underwent the deepest agony of spirit in mortal combat with the powers of darkness. Was it not fitting that this suffering should be followed by Jesus' triumphant Ascension? Was it not appropriate that this mount, which saw Jesus in His deep humiliation when He was weak and trembling like a human being, should also see Him ascending to heaven as Victor over the laws of nature and all powers of darkness?

From the Mount of Olives Jesus returned to the Father to sit at the right hand of God as King of kings. Worshipping choirs of angels must have accompanied Him with their anthems of praise as they paid Him homage. They must have held a triumphant reception for Him. How different was Jesus' Ascension to heaven from His departure! To the amazement of all the angelic hosts, Jesus, whom they worship as their Creator, returned home with woundmarks, which tell of the bitter struggle it cost Him on earth to ransom the sons of men. From that time on the wounds of the ascended Lord, the Lamb of God on the highest throne, shone like rubies throughout the heavens as the sign of His victory. They are His highest honours, attesting to His kingship, proclaiming that He is the Lord, who defeated Satan in mortal combat and entered heaven as Victor.

Yet Jesus, our Lord and King, will not always remain in heaven. At the close of the age His love will constrain Him to come again to us as it is written, "This Jesus, who was taken up from you into heaven, will come in the same way as you saw him go into heaven" (Acts 1 : 11). But He will not only come in the clouds of heaven to gather His own to Himself (1 Thessalonians 4 : 16 f.), He will also come to the Mount of Olives, to His chosen people. The Prophet Zechariah foretells that in the last times the Lord will stand on the Mount of Olives, which will split open (Zechariah 14 : 4) and provide a place of refuge for His people. Thus it is not surprising that here on the Mount of Olives Jesus held His eschatological discourses for His disciples and His future Church.

Now that we have entered the nuclear age, these discourses of Jesus have become most relevant. The end times, which Jesus referred to on the Mount of Olives, have begun. With unmistakable clarity and realism physicists cite facts that prove we are living in an age like none before. For the first time in history, the necessary conditions exist for disasters, triggered off by man, to annihilate the whole world. The time is drawing near when men will be "fainting with fear and with foreboding of what is coming on the world" (Luke 21 : 26) as Jesus prophesied for the last days. The other signs that Jesus mentioned on the Mount of Olives when He spoke of His return are also being visibly fulfilled in our times – especially with regard to the anti-Christian powers, which are gathering force (Matthew 24 : 9-12), and the preaching of the Gospel throughout the whole world (Matthew 24 : 14).

Never before have Jesus' discourses for His disciples on the Mount of Olives about the last times been so significant for us as they are today. The close of the age is a time of division and therefore a time of decision. Then the words that Jesus spoke on this mount will be fulfilled. "Two women will be grinding at the mill; one is taken and one is left" (Matthew 24 : 41). Or, as Jesus illustrates in the parable of the ten virgins, all ten have set out to meet the Bridegroom, but the dividing line cuts through the midst of these believers. Only five are received by the Lord. To the others Jesus says, "I do not know you."

Now at the close of the age there is no longer a middle course, where we can abide in "cheap grace" and lead a self-satisfied, comfortable Christian life. Jesus compares the last days with the days of Noah preceding the Great Flood (Matthew 24 : 37-39). At such a time when the earth is threatened with destruction, we cannot live as in more normal times. In this time before the nuclear war, as in the time before the Flood, things have become sin which were not sin before. To go on living as though we were not standing on the brink of disaster is a sin in itself. According to Jesus' words, this attitude was the downfall of the people in Noah's day; it brought them the Flood as God's judgment.

This also applies today when devastation is imminent. As Jesus says, we shall suffer the same fate if we do not break every earthly tie and bind ourselves to Him alone, surrendering our lives to Him and abiding in total obedience to God's commandments, His Word and His will. Indeed, if we do not take up Jesus' challenge now, if we do not want to lose our lives and all that we regard as essential for them, we shall perish like Lot's wife (Luke 17:32 f.). If we are not wholehearted and earnest about our discipleship to Jesus, we are ignoring the fact that we are living in a nuclear age in which God's judgments could suddenly descend and destruction swiftly overtake us.

Today we are faced with the vital question of how we shall go through the coming time of destruction. Now the die is being cast as to whether we shall be among those whom the returning Lord will deliver out of the great tribulation to be with Him in glory at the sound of the last trumpet as it is written in 1 Corinthians 15 : 51 f.

The Mount of Olives with its site commemorating Jesus' eschatological discourses sounds the trumpet blast, "Behold, the Bridegroom is coming; prepare yourselves!" Only those who submit to chastening and prepare themselves through daily contrition and repentance, through much prayer and much love, are counted worthy "to escape all these things that will take place, and to stand before the Son of man" (Luke 21 : 36). In reference to the last times Jesus encourages His own, "When these things begin to take place, look up and raise your heads, because your redemption is drawing near" (Luke 21 : 28). But only those who wait in love and expectation for the coming of the Bridegroom will be able to "raise their heads" when fear befalls them in view of the coming times and when "these things begin to take place".*

* For further reading: *Countdown to World Disaster — Hope and Protection for the Future* and *The Eve of Persecution*.

PRAYER ON THE MOUNT OF OLIVES

Dear Lord Jesus,

I thank You that You will come when the world is at its darkest. And I thank You for the assurance that the more swiftly we approach midnight hour on earth, the sooner the day of Your coming will dawn.

Fix my gaze firmly on Your return, that day of supreme joy, so that the promise of Your return at the end of time will shine like a bright light in my heart. I pray, do not let me be preoccupied with the thought of the coming destruction or with my tasks in everyday life. Instead let me concentrate on the all-important fact that You are coming soon and that I must be prepared for that day, freed from all earthly things, purified and transformed into Your image.

May I be prepared for the hour of Your coming. Help me to live with this one goal in mind. But let me also be realistic in the knowledge that this hour will be preceded by war, devastation and affliction, such as the world has never known. Therefore, I dedicate myself now to abide wholly in You and to spend myself for You, so that in the horrors and darkness of the threatening nuclear war You can be my source of light, comfort and joy and that in You I shall be as secure as in a fortress.

But You have also said that we should watch and pray, in order that we may be counted worthy to escape all these things and to stand before the Son of man. Help me to act according to Your command, so that I may experience the fulfilment of Your promise and be able to "escape all these things", having been freed from this world and bound to You alone. All my love shall be Yours, so that when You come again I shall be drawn to You as if by a magnet. Lord, prepare me, that I may behold You when You appear in glory as the Bridegroom, for then You will deliver me out of the great tribulation to take me to Yourself at the rapture.

Amen.

When the trumpet call sounds at midnight, only those whose hearts are tuned to the sound will hear it. These are people who love Jesus, who wait expectantly for Him, whose hearts are always with Him and whose lives are surrendered to Him. They will be gathered to Jesus when He appears as the Bridegroom.

King of Glory

7. 7. 7. 7.

King of Glo - ry, Je - sus, Lord, /

He shall ev - er be a - dored! /

Heav'nly hosts His prais-es sing,/
Hail in Him their glorious King.

Home again with wounds so bright,
Bathed in resurrection light,
Peerless in His vict'ry won,
Joyfully returns God's Son.

Sovereign Lord of all the world,
Lamb of God with flag unfurled,
Mightily the foe o'ercame.
Honour now His glorious name!

Mighty Victor, Lord of all,
Earth and heav'n in homage fall.
See! exulting angels come,
Bringing Him in triumph home.

Jesus on the highest throne
With the Father now is one.
He reaps glory evermore
For the suff'ring He once bore.

Sovereign might and pow'r are His,
Endless glory, ceaseless bliss.
Him for e'er enthroned we see,
Jesus, King eternally.

Can also be sung to the melody, "Let Us, with a Gladsome Mind"

The King Draws Near

8. 8. 8. 8. 8. 8. 8. 7.

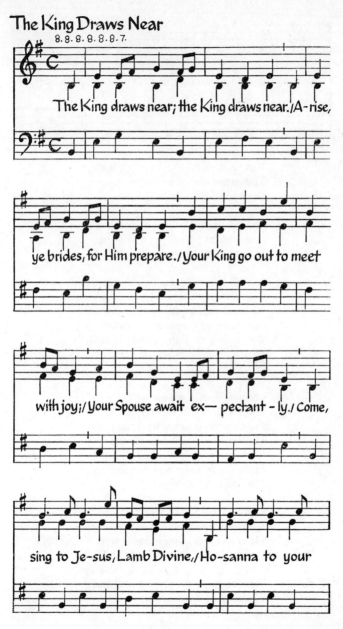

The King draws near; the King draws near./A-rise,

ye brides, for Him prepare./Your King go out to meet

with joy;/Your Spouse await ex— pectant-ly./Come,

sing to Je-sus, Lamb Divine,/Ho-sanna to your

Spouse sublime,/ Ho-sanna in the high-est!

Now put ye on the wedding dress,
The garment of His righteousness;
Be clothèd with humility,
And robe yourself with purity.
Come, sing to Jesus, Lamb Divine,
Hosanna to your Spouse sublime,
Hosanna in the highest!

The King now comes with us to dwell.
Our perfect bliss what voice could tell?
As handmaids spread we as is meet
Our robes as carpet for His feet.
Come, sing to Jesus, Lamb Divine,
Hosanna to your Spouse sublime,
Hosanna in the highest!

He long ago upon an ass
From Olivet did meekly pass;
But now on charger white to reign
He comes with all His glorious train.
Come, sing to Jesus, Lamb Divine,
Hosanna to your Spouse sublime,
Hosanna in the highest!

Come, wave the vict'ry palm on high,
And ceaseless raise the vict'ry cry:
He comes, He comes, our Spouse divine!
Come, sing to Jesus, Lamb Divine!
Come, sing to Jesus, Lamb Divine,
Hosanna to your Spouse sublime,
Hosanna in the highest!

Well-spring of Joy 10

DOMINUS FLEVIT

THE HISTORICAL ASPECT

As early as the Byzantine times, in the sixth century, a small chapel and monastery stood here on the slope of the Mount of Olives, near the present chapel of Dominus Flevit (The Lord wept), as recent excavations have revealed. In A.D. 400 there were altogether twenty-four monasteries and convents on the Mount of Olives. But not until after the time of the Crusaders do we have any record of the tradition that Jesus wept on this spot. The Franciscans, who have had a branch and a small chapel here since 1891, discovered the remains of the Byzantine monastery in 1953 when excavations were made, and later they erected a tear-shaped chapel on this site with a large window above the altar looking out over Jerusalem. During the excavations ancient tombs were also brought to light in the vicinity.

The tradition that Jesus wept here before His entry into Jerusalem is questioned by some, because the steepness of the slope would have been unfavourable for a procession, but no other place has this tradition. Yet to remember Jesus' tears over Jerusalem it is surely not so important to know the actual spot as it is to have a view of His city from the western slope of the Mount of Olives, and Dominus Flevit fulfils this requirement especially well.

FROM THE HOLY BIBLE

When Jesus came down from the Mount of Olives and saw the city, he wept over it, saying, "Would that even today you knew the things that make for peace! For the days shall come upon you, when your enemies will cast up a bank about you and surround you, and hem you in on every side, and dash you to the ground and they will not leave one stone upon another in you; because you did not know the time of your visitation."   cf. Luke 19 : 37, 41-44

"O Jerusalem, Jerusalem, killing the prophets and stoning those who are sent to you! How often would I have gathered your children together as a hen gathers her brood under her wings, and you would not!"   Luke 13 : 34

DOMINUS FLEVIT –
A MESSAGE FOR US

Dominus Flevit lies on the western slope of the Mount of Olives, a mountain that had seen so many tears of our Lord Jesus Christ. At the foot of the Mount of Olives in Gethsemane as the powers of darkness oppressed Him greatly, Jesus prayed with "loud cries and tears" to His Father, "who was able to save him from death" (Hebrews 5 : 7). Only a few days earlier when Jesus was about to enter Jerusalem, He also shed tears here on the Mount of Olives – a short distance above Gethsemane. He wept over Jerusalem, the city of God, the city of the great King, which, although it was called "His city", refused to accept Him and would even thrust Him outside the city walls a few days later in order to crucify Him.

Jesus lamented and wept over Jerusalem. This was the chosen city, destined to be the pride of all cities and nations, surpassing them in beauty and splendour, but now it was heading towards destruction. God's very nature was to radiate from this city, for a holy people would live there (Isaiah 62 : 12). Destined to be a blessing for all nations, this people was to bring healing to the whole world. God had given wonderful promises concerning the city of Jerusalem. The law was to proceed from it into every land (Isaiah 2 : 3) and Jerusalem was to be like a blazing torch for all the world to see (Isaiah 62 : 1).

And now Jesus could only weep over Jerusalem and its citizens. Instead of being a light to all the nations, it was veiled in darkness. Instead of radiating love, it emanated strife, hatred and spiritual death; wicked deeds were committed within its walls. Only a few days earlier hands were raised to stone Jesus in the Temple, the holiest part of the city (John 10 : 31). "O Jerusalem, Jerusalem, killing the prophets and stoning those who are sent to you!" This was Jesus' lament. Like a mother who can scarcely believe it when her favourite child has gone astray, Jesus must have found it hard to grasp what had happened to this city, which had a special place in God's heart. The high and lofty God had made His dwelling in the Temple; there He revealed Himself. But what did man do? He turned the Temple into a den of thieves!

Only a person who loves a city and its citizens can weep and lament to see it rushing headlong into destruction. Jesus wept and lamented as He beheld His city Jerusalem, because it was especially dear to Him. And even though the people who lived in the city were not "righteous" men (Isaiah 60:21) but sinners, who hated and rejected the Son of God, Jesus continued to love them with a deep love.

Who wept with Jesus then? Hardly a soul! Jesus' tears and lament over man, whom He created, are meant to rouse us and evoke a response from us. When our Lord God is weeping and lamenting, how can we, who call ourselves His own, not join in this lament, especially since we have every cause to weep and lament over the evil in us and the judgment that will ensue?

Dominus Flevit waits for a response from all who come its way. It waits for tears of repentance from each one of us, since Jesus has wept over us too, over our sins and unwillingness. Did He not weep over us, because we did not know the things that make for our peace, when He called and beckoned us or intervened in our lives? How often did we resist when Jesus tried to draw us back to Himself? How often did we adhere to our own wills, persisting in rebellion and defiance, and continue to complain about His leadings? Like His people long ago we did not heed His beckoning and follow Him; we despised His pathway of lowliness and obedience.

Dominus Flevit has yet another message for us. Not only does it remind us of the tears Jesus shed at His first coming when He was not accepted, but it tells us of the tears that will be shed at His second coming, though this time not by Him. At the close of the age when Jesus appears in glory on the Mount of Olives, which will be split in two (Zechariah 14:4) to provide a refuge for His people, they will raise a great lament over what they have done to Him. At last Jesus' tears will find a response; there will be lamenting and weeping such as the world has never seen before. But the lamentation will soon be turned into cries of joy and exultation when Jesus is honoured and worshipped as King. Jesus' tears will be rewarded and all the promises concerning His city will come true and the law will indeed proceed from Jerusalem into all the world.

Yet preparations must be made for this day. The way

must be paved for His second coming as it was for His first coming. And who should prepare His way but those who already know Him and call upon His name? Jesus is waiting now for our contrition and repentance, for our heartfelt lamentation over all our defiance and persistence in sin. He waits for this as a response to the tears He shed over us. Then His heart will be consoled and filled with joy at the thought of the day when all His children turn to Him in repentance.

PRAYER AT DOMINUS FLEVIT

Dear Lord Jesus,

We humble ourselves that You wept here because of us stubborn sinners. And ever anew You must weep, since we ignore Your loving shepherd's call as You beckon us, and since we refuse to break with sin and to follow in Your footsteps in everyday life.

Grant that through the power of the Holy Spirit Your tears may touch the depths of my heart, drawing tears of repentance from me for every time I have grieved You by my defiance and disobedience. Lord Jesus, since You continually pour out such love upon us all, it is my fervent longing that You will no longer grieve but rejoice over us. Take my life that I may be a joy and a comfort to You in the grief and suffering You still bear today because of mankind, whom You created.

Take my will. From now on I would heed Your call and walk in humility, self-denial and obedience – the path You walked before us. By faith in the power of Your redemption I want to heed every admonishment of the Spirit, so that through repentance and dedication I may help to pave the way for Your coming.

Amen.

My Saviour Weeps

8. 8. 7. D.

My Saviour weeps; His heart is rent. / J hear His loving, sad la-ment / Up-on the Mount of Ol - ives. / "Come home! Come home!" J called and pled, / But you chose other paths instead / And did not want to fol - low."

My Saviour weeps; His heart is rent.
I hear His loving, sad lament
Upon the Mount of Olives.
"I yearned to save and set you free.
If you had only turned to Me!
But you preferred the judgment."

My Saviour weeps; His heart is rent.
I hear His loving, sad lament
Upon the Mount of Olives.
"Come home! The Father's waiting there.
What bliss and joy is yours to share!
And yet you would not listen."

My Saviour weeps; His heart is rent.
I hear His loving, sad lament
Upon the Mount of Olives.
"My own are blind and deaf to Me.
Though they God's children claim to be,
They do not see My suffering."

My Saviour weeps; His heart is rent.
I hear His loving, sad lament
Upon the Mount of Olives.
"Come home, My children, come to Me.
I wait and yearn so fervently;
For you My heart is open!"

"Come, come unto Me ..."
Hear the voice of Love calling ever,
"O My children, come! I wait for you."

Come, gather round the staff of the Good Shepherd.
Lie down at His feet.
Come in sorrow and contrition to the One who loves you.

Listen,
Listen to the Good Shepherd's call,
"Come to Me, My little ones.
Here alone you will find the open door
To pleasant pastures.
Come, come unto Me.
The doors to the Father's house are
Wide open for you.
He has chosen you before the foundation of the world
To be His own.
O come, come home to Me!"

See how His heart in grief is weeping
On the Mount of Olives.
He weeps today as once long ago.
O belovèd of the Lord,
Turn to Him, for it is time.
This will soothe His wounded heart.

Dominus Flevit, October 29, 1959

GETHSEMANE

THE HISTORICAL ASPECT

John, in his report of the events of the eve of Good Friday,
records that after the Last Supper Jesus crossed the Kidron
Valley with His disciples and entered a garden there. The other
Evangelists relate that Jesus went as was His custom to the Mount
of Olives, to a place called Gethsemane. These descriptions seem
to fit the location of the present Gethsemane Basilica of the
Agony, for the road crossing the Kidron meets the Mount of
Olives at this point. Thus it is highly probable that this is the
site of Jesus' Agony, especially since an ancient tradition is
associated with it.

According to the testimony of the historian Eusebius about
the year 330, the Christians in Jerusalem still had a vivid rec-
ollection of the place Gethsemane (referred to in Matthew 26 : 36
and Mark 14 : 32) as being the site of Jesus' Agony and Betrayal.
Eusebius describes it as lying on the Mount of Olives. Yet according to various ancient sources only an enclosed portion of
the olive gardens was called Gethsemane up to the end of the
fourth century. This enclosure contained the cave where the
disciples slept and where Jesus was betrayed (see chapter on The
Cave of Betrayal). The tradition that Jesus was taken prisoner
before this cave has been well established ever since Early Christian times. For this reason the site was deeply impressed upon
the memory of the people of Jerusalem and the Agony was probably also commemorated here.

About the year 400 the Church Father Jerome refers to the
report of Eusebius, but defines the location of the place Gethsemane more exactly, stating that it lies at the foot of the Mount
of Olives. He applies the name "Gethsemane" to the whole area
and adds that a church was built on it. According to the report
of the nun Etheria in 385, this church or "Ecclesia elegans" (the
elegant church) as she called it, which was connected by a path
to the Cave of Betrayal, was where the Agony was commemorated. This place was venerated as the site of Jesus' struggle with
Death, a stone's throw away from the cave where the Apostles
slept and the Betrayal took place.

The church mentioned by Jerome is surely evidence of the
authenticity of the place, since this sanctuary was built over the
site of Jesus' Agony as early as the fourth century. This magnificent church was destroyed with many others by the Persians in
the year 614. A small church, which was built on the same spot
in the eighth century, and a larger one erected during the time

of the Crusaders were also devastated, and by the middle of the fourteenth century no trace could be found of them.

However, the statements made about the earliest church and the authenticity of the site were confirmed when in 1909 the Franciscans unearthed the foundations of both the Crusader church and the fourth century one. During the building of the fourth century Byzantine church the roof and sides of the cave where Jesus had prayed were apparently removed so that only the far wall remained and the ground on which Jesus had knelt. The high altar was placed against this cave wall, with the Rock of the Agony visible in the foreground. This arrangement has been retained in the present Basilica of the Agony, which was built by the Franciscans over the foundations of the Byzantine church. Before us lies the light-coloured limestone rock on which Jesus' tears and sweat of blood probably fell as He fought in the agony of death. The Basilica of the Agony, constructed between 1919 and 1924, is also called the Church of All Nations, since it was built with the funds donated by Roman Catholics of all nations. Behind the basilica a part of the original rocky landscape, probably as it was in Jesus' day, has been preserved.

In front of the basilica is a small flower garden, lovingly tended by the Franciscans, who acquired it in 1666. Here we find eight ancient olive trees, which are like a relic of the past, reminding us of Jesus' day. The olive tree does not die, but continues to live by producing new shoots. Thus it is possible that the trunk of the tree venerated as the Tree of the Agony dates from the time when Jesus wrestled in prayer here.

FROM THE HOLY BIBLE

The Lord left the city and went, as was his custom, to the Mount of Olives; and the disciples followed him. And when he came to the place he said to them, "Pray that you may not enter into temptation." And he withdrew from them about a stone's throw, and knelt down and prayed, "Father, if thou art willing, remove this cup from me; nevertheless not my will, but thine, be done." And there appeared to him an angel from heaven, strengthening him. And being in an agony he prayed more earnestly. "My Father, if this cannot pass unless I drink it, thy will be done." And his sweat became like great drops of blood falling down upon the ground. And when he rose from prayer, he came to the disciples and found them sleeping for sorrow, and he said to them, "Why do you sleep? Rise and pray that you may not enter into temptation."

cf. Luke 22 : 39-46 and Matthew 26 : 42

GETHSEMANE – A MESSAGE FOR US

That Jesus often went to the Garden of Gethsemane, whose name means "oil press", we know from the words in the Bible, "He came out, and went, as was his custom, to the Mount of Olives" (Luke 22 : 39). In this garden at the foot of the Mount of Olives He spent much time in prayer, conversing with His Father in the solitude of the night. And many a time the angels from heaven must have descended upon the Son of man, as Jesus had told His disciples, "You will see heaven opened, and the angels of God ascending and descending upon the Son of man" (John 1 : 51).

Gethsemane must have been an oasis for Jesus. Here under the olive trees Jesus could find a quiet spot after the long day with all its demands – the pressing crowd, the disputes of the Pharisees and their harassments. Indeed, Gethsemane was His refuge where He could be completely alone with His heavenly Father. No doubt He would retire to one of the many caves on the Mount of Olives, which were frequently used as places of prayer in those days.

On Maundy Thursday Jesus must have gone to the cave He knew so well. But this time as He began to pray, He did not find the Father waiting for Him, nor hosts of angels and an open heaven. Instead, He found the hordes of hell lined up with the prince of hell, Death himself, waiting to engage Him, the Son of man and Son of God, in a battle that would cost Him sweat of blood.

This time Gethsemane was to become a true Gethsemane for Jesus according to the meaning of its name "oil press". God Himself treads the oil press. He beats His Son, using the most horrible instrument of all – Satan, together with his hordes from hell. For our sakes God thrashes His only-begotten Son, although as sinful children we deserve to be disciplined and chastened and beaten by our heavenly Father. Indeed, the Father delivers Jesus into the power of Satan, who appears in this hour in his mightiest and most terrible form as the prince of death, "who has the power of death" (Hebrews 2 : 14).

And now at this site began the most dreadful and yet the most crucial battle that the world has ever seen. Only once before had there been a similar occasion – and that was in the Garden of Eden when Satan entered a battle with the first two human beings. But that time he did not have to exert himself. Though it was a matter of life and death for the entire human race, the incredible occurred – Adam and Eve showed hardly any sign of resistance and therefore they had no need to sweat blood. However, their unwillingness to put up a struggle in the face of this assault of the enemy proved disastrous – a fatal defeat was inevitable. From that time on Death reigned over mankind and no one could save the human race from his clutches.

Now the time had come when Jesus, who is the very essence of life, had to confront the prince of death, who had assembled all the forces of his kingdom, the entire host of evil spirits. In this crucial hour, would Jesus in His human frailty abandon the struggle as Adam and Eve once did? Would the extreme pressure of His diabolical enemies drive Him to capitulate? Satan staged three major attacks to make the Son of God abandon the fight, so that he, Satan, could conquer Him.

However, Jesus took up Satan's challenge and entered this terrible battle with hell, Death and sin. He struggled with Satan in mortal terror at the Rock of the Agony, from which the Gethsemane Basilica takes its name. He fought for us to the utmost, even sweating blood. He fought on behalf of those who were once unwilling to fight the enemy, since they treated sin so lightly.

Why was this terrible struggle raging between heaven and hell? Satan's objective was to force a word from the lips of Jesus such as Adam and Eve once uttered – a word of mistrust, of doubt about the love of God, of rebellion against His will. But every attack of the enemy had the opposite effect. Each time Jesus replied, "My Father". "My Father, if it be possible, let this cup pass from me; nevertheless, not as I will, but as thou wilt."

"My Father", said Jesus at a time when in His heart He could no longer understand God and could have lost

65

confidence in Him. Satan must have suggested everything possible to Him, using the same tactics he used with the first two human beings – "Did God say ...?" Now that the hand of Death reached out to take Jesus, did it not seem as though His whole act of redemption would be ruined, since He would be prevented from dying on the Cross in expiation for the sins of man? Yet in this mighty battle Jesus uttered two words that put Satan to flight. In the throes of deepest agony and inner conflict Jesus expressed His trust in the love of God. "My Father", He said, and with these powerful words, which were like a mighty sword thrust, Jesus overcame Satan.

The words "My Father" must have echoed throughout the regions of hell, making the fiendish spirits tremble with fright, for it was the signal of their defeat. Reverberating a thousand times over throughout the heavens, these words must have caused the angels to fall down in worship and consoled the heart of the Father, who must have been moved to say again, "Thou art My beloved Son, with whom I am well pleased." In this agonizing hour when the enemy oppressed Him, Jesus not only fought to the point of shedding blood, but He fought with the right weapon – loving trust in the love of God.

Truly, God did not tread the oil press in Gethsemane in vain. He aimed blow after blow at His Son, using many different instruments until His Son lay on the ground, tortured and sorely wounded in body, soul and spirit. Now the juice could be squeezed from the fruit in the oil press. Streams of blessing flowed forth into all the world and continue to flow. Weak and sinful people are able to overcome in their temptations and struggles with Satan by following Jesus' example and fighting to the point of shedding blood when Satan attacks. In hours of combat they are able to repeat Jesus' words, "My Father, Thy will be done." They can say, "My Father, I do not understand Thee, but I trust Thee."

Today Jesus is waiting for such disciples and warriors as the fruit of His battle and agony in Gethsemane, for when we fight like this during hours of temptation, we shall emerge as victors to the glory of Jesus.

PRAYER IN THE BASILICA OF THE AGONY

Dear Lord Jesus,

I thank You for undergoing such a terrible night of temptation and for grappling with the powers of hell in a mortal combat that cost You tears and sweat of blood. I thank You for suffering this agony out of love for us. I thank You for overcoming in temptation by saying, "Yes, Father". Lord, I worship You for humbling Yourself beneath the will of God when You were in utter darkness and probably no longer able to understand the Father.

At this holy place of Your Agony, accept my life as a token of my gratitude for Your immeasurable suffering, accept my dedication to say "Yes, Father" at all times. I want to humble myself under the mighty hand of God when He chastens me. When I no longer understand Him, I want to trust in His fatherly love. In this way let me overcome in my trials and temptations. Grant that I may one day be crowned as victor to Your joy and be a reward for Your Agony in Gethsemane, having resisted the adversary and sin to the point of bloodshed as a true follower of Yours.

Amen.

THE WAY TO VICTORY IN TEMPTATION IS

to pay no heed to temptation.
to trust in God's love, even when we do not understand Him.
to submit humbly to God's incomprehensible leadings.
to acknowledge that God's thoughts are higher than ours.
not to seek to understand God with our fallen intellect.
to honour God's commandments and His holy will.
to obey God absolutely, seeking nothing but His will.
to cling to His promises.
to believe that God is Yea and Amen and keeps His promises.
to hope against hope and to be steadfast in faith to the end.
to be able to wait for God to act, since His timing is always
perfect.
to believe that God's plans are always marvellous.
to trust implicitly that God is Love and only has the very
best intentions for His child.
to remember that temptation brings forth glory.

Gethsemane! Who Hears His Pleading

9. 9. 8. 8. 7.

Gethsem-ane! Who hears His pleading,/ His
fearful crying and entreating? / The Son of
God in anguished fear/With none to sol-ace
Him is here./ He is alone, for-sak-en.

Gethsemane! Who notes His yearning,
Who sees Him to His friends now turning,
That He may all His grief impart,
And they may cheer, console His heart?
Alas! His friends are sleeping.

Gethsemane! Who sees Him wrestling,
With evil pow'rs around Him pressing,
Tormenting Him with all their might?
And in His soul He sees no light,
By God and man forsaken!

Gethsemane! Where Christ so suffered,
My praise a thousandfold be offered.
For me Christ all this pain endured,
Freedom from death and hell secured.
How can I ever thank Him!

Well-spring of Joy 53

✝

My Jesus, here will I kneel beside You
At this rock of Your fear and agony.
Out of love will I stay with You
When You lead me through the dark valley.
I will stay by You. I will endure to the end with
    You,
Prepared to battle through the darkest night
Until You lead me home to dwell with You,
To live in glory and eternal light.

Highest Praises, Love and Honour

8. 8. 7. D.

Highest praises, love and honour/ Be to Thee,
our Lord and Saviour,/ for Thy lips "Yes, Father" say. /
Though the chalice He is off'ring/ Bringeth pain, disgrace
and suff'ring,/ Thou dost pray, "Thy will be done."

Jesus, here I long to praise Thee
And my highest homage bring Thee,
Lying at Thy feet in love.
Should not I, a sinner, humbly
Bow before Thee and obey Thee,
Fully yielding to Thy will?

✝

With His prayer, "Yes, Father!", the total surrender of His
will, Jesus triumphed in the darkest night of temptation.
Thus He showed us that by consenting to the will of God
in obedience, we too shall be led out of the darkness into the
light of victory.

THE CAVE OF BETRAYAL
(also known as The Grotto of Gethsemane)

THE HISTORICAL ASPECT

This important station along Jesus' pathway of sorrow is mentioned in ancient reports. From the historian Eusebius we learn
that ca. A.D. 330 the place at the foot of the Mount of Olives
where Jesus suffered His Agony and was betrayed was still very
present in the minds of the people of Jerusalem. And the Pilgrim
of Bordeaux (ca. 333), from whom we have the earliest pilgrim
report extant, describes the same cave that is still pointed out
today as the site of the Betrayal. In the fourth century the name
"Gethsemane" was applied only to this cave where both the
Agony and the Betrayal were commemorated. Later, ca. A.D. 385,
a magnificent church was erected a short distance south of the
cave to commemorate the Agony (see chapter on Gethsemane),
whereas the Betrayal and Arrest of Jesus continued to be commemorated at this cave. Only when the church was destroyed,
did the cave temporarily resume its former role for the commemoration of the Agony as well. From the description given by
the nun Etheria about the year 385 we can see how vivid the
memory of Jesus' Arrest here was for the people of Jerusalem.
As the relevant passages from the Gospel narrative were read
aloud at this site during the Maundy Thursday procession, the
crowd would burst into tears, lamenting and weeping loud enough
to be heard in the city.

The tradition that Jesus was arrested before the Cave of
Betrayal continued without interruption, so that the Crusaders
accepted it without question, but the tradition that the cave was
also the place where the Apostles slept did not come into being
until later. Before the time of the Crusaders no definite site had
been determined. However, we know that in the twelfth century
the cave was regarded as the place where the three Apostles
slept, for in 1102 the English pilgrim Saewulf wrote that "here
in Gethsemane is a place of prayer where the Lord left Peter,
James and John". In his day the grotto was considered the place
where the three Apostles slept. Later the other eight Apostles
were thought to have been there also. Consequently, it is difficult
to ascertain the exact place where the three Apostles slept. At
one time tradition — no doubt incorrectly — transferred the
site of the Last Supper to this cave, where tables and benches
made out of stone could be seen. It is uncertain whether a church
was ever built over the cave, although we could draw this con-
clusion from some ancient reports. Today the cave has been

turned into a chapel and, unlike the cave in the Gethsemane Basilica of the Agony, the natural roof has been retained, so that the bare rock still forms the roof of the chapel. It is under the guardianship of the Franciscans.

In order to reach the Cave of Betrayal, we cross the sunken courtyard of Mary's Tomb, an ancient sanctuary, which has commemorated the burial place of the Mother Mary since the fifth century.

FROM THE HOLY BIBLE

And Jesus came the third time, and said to his disciples, "Are you still sleeping and taking your rest? It is enough; the hour has come; the Son of man is betrayed into the hands of sinners. Rise, let us be going; see, my betrayer is at hand." Now Judas, who betrayed him, also knew the place; for Jesus often met there with his disciples. So Judas, procuring a band of soldiers and some officers from the chief priests and the Pharisees, went there with lanterns and torches and weapons. And when he came, he went up to Jesus at once, and said, "Master!" And he kissed him. And they laid hands on him and seized him. And the disciples all forsook him, and fled.   cf. Mark 14 : 41-50 and John 18 : 2 f.

THE CAVE OF BETRAYAL –
A MESSAGE FOR US

That the Cave of Betrayal is also known as the place where the Apostles slept and as the site of the Arrest has a deep meaning. Different events are interwoven here, thus helping us to see the true significance of what happened. No one event could have taken place apart from the other. Jesus could only be arrested, because Judas, one of the Twelve, had turned traitor. Again, at the Arrest Jesus' grief would not have been so great if His disciples had not disappointed Him bitterly by sleeping while He fought His hardest battle.

In Gethsemane they had the chance for once to perform a service for their Lord. But Jesus was abandoned by the disciples – the very ones who should have stood by Him in

73

His deepest distress, who could have consoled Him in this hour of extreme anguish by their readiness to place themselves at His disposal and to watch and pray with Him.

Their inability and failure to suffer with Jesus and stand by His side in this crucial hour had a special reason. Previously the disciples did not wish to hear anything about the cross and suffering, and once Peter, hearing Jesus speak about His Passion, even cried out, "God forbid, Lord! This shall never happen to you" (Matthew 16 : 22). Because of their attitude the disciples failed to recognize Jesus beforehand as the Lamb of God, although John the Baptist had called Him by this name. They did not wish to face the fact that Jesus had to enter death on account of our sins and therefore go the way of the Lamb, of sacrifice and suffering, a pathway that would end in defeat and not in victory – at least at first. Consequently, they could not understand Him when they saw Him in weakness and temptation in Gethsemane. They lost their confidence in Him just as He had warned them in advance, for they had wanted to see Him only as the all-powerful Messiah, who would establish the Kingdom of God on earth and secure honours for them.

Instead of suffering and lowliness they desired recognition and honour. Instead of giving themselves willingly to suffering, and losing their lives and all that made life worthwhile for them, they wanted to save their lives. This impulse was so strong in them that Jesus' words, "If any man would come after Me, let him take up his cross", left them unmoved. They did not take them to heart, since this way seemed too hard and therefore impossible to them.

This could be the only explanation why the disciples were so apathetic and unfeeling in Jesus' hour of suffering and fell asleep. It was inevitable that the moment Jesus was arrested and the cross loomed before them they fled in all directions. But in doing so, they made the Arrest even more disgraceful for Jesus. Abandoned, without a single disciple to acknowledge Him, Jesus stood before the guards and the Pharisees, as though He were not even worthy of His disciples' loyalty. What grief the disciples caused Jesus with their reluctance to suffer!

The cave where the Apostles slept, the site of the Betrayal and Arrest of Jesus, is a warning to us. It shows us the frightening outcome of our fear of the cross. It shows us that our faith in Jesus is only genuine when we take Him into our hearts as the Man of Sorrows and prove that we belong to Him by surrendering our lives and following in His footsteps. Indeed, this place tells us that we only love Jesus in truth when we take His words as binding for our lives. "Whoever does not bear his own cross and come after Me, cannot be My disciple."

How important it is that in our everyday lives we practise taking up our cross, accepting it from God's hand – whether it be the cross of humiliation, insults, injustice, contempt, disappointments or the loss of material goods. It is vital that we humble ourselves beneath the hand of God in the knowledge that the blessing of the cross will then be poured out upon us. In Judas' case we can see what the ultimate result is when we crave for honour and wealth under a pious guise, and refuse to follow Jesus' pathway, the path of poverty and lowliness. In the end this attitude made Judas turn traitor. And if we take such an attitude, we too shall fail miserably in times of severe testing, either deserting Jesus or betraying Him.

In the hour of Gethsemane long ago the disciples did not yet know Jesus as the Prince of Victory, who rose from the grave. But we know Him as the risen Lord. We know that suffering is turned into glory, disgrace into honour, tears into laughter. Indeed, we know that whoever loses his life for Jesus' sake will gain far, far more in return even in this lifetime. Consequently, Jesus is waiting today for disciples who will not disappoint Him and cause Him immeasurable grief by forsaking Him, but who will follow Him on the way of the cross and lose their lives day by day. This is what Jesus expects of us, and rightly so. In practice this discipleship entails following Him especially when His leadings run counter to our wishes and desires. Then when the hour of testing comes, we shall prove ourselves as true disciples, who stand by Him no matter what the cost – prepared, if necessary, to go with Him into imprisonment and death.

✝

Whoever commits himself to the Lord ever anew and daily practises losing his life will be faithful to Jesus in the hour of testing and able to give his life for Him.

O Jesus, Lonely While Men Sleep

8. 8. 7. 7.

O Jesus, lonely while men sleep,/ For none with you their watch will keep./ You are a-lone, for-sak-en;/ This lonely path You've tak—en.

Abandonment the path You tread,
To loneliness Your soul is wed.
You are alone, forsaken;
This lonely path You've taken.

You knock, You plead and You implore;
Your friends go with You now no more.
You are alone, forsaken;
This lonely path You've taken.

Foreboding sore burns in Your heart.
Will none in pity take Your part?
That You no more be lonely,
We'll take with You this pathway.

Well-spring of Joy 51

☩

Judas considered Jesus only worth thirty pieces of silver;
the other disciples esteemed Him so little that they forsook
Him at His Arrest. Today Jesus is waiting for disciples who
love Him so dearly that they will follow Him whatever the
cost.

☩

Here You were taken prisoner,
O dearest Lord,
Bound with ropes,
Deprived of Your honour.
Here You let Yourself be bound,
O my King and my God;
Surrendering Your freedom,
You submitted to those who led You to death.

Here let us worship the Lord of the universe,
Who chose to be bound
For the sake of man, whom He created,
Paying the ransom to set him free.

The Cave of Betrayal, February 6, 1961

PRAYER IN THE CAVE OF BETRAYAL

Dear Lord Jesus,

We humble ourselves before You, because it was Your disciples who betrayed and forsook You at the hour of Your Arrest, thus causing You even more sorrow in Your bitter Passion. And we, who long to be Your disciples today, are no different. Time and again we treat You in the same way when You lovingly beseech us to accompany You along the way of the cross. Forgive us our reluctance to take up the cross, for this brings You immeasurable grief, today as long ago, and it so often causes us to forsake and betray You in the hour of testing.

Jesus, I want to endure with You now; I want to accompany You and never leave You all alone again. So I commit myself to accept willingly the small hardships and crosses that You give me in everyday life. Help me to renew this dedication daily, that I may gain practice in suffering and be strong and faithful in the hour of testing as Your true disciple. May I be found at Your side at all times, even in affliction, imprisonment and death.

Amen.

In their fear of the cross Jesus' disciples slept through the holiest of all hours when God's Son yearned to reveal to them the deep pain and agony in His heart. Only those who open their hearts to suffering can understand Jesus' heart.

THE VALLEY OF KIDRON

In visiting the Mount of Olives, we have already entered the realm of Jesus' Passion. As we now trace the footsteps of our betrayed and arrested Lord on the eve before His death, we come to the Valley of Kidron. Jesus was led through this valley by the band of guards and the Pharisees on the way to the palace of Annas and Caiaphas. Leaving the Cave of Betrayal, we take the broad Jericho Road and follow it for about 100 m. At this point a road forks off to the right, making a sharp descent into the Kidron Valley (see sketch-map).

The valley begins north of the Old City. First it runs to the southeast and then makes a slight bend, continuing in a southerly direction parallel to the eastern city wall. Since there is no spring feeding the Kidron, the valley is dry for the greater part of the year; only in the rainy season does water pour down the steep valley sides and run through the Judean Desert towards the Dead Sea. Owing to the accumulation of debris from the Temple wall, which was destroyed several times, the level of the river bed has been raised considerably since the time of Jesus. Nevertheless the narrow, stony valley paths remind us of the way taken by Jesus as a captive.

Since the fourth century the section of the valley that separates the city from the Mount of Olives has also been called the Valley of Jehoshaphat in reference to Joel 3 : 2. Thus this valley of Jesus' suffering, which beheld Him in His deepest humiliation, has yet another significance. According to Joel 3 Jesus will appear here to judge the Antichristian world. Tradition interprets this passage from the Bible by saying that the Valley of Jehoshaphat will be the site of the Last Judgment. In the course of time many Jews as well as Christians and Moslems have let themselves be buried here, since they desired to be at hand when the angels sound the trumpets. The Jewish graves are on the western slope of the Mount of Olives, and on the opposite slope are the Moslem ones just below the Temple Site. Above all, many Jews from Eastern Europe immigrated to Jerusalem, often at a very advanced age, so as to be buried here, for they held fast to the promise in Joel 2 : 32 made in reference to this place, "All who call upon the name of the Lord [here] shall be delivered".

The slope of the Mount of Olives is strewn with tens of thousands of Jewish graves. The sight of this vast cemetery turns our thoughts to the future. An unusual atmosphere of expectancy seems to rest here, giving the valley a deeper dimension, especially when we contemplate the events that are to take place here.

On the left, opposite the high southeast corner of the city wall called the Temple Pinnacle, lies the Pillar of Absalom, which is easily identified by its narrow cone. Nearby in the rock cliffs are what are known as the tombs of James, Zechariah and Jehoshaphat, which date from 100 or 200 B.C. Since they stood there on the side of the road even in Jesus' time, they probably witnessed the sad procession that led Jesus off on the night of the Arrest.

Both sides of the valley are covered with rocks and stones. We catch sight of the village of Silwan lying on the slope of the Mount of Offence, and after the road curves, we can pick out the village Ophel to the right of the valley on the southern spur of the Temple Mount. High above the rooftops the church St. Peter in Gallicantu (cock crow) can be seen on the eastern slope of Mount Zion, towering into the sky.

By now the road has reached the bed of the valley. To the right are two school buildings and behind them are steps leading down to the Gihon Spring, also known as the Fountain of the Virgin, which was the only spring near ancient Jerusalem. Here various Old Testament scenes come alive for us. It was from here that David captured Jerusalem when Joab, his captain, went up the "water shaft", an underground waterway leading into the city (2 Samuel 5 : 8). This was also where Solomon was anointed king (1 Kings 1 : 38 f.). The view now opens out to the south and in front of us lies the Mount of Evil Counsel, with its tree-clad summit. The name is derived from the tradition that here, in his country house, Caiaphas is said to have given the counsel that Jesus must be put to death (John 11 : 47-53).

At the bottom of the valley, on the left-hand side of the road, the landscape is a deep, rich green. This is what is known as the Garden of the King, which is irrigated by a stream flowing from the Pool of Siloam. Here there is a dense grove of fig trees; the grass is lush and the vegetables are profuse. Soon we pass by the rushing water that comes from the Pool of Siloam, which lies to the right of the road. We follow the Kidron Valley a little farther south and from there we have a view of another site known to us from the Passion narrative. A steep-sided rocky ravine runs into the Kidron Valley from the west. It is the beginning of the Valley of Hinnom. Above it on the slope we see Haceldama, the Field of Blood (Matthew 27 : 7 f.; Acts 1 : 18 f.), which was a cemetery for pilgrims in medieval times. Today a Greek Orthodox convent marks the site and a little farther to

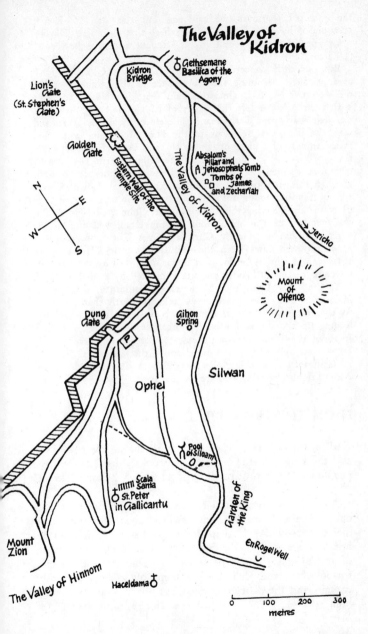

The Valley of Kidron

Lion's Gate (St. Stephen's Gate)

Golden Gate

Kidron Bridge

Gethsemane Basilica of the Agony

Eastern Wall of the Temple Site

The Valley of Kidron

Absalom's Pillar and Jehosophat's Tomb
Tombs of James and Zechariah

→ Jericho

N E W S

Dung Gate

P

Gihon Spring

Mount of Offence

Ophel

Silwan

Pool of Siloam

Scala Santa
St. Peter in Gallicantu

Garden of the King

Mount Zion

En Rogel Well

The Valley of Hinnom

Haceldama

0   100   200   300
metres

81

the left, off the road we can pick out the well En Rogel, surrounded by some houses. It was here that Adonijah, David's son, appealed to the people in his attempt to usurp the throne (1 Kings 1 : 9).

But our chief concern is to follow the route taken by Jesus as a prisoner. Assuming that the palace of the High Priest lay on Mount Zion, it is almost certain that the soldiers together with their prisoner left the Valley of Kidron at an earlier point on their way from Gethsemane. Therefore, let us also turn and take the path that leads us to the Pool of Siloam, which lies in the middle of a piece of land with trees. As in Hezekiah's day the pool is still connected with the Gihon Spring by a subterranean channel (2 Kings 20 : 20), and it is possible to walk through this ancient underground waterway. The Pool of Siloam will be familiar to us, for this is where Jesus sent a blind man to wash, after having ministered to him (John 9 : 7). No doubt, the memory of this miraculous healing established the site as a place of prayer in early Christian times. The first record of a basilica here dates from the mid fifth century. However, in the year 614 this Byzantine church was destroyed by the Persians, never to be rebuilt. Today the site is marked by a small mosque.

To reach the Church of St. Peter in Gallicantu, which commemorates Peter's repentance, we take the path that forks off to the left behind the mosque. It is a steep and stony path, leading up the slope of Mount Zion, past the houses of Ophel. In about 10 minutes we reach the motor road that comes from the Dung Gate and leads past a hotel above the Church of St. Peter in Gallicantu. The church lies in the park-like grounds of the Assumptionist Fathers, who are its guardians.

FROM THE HOLY BIBLE

And all the country wept aloud as all the people passed by, and the king [David] crossed the brook Kidron, and all the people passed on toward the wilderness.   2 Samuel 15 : 23

At that hour Jesus said to the crowds, "Have you come out as against a robber, with swords and clubs to capture me? Day after day I sat in the temple teaching, and you did not seize me. But all this has taken place, that the scriptures of the prophets might be fulfilled." Then all the disciples forsook him and fled. So the band of soldiers and their captain and the officers of the Jews seized Jesus and bound him.   Matthew 26 : 55 f. and John 18 : 12

My Saviour goes to suffer,
Belovèd Lamb of God.
O let me stay close by You
And share Your way, dear Lord.
Because of me You suffered
And for my sake You died.
Let me lament my sinning
And stay close by Your side.
O let me now go with You,
My dearest Lord and King;
Filled with contrition join You
In Your night of suffering.

THE VALLEY OF KIDRON –
A MESSAGE FOR US

Kidron Valley, a vale of tears, where King David wept as he crossed the Kidron Brook, prefiguring the one true King, Jesus Christ, who would pass through this valley on His way of suffering.

King David was followed by a weeping crowd of subjects, who strengthened and consoled him with their sympathy. But when Jesus, our Lord and King, Saviour of mankind, went through the Kidron Valley in the hour of deepest affliction, He was all alone. Not one of His disciples was in sight. Surrounded by guards, Jesus was led off under the mocking eyes of the scribes and Pharisees. King David took this path when he had to flee from his son Absalom, and the Son of God took the same path, persecuted by man, whom He had created – by His people, whom He loved. David went as a free man, but Jesus as a prisoner. With His hands bound like a criminal He was conducted through the Kidron Valley to His judges, like a beast led to the slaughter.

What must this procession have been like? The sharp stones of the narrow paths in the Kidron Valley must have bruised and cut Jesus' feet. Every step must have brought immeasurable agony to His utterly exhausted body, for, but a few hours earlier, He had struggled in mortal combat, sweating blood. Perhaps the words of Psalm 110:7, "He will drink from the brook by the way", were fulfilled that night and He was able to take a fleeting drink at the Gihon Spring.

Jesus, who has the might and power to bind others, to lead and govern them, voluntarily submitted to the wicked will of man, whom He created, letting Himself be bound in shackles, dragged along and yanked from side to side. Why? Because the sons of men, the scribes and Pharisees and many others, did not allow themselves to be bound by the good and omnipotent will of God, which Jesus proclaimed. Despite the power of Jesus' words we, like the men of long ago, refuse to accept the will of God time and again. Therefore, by His very life and example as a prisoner bound in chains, Jesus wished to impress upon us for evermore His image of humble submission. In this way Jesus beseeches us even more earnestly. "Let yourselves be bound to the will of God and follow His guidance. Accept His sovereignty by looking at Me, the Prisoner, and seeing how I submitted to the chains and fetters placed on Me by men, whom I created. Though I am their God, I let them do with Me according to their will. Should this not move you deeply and give you a change of heart, so that you surrender your wills to Me? Won't you give Me your hands, so that I can bind them and guide you, leading you even where you do not want to go? And when I lead you along hard paths, remember that they are the very best ones, for they have been planned by the wise and loving heart of My Father. Such pathways lead you to a wonderful destination, for they end in everlasting glory. By following them, you will be purified and prepared to live in My kingdom of eternal peace and joy, love and bliss."

Here in the Valley of Kidron let us hear the plea of our meek and silent Lord, bound in chains.

✝

Surrendering our will to God makes us strong, for then we are united with the living Lord, for whom nothing is impossible.

Whoever surrenders his will to God has made the best choice, for then he is subject to the will of Him who alone is wise and good, and he will be led along the very best path.

Love surrenders its wishes and desires to the beloved as its most precious gift. How could we withhold this gift from God when His Son let Himself be bound by the will of man and led along the path of suffering for love of us?

PRAYER IN THE VALLEY OF KIDRON

Dear Lord Jesus,

Thank You for taking this bitter path of suffering through the Valley of Kidron for our sakes. Lord, we thank You, for though You have power over all men and the shackles they impose, You let Your enemies bind You with fetters in order to free us from the fetters of our self-will. You see how bound I am to my own desires, wishes and opinions, repeatedly refusing to submit to Your will and the will of those whom You have placed in authority over me. Forgive me for always wanting to be free and able to decide for myself. Lord, deliver me from servitude to my sinful self-will, which is my ruin.

At this place I surrender my will and all my desires to You. From now on I want to be bound to You, Lord Jesus, and to Your divine will, which alone is wise and good, and I want to obey Your will in whatever form it comes to me through those whom You have set in authority over me. By faith in the power of Your redemption I want to be wholly obedient to Your will. Through Your bitter suffering here You won us this obedience. I praise You for setting me free from bondage to my sinful ego and my self-will and for binding me to You and Your will alone, that I may obey You out of love.

Amen.

Through Kidron Valley

10. 10.

Through Kidron Valley, Lord, You now go bound,
Where tears, distress and suf-fer-ing a-bound.

You go alone, for none dares with You go.
The angels weep, their Maker's fate to know.

Your path of grief and torture now begins,
Which leads to death to free us from our sins.

'Tis love alone that drives You on this way,
And so no grief or pain can You dismay.

Humbly, submissively, You tread this way,
As though for Your own sins, Lord,
    You must pay.

Who ever thanks You for this, dearest Lord?
Accept my ardent love for You outpoured.

Jesus, in Fetters Bound

6. 6. 7. D.

Jesus, in fetters bound, / Why jostled thus a-round? / Man always wants to be free, / Free e'en to dis-o-bey / What-ever God may say, / All fett'ring bonds tears a-way.

Jesus now shows to me,
Though bound we can be free,
Christ pioneering the way.
All that His Father willed
Jesus in love fulfilled
To set us free from our chains.

Bound as a lamb He's led,
Crucified in our stead.
Watch how He goes to His death.
Lo, God in fetters see;
He waits for those who'll be
Willing to wear chains like Him.

Well-spring of Joy 57

ST. PETER IN GALLICANTU

This place commemorating Peter's repentance lies on the eastern slope of Mount Zion. Apart from taking the path through the Valley of Kidron, we can reach St. Peter in Gallicantu directly from the Old City, by passing through the Dung Gate in the southern end of the city wall. Bearing south, we follow the asphalt road, which leads to the property of the Assumptionist Fathers where many pines and cypress, olive and pepper trees grow in park-like grounds. The road continues to the hotel just above the church. But before that a footpath forks off to the left through the park. Since we wish to remember Jesus' way of sorrows on the eve of His Passion, we take this path to the church. It first leads us to the excavated steps called the Scala Santa (the Holy Stairs), which Jesus must almost certainly have trodden when He was led as a prisoner to the palace of Caiaphas. According to archaeological reports the stairs were in existence in Jesus' day, probably dating from an even earlier period. Close by the church and underneath it further excavations can be seen.

Even if there is no proof that Jesus was imprisoned here, the dungeon that lies deep beneath the church nevertheless helps us to visualize Jesus' imprisonment after the trial before Annas and Caiaphas when He spent the rest of the night in deep suffering.

The church is open Monday to Saturday from 8:30 a.m. till noon and 2 p.m. — 5:30 p.m.

THE HISTORICAL ASPECT

The church commemorating Peter's repentance after his denial brings to life the events of Maundy Thursday night when Jesus was put on trial before Caiaphas. The house of Caiaphas lay on Mount Zion according to ancient pilgrim reports such as the account given by the Pilgrim of Bordeaux in 333. St. Cyril, Bishop of Jerusalem in 348, also refers to this place saying that it was known to all. On the ruins of the house of Caiaphas the Empress Eudoxia is said to have had a church built in about 460 to commemorate the Apostle's denial and repentance.

Reports from the sixth to the ninth century confirm that a basilica was built on the site of Caiaphas' house in memory of the Apostle Peter. Probably it was destroyed by the Persians in 614, but in 630 it reappears in the liturgical calendar of Jerusalem as part of the Maundy Thursday procession to the places where Jesus suffered. The calendar relates that the procession also went to "St. Peter's where the house of Caiaphas formerly stood".

As to the subsequent history of this holy place and its exact location, the ancient reports give no clear information, and accordingly different opinions have arisen. In the seventh century various reports mention a church that commemorated Peter's tears of repentance but not his denial. This church is considered by the guardians of the present Church of St. Peter in Gallicantu to be the church that was rebuilt after the Persian destruction on the site of Caiaphas' house and renamed the Church of Repentance. In the tenth century it was destroyed again, but later rebuilt by the Crusaders. The English pilgrim Saewulf mentions this church in 1102, for the first time giving it the additional name Gallicantu (cock crow). According to this version the Crusader church was erected on the site of the ancient basilica and perpetuated the memory of the Apostle's repentance, but no longer that of his denial. In 1330 this church was destroyed.

However, others, such as Clemens Kopp in *Stätten des Evangeliums,* consider that the Church of Repentance was not built on the site of Caiaphas' house, but was a different holy place that came into recognition in the seventh century. They believe that after the place of repentance was separated from the place of the denial, it was shifted to the southeastern slope of Mount Zion where the present church St. Peter in Gallicantu stands. In their opinion the house of Caiaphas, in whose courtyard the denial took place, as well as the ancient St. Peter's basilica built on its site stood on Mount Zion proper. They suggest that the ruins inside an Armenian monastery, north of the Upper Room, are the remains of these buildings.

The Church of St. Peter in Gallicantu was rebuilt in 1931 by the Assumptionist Fathers, who are its guardians to this day. In 1888 when they began excavating here, they discovered the Scala Santa, an ancient stone stairway. Tombs and many other vestiges of ancient Jewish and Christian times also came to light.

FROM THE HOLY BIBLE

Then they seized Jesus and led him away, bringing him into
the high priest's house. Peter followed at a distance; and
when they had kindled a fire in the middle of the courtyard
and sat down together, Peter sat among them. Then a maid,
seeing him as he sat in the light and gazing at him, said,
"This man also was with him." But he denied it, saying,
"Woman, I do not know him." And a little later some one
else saw him and said, "You also are one of them." But
Peter said, "Man, I am not." And after an interval of about
an hour still another insisted, saying, "Certainly this man
also was with him; for he is a Galilean." But Peter said,
"Man, I do not know what you are saying." And immediately, while he was still speaking, the cock crowed. And
the Lord turned and looked at Peter. And Peter remembered
the word of the Lord, how he had said to him, "Before
the cock crows today, you will deny me three times." And
he went out and wept bitterly.   cf. Luke 22 : 54-62

ST. PETER IN GALLICANTU –
A MESSAGE FOR US

That Peter should weep tears of repentance here on the slope
of Mount Zion has a deep significance. It was probably not
far from this spot that Peter had sworn but a few hours
earlier, "Though they all fall away because of you, I will
never fall away" (Matthew 26 : 33). After the Last Supper
when Peter, our Lord and the other ten disciples were descending Mount Zion and passing through the Kidron Valley
to Gethsemane, these words might have been spoken on the
way. Jesus warned them about the night, telling them that
He, the Shepherd, would be struck and that His sheep instead
of gathering round Him would be scattered in all directions.
But Peter, in spite of the Lord's personal warning to him,
insisted again, "Even if I must die with you, I will not deny
you."

It was a few hours later. Jesus had been arrested and Peter
had denied his Master. In his deep grief Peter may well have

91

hurried away to this spot in order to be alone. Looking down from the hill upon the path leading to the Valley of Kidron, he suddenly recalls the conversation on the way to Gethsemane and is deeply shocked now that his Master's gaze had fallen upon him. It was a gaze of inexpressible sadness, so full of sorrow and yet so loving. A gaze that could come only from Jesus' heart of love.

Can Peter really grasp what has happened? Was he really the same person who had stood at the side of his Master about six hours earlier down below in the Kidron Valley and boldly declared that he would never deny Him? In the meantime the terrible has occurred. Peter has denied his Lord. He has denied the One he loves above all, for whom he had left his family and job, and to whom he had dedicated his whole life. In that hour when for once he could have demonstrated his loyalty to his beloved Master, Peter not only failed miserably, but he denied his Lord. Yet is it not at such times of dire distress that we should prove our loyalty? And to think that he had fled in Gethsemane instead of letting himself be bound with his Lord! Peter now looks down at the paths along which his Lord and Master had been led to His judges only a few hours earlier by a jeering mob of guards. He had not been at Jesus' side. He had not even been in sight, but had kept a safe distance, watching the procession from afar.

Later he stood outside in the courtyard while his Master faced His judges and bore all the wicked and unjust accusations like a lamb. Not one of the judges came to Peter, only an insignificant maid, who merely stated that he had been with the accused, and pronounced, so to speak, a verdict on him. But Peter, who did not receive an unfair judgment such as his Master had to bear, could not even accept a true word. Though it was said in a tone of reproach and scornful amazement, it was the truth. Alas, Peter rejected it, and in doing so committed a serious crime – he denied his Lord, whom he loved so dearly. He denied Jesus – now at a time when He was disgraced, forsaken by all, and undergoing immeasurable suffering.

His Master was able to accept the false accusations, because He was willing to bear the Cross. In His deep humility He accepted the sentence pronounced upon Him, thus consenting to the Crucifixion. But he, Peter, who deserved to be condemned as a sinner, did not want the cross. To suffer disgrace and persecution with his Master was too hard for Peter and therefore he denied all knowledge of the Lord, rejecting the condemnation that was behind the maid's words. Oh, how wretched he is! He has forsaken and denied his beloved Lord. There on the slope of Mount Zion brave Peter breaks down and weeps bitterly.

This slope had seen much of the disciples' sin when Jesus walked along its paths alone, deserted by His own, who did not want to follow Him into humiliation, disgrace and captivity. But now it also witnessed a disciple's tears of repentance over his sin, tears that gave rise to new life. Out of these tears was born a love stronger than ever before, love that had the power to remain faithful even unto death for the sake of the beloved Master as Peter later proved.

Jesus was still standing before His judges in the house of Caiaphas; the hardest part of His path of sorrows was yet to come. But at that moment He received strengthening and consolation from the very person who had denied Him. Jesus, who sees and knows all things, probably saw Peter from afar weeping in repentance, and these tears of repentance comforted and strengthened Jesus for the hard way that lay ahead. A person who had sinned grievously against Jesus now wept bitterly in contrition, thus becoming a true follower of Jesus, loving Him with all his heart. Jesus' Passion, the suffering He underwent in atonement for our sins, had not been in vain.

At this site commemorating Peter's tears of repentance, Jesus, who still suffers and wrestles on behalf of mankind, waits today for those who will respond to His suffering by weeping bitterly over their sins, not only once, but ever anew. He waits for those who will weep out of genuine repentance, which does not lead to death but to life and love, for they weep over what they have done to Jesus and at the same time reach out in faith to grasp His forgiving love. How precious are such tears of repentance!

PRAYER AT ST. PETER IN GALLICANTU

Our Lord Jesus,

We thank You for the words You spoke at the Arrest, "I am he." With these words You surrendered Yourself to the guards and to Your judges as though You were the wanted man, the guilty one. This You did, so that Your disciples could go free. You did not vindicate Yourself and Your innocence. Instead You shielded us and covered our guilt.

Lord Jesus, we worship You and humbly confess that we have so often been like Peter, who acted completely differently from You, denying his Master to protect himself and refusing to accept even a maid's verdict.

Lord, You gave Peter the grace to repent and weep bitterly over his sin. Grant me also the grace of repentance for every time I have thought or said, "I am not the one." Forgive me, for in doing so, I protected and shielded myself from all reproach, but denied You. Let me always accept Your verdict upon me, for it is right; help me to accept it even when it comes to me through others who are Your instruments. Grant me like Peter the grace of repentance. Grant me a broken and contrite heart, convicted of sin, that I may love You more than ever and follow You on the way of the cross to the end.

Amen.

O Holy Ghost, Please Give to Me

8. 8. 7. D.

O Holy Ghost, please give to me / A penitent humil-i-ty,/ The greatest of Your graces./ for
all my sins You will impart / Abundant sorrow
to my heart,/To make me tru-ly hum — ble.

O Holy Ghost, please make me see
My lukewarm heart's complacency,
And bring me to repentance.
Help me lament for all my sins,
The cause of my dear Saviour's pains,
Who all my guilt is bearing.

Come, Holy Ghost, I pray, to me,
That You my Advocate may be,
and plead my wordless longing.
You see, as hard as stone, my heart;
Repentance deep to me impart;
Help me to hate my sinning.

Spirit of penitence, I pray,
Give me another heart today,
A broken heart, most humble,
That will not hide, but make it plain,
My sin caused Jesus such great pain.
I mourn that I have grieved Him.

You are the One who shall impart
A truly contrite, lowly heart,
As promised by my Saviour.
Show me my sins and humble me,
That I by grace may pardoned be,
Restored to loving favour.

Well-spring of Joy 173

+

Jesus, once filled with sorrow because of Peter's sin, is now
gazing at us. He longs that we too may shed tears of
repentance over our sins. The more we weep in contrition
for having grieved Jesus, the more fervent our love for Him
will be.

I mourn about my sinning
That caused You, Lord, such pain.
It brought You grievous suff'ring;
I sinned and sinned again.
I'm only just beginning
My depths of sin to see,
And thank You for forgiving
A sinner such as me.

You have, O dearest Saviour,
In mercy looked on me.
You have to grace restored me
And now with joy I see
That You for me salvation
Have won on Calvary.
My thankful heart rejoices;
I am from sin set free!

Now to Your praise and glory
My life for You I live.
In mercy You forgave me;
So ardent love I give.
It is beyond man's thinking
That sin such gain could bring,
Such wondrous love me bringing;
Rejoice, my soul and sing!

Well-spring of Joy 170
Can also be sung to the melody,
"The Church's One Foundation"
7.6.7.6.D.

Jesus, My Dearest Lord

6. 4. 6. 6. 4. 8. 4.

Jesus, my dear-est Lord, look now on me, / That I may under-stand / What I have done to You, / Lord, look on me. / As once You did on Pe-ter gaze, / Lord, look on me.

Jesus, my dearest Lord,
Look now on me.
Lord, Your sad look has pow'r,
Can penitence impart,
Wholly transform
My sinful heart, make all things new.
Lord, look on me.

Jesus, my dearest Lord,
Look now on me,
That I, like Peter, too
May weep so bitterly,
Love You so much,
I never more Your love may grieve.
Lord, look on me.

Well-spring of Joy 168
St. Peter in Gallicantu
April 28, 1965

THE FORTRESS OF ANTONIA

(the sites of the Scourging, Crowning with Thorns,
Condemnation and the Laying On of the Cross)

After making our way through the Valley of Kidron, we now
trace the steps of our suffering Lord within the city wall. Starting
at the Lion's Gate (St. Stephen's Gate), we once more take
the road that passes by St. Anne's Church. This road is wider
than most streets in the Old City. After about 200 m. we come
to a narrow, overgrown arch. Here begins the Via Dolorosa, the
way of sorrows, the street in Jerusalem that we long to tread
more than any other. The Via Dolorosa leads first of all to
the site of the Fortress of Antonia, which in Jesus' day was
located northwest of the Temple premises. At first glance the
various buildings erected over the place are not suggestive of the
ancient fortress, but in them we find the sites commemorating
the Scourging, the Crowning with Thorns and the Condemnation.

Just beyond the archway, on the left-hand side of the street,
a ramp leads into the courtyard of El Omariyeh College, where
the processions to the Stations of the Cross begin (see chapter on
the Via Dolorosa). A chapel commemorating the Crowning with
Thorns, which could previously be reached via this courtyard, is
no longer accessible. Let us now cross the road to visit the
Chapel of Flagellation and the Chapel of Condemnation, both
of which lie within the Franciscan property, usually known as
the Convent of the Flagellation. The main entrance to the Franciscan property is just beside the arch. After passing through the
inner court with its flower garden, we turn right and come to
the Chapel of Flagellation, which lies to the east. As we tarry
here in silent contemplation, a huge crown of thorns over the
sanctuary helps us also to remember our Lord's suffering when
He was crowned with thorns. The Chapel of Condemnation,
which is on the left side of the courtyard, commemorates both
the Condemnation and the Laying On of the Cross. Part of the
ancient pavement of the Fortress of Antonia, called Lithostrotos,
which extends to the west, is visible here. In these chapels we
become very conscious of the suffering our Lord and Saviour
underwent when He was scourged, condemned and given the Cross
to bear.

In particular the building next door to the Franciscan Compound on the same side of the street speaks to us of Jesus'

sufferings. It is the Ecce Homo Basilica belonging to the Convent of the Sisters of Zion. The Ecce Homo Arch, which spans the street and extends into the basilica, derives its name from Pilate's words, "Behold the man." Actually, the arch was not built until the second century after Christ, but in the sixteenth century it was given this name, since the pavement stones on which Jesus is said to have stood when Pilate spoke these words were built into it.

Beneath the Convent of the Sisters of Zion we can see the excavated portion of the Lithostrotos. Our attention will be especially caught by the significant symbols of the Game of the King carved on the surface of the large flagstones. *(For additional information see The Historical Aspect.)*

We can find some more of the pavement beneath the adjoining building, a Greek Orthodox monastery, which bears the inscription "Prison of Christ" over its portal.

Times of opening:

Chapel of Flagellation (R.C.)	open all day
Chapel of Condemnation (R.C.)	will be opened upon request
Lithostrotos (R.C.)	8 a.m. till noon 2 p.m. — 6 p.m.
"Prison of Christ" (Greek Orthodox)	will be opened upon request

THE HISTORICAL ASPECT

According to the Gospels the site where Jesus was scourged, mocked, crowned with thorns and condemned was the Praetorium, the palace of the Roman governor. But where did Pilate reside when he condemned Jesus to death? Where was the pavement that heard the cry, "Crucify him"? Over the course of the centuries there have been various opinions. When Pilate came to Jerusalem, he usually took up residence in Herod's palace, for according to Roman custom the governor took over the royal residence of the former ruler. Herod's palace stood in the western part of the city, near the Jaffa Gate, where remains of its most imposing tower, the Tower of Phasael, can still be seen at the base of the tower that is now known as David's Tower. On the basis of various sources some scholars think that Jesus' trial before Pilate took place here; they conclude that the Lithostrotos

(The Pavement, John 19 : 13) lies buried beneath the debris in this part of the city. According to this version Jesus' way of sorrows began in Herod's palace.

However, Pilate also resided in the Fortress of Antonia, especially when there was a threat of an uprising in the Temple area. The Fortress of Antonia, a powerful citadel, was the military headquarters of the Romans here at the time of Jesus. Its southeast tower, almost 9 m. higher than the other towers, provided the Romans with a lookout over the entire Temple area, and a stairway led directly from the fortress into the Temple court. Since large crowds always came to the Temple in Jerusalem for the Feast of the Passover, the Roman procurator would have naturally been suspicious and have taken precautions in the event of an uprising. Thus we can well assume that Pilate was residing in the Fortress of Antonia at the time of Jesus' Passion.

This last version tallies with an old tradition from the early fourth century, which regarded this place as the beginning of Jesus' way of sorrows, the Via Dolorosa, although all memory of the fortress at this site had vanished by then. In A.D. 70 the Fortress of Antonia was completely destroyed and in the course of the centuries the place was built over; thus the location of the fortress was forgotten. But the tradition that here, in the Fortress of Antonia, Jesus was scourged, crowned with thorns, condemned to death and given the Cross was confirmed by excavations. In the latter half of the nineteenth century the foundations of the Fortress of Antonia were brought to light, and thus it was possible to reconstruct the plan of the vast fortress.

When in 1857 Father Ratisbonne, the founder of the order of the Sisters of Zion, began to build a convent for the Sisters beside the Ecce Homo Arch, portions of an ancient pavement were discovered. On the flagstones were found rough carvings of geometrical patterns. Among them was the symbol of a diadem surrounded by rays with the letter B (probably standing for "Basileus", the Greek word for "king"), all of which was part of the Game of the King, a popular pastime for Roman soldiers, as excavations in other Roman garrisons have also revealed. At this particular site the Game of the King may well have been associated with the cruel mockery and the Crowning with Thorns during Jesus' Passion. The pavement extends throughout the entire western part of the site of the Fortress of Antonia and probably formed the fortress' outer courtyard, to which the public had access.

While we tarry at these sites, we can hear the distant noise from the street and the penetrating call from the minarets. But louder still is the entreaty of these silent stones, challenging us to bring honour and glory to our Lord, who is so dishonoured.

FROM THE HOLY BIBLE

Then the whole company of them arose, and brought Jesus before Pilate, to the praetorium. And they began to accuse him. Pilate went out to the Jews and told them, "I find no crime in him. But you have a custom that I should release one man for you at the Passover; will you have me release for you the King of the Jews?" They cried out, "Not this man, but Barabbas!" Now Barabbas was a murderer.

Pilate addressed them once more, "Why, what evil has he done? I have found in him no crime deserving death; I will therefore chastise him and release him." But they were urgent, demanding with loud cries that he should be crucified. And their voices prevailed.

So when Pilate saw that he was gaining nothing, but rather that a riot was beginning, he took water and washed his hands before the crowd, saying, "I am innocent of this righteous man's blood; see to it yourselves." Then he released for them Barabbas, and took Jesus and scourged him.

Then the soldiers of the governor took Jesus into the praetorium, and they gathered the whole battalion before him. And they stripped him and put a scarlet robe upon him, and plaiting a crown of thorns they put it on his head, and put a reed in his right hand. And kneeling before him they mocked him, saying, "Hail, King of the Jews!" And they spat upon him, and took the reed and struck him on the head.

So Jesus came out, wearing the crown of thorns and the purple robe. Pilate said to them, "Behold the man! Take him yourselves and crucify him, for I find no crime in him." But the Jews cried out, "If you release this man, you are not Caesar's friend." When Pilate heard these words, he brought Jesus out and sat down on the judgment seat at a place called The Pavement. Now it was the day of Preparation for the Passover; it was about the sixth hour. They cried out, "Away with him, away with him, crucify him!" Then he handed Jesus over to be crucified.

cf. Matthew 27, Luke 23 and John 18 & 19

LITHOSTROTOS – A MESSAGE FOR US

Lithostrotos! At this site we remember how Jesus was mocked and crowned with thorns. Mute but eloquent the figures of the Game of the King, carved in the flagstones, take on a deep meaning as we now contemplate this event.

Simple, ordinary soldiers whiled away the time with the Game of the King, hoping to make some gain. Perhaps they also played it because of the desire to be great, which dwells in every human heart, the desire to be first, yes, even king. And since they were not permitted to be lords in real life, they tried to assume the role in their game.

Then Someone who really was a king was brought into their guardroom, perhaps here on the Lithostrotos. This was their Lord, the king of all nations and of the entire human race. But although they were so filled with ideas about kingship, they failed to recognize the one true King, who now stood in their presence. They included Him in their game and made Him a mock king, reducing Him to a figure of ridicule. They felt justified in taunting Him. Did He not call Himself King, but had neither realm nor subjects? Had not His own people rejected Him? It could only be madness if He still called Himself King.

They scoffed at Jesus instead of scoffing at themselves and their deep-rooted desire for greatness, which so preoccupied them. Their "greatness" was entirely unfounded and therefore their pretentious behaviour was absurd. These soldiers, like all of us, were wretched human beings with nothing kingly about them. Even so they mocked this king, whom they considered a sorry figure, for blindness about themselves made them blind to Jesus.

Yet, like Pilate and the others who had seen Jesus in His immeasurable suffering, they could have realized that Someone completely different had come to them. They could have recognized His true worth and nobility. Certainly, some dimly perceived who Jesus was, but this incited them all the more to degrade our Lord so as to destroy this nobility. Today as long ago we are not content until we have reduced Jesus to a figure of ridicule and folly before our eyes. Then we have proven that He is not lord and king and that He has no right to rule over us. Then we do not need to submit to Him or surrender our will and personal greatness to Him.

Yet Jesus, who is King of kings freely endured such derision and contempt. He humbled Himself before man, whom He had created, and like a lamb He patiently suffered His royal honour and dignity to be dragged in the dust. He permitted His divine glory to be ridiculed and derided so as to make atonement not only for the sins of the soldiers and of those who goaded them on in this cruel game of the Crowning with Thorns, but for the sin of pride and arrogance that is present in us all.

To this very day Jesus is degraded ever anew by man in his pursuit of recognition and greatness, but especially by the devout when they seek honour. Today as long ago Jesus is so often scoffed at and ridiculed because of His claim to be King. He is mocked silently and even aloud as taunting voices ask the same questions as in those days. "Where is Your power if You cannot prevent wars and suffering? Where are Your subjects, Your kingdom, Your throne? The nations, even the Christian ones, do not acknowledge You. They laugh at the laws You laid down for Your kingdom, for example, those in the Sermon on the Mount, and they call them the laws of an unrealistic fool. To this day You have not been accepted as King by Your own people and You receive little homage from the New Testament people."

What a grief for Jesus that even today He receives so few royal honours, because there are so few humble people, who will sacrifice their pride, prestige and their desire to rule. God finds so few who humble themselves before Him and man and who submit wholeheartedly to His sovereignty and His leadings for their lives, and thereby acknowledge Him as King.

Here at the site that commemorates the Crowning with Thorns, God wants to imprint on our hearts the image of His Son humiliated to the dust. Jesus crowned with thorns! At this sight heaven fell silent. God had appointed the angels to worship the Son in His glory, but in this hour when they beheld their Lord disgraced and robbed of all honour, they must have prostrated themselves in deep grief. They must have been unable to comprehend that the sons of men are so loved that their Lord and God humbled Himself beneath the level of human dignity, letting Himself be made a figure of derision. Yet we can comprehend it. For our sakes Jesus suffered such disgrace and humiliation so as to win back for us the noblest virtue of all – humility, which we lost at the Fall of man.

As we inwardly behold our Lord with the crown of thorns, we cannot but sink into the dust, where He lay for us, and humble ourselves in shame. Our pride was the cause of His suffering when He was crowned with thorns. Surely words of gratitude must pour from our lips for all He endured for us. Jesus beneath the crown of thorns humbly bearing the pain and gazing lovingly at His mockers and tormentors – does not this sight cut us to the heart? Are we not ashamed of our arrogance, our aspirations for greatness, recognition and glory?

If we bear within our hearts the image of Jesus crowned with thorns, it will continually convict us of our desire for honour and recognition and move us to renounce this sin. And we shall be constrained to take our place at the side of Jesus, our degraded Lord, saying, "I will stand beside You here. I will tread the path You trod."

PRAYER IN LITHOSTROTOS

Dear Lord Jesus,

I humble myself deeply before You, my Creator, Lord and God, King of heaven and earth. I thank You that at this place You let Yourself be crowned with the crown of thorns, the crown of disgrace, amid ridicule and blasphemy, because of our pride, our desire to dominate and to win recognition. Forgive us that we, like the men of long ago, are unwilling to humble ourselves before God and man. Instead we seek recognition, honour and esteem, and therefore You had to suffer deep humiliation when a mockery was made of Your kingship and when Your honour was profaned. Lord, forgive us. In deep shame I confess that even though I know that You bore a crown of thorns, time and again I dare to strive for first place in order to receive recognition, be superior to others and rule over them.

Jesus, through Your bitter suffering when You were crowned with thorns, You have redeemed us from this craving for honour, importance and superiority. You have redeemed us from this desire of Lucifer's, which binds us to him. I believe in Your act of redemption, which will remould me into Your image of humility, provided that I commit myself to following pathways of humiliation. In beholding Your degradation, I make my committal here. I no longer wish to be important. I renounce all my aspirations for recognition and esteem. I want to choose Your path, O humble Lamb of God, the path of lowliness and humility. Out of gratitude for the deep humiliation You suffered, I want to glorify You with my whole life. For us You suffered immeasurably under the crown of thorns, but now You must be glorified and adored – till the day You establish Your royal dominion in our midst and every knee bows before You.

Amen.

✝

Jesus, scorned, ridiculed and crowned with thorns – this is the image presented of Him nowadays as long ago. Thus He is waiting today for disciples who will glorify Him. But only from the depths of a contrite heart can we give Jesus the true homage that is His due as King of kings.

Because so few are willing to choose abasement and take their rightful place, Jesus took this place in our stead. If we truly love Jesus, we shall make this choice too.

O Sight Demanding Silence

7. 7. 6. 7. 7. 8.

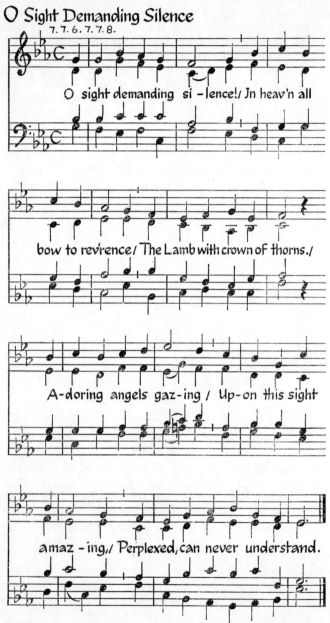

O sight demanding si-lence!/ In heav'n all bow to rev'rence/ The Lamb with crown of thorns./ A-doring angels gaz-ing / Up-on this sight amaz-ing,/ Perplexed, can never understand.

O pain beyond conceiving,
Lamenting angels grieving
Around their Maker, Lord!
Scarcely a man He stands there.
How can we God discern here
Beneath the shameful crown of thorns?

O sight such sorrow bringing,
With burning anguish wringing
The very heart of God!
His only Son a Victim
Of men, who sore afflict Him
With bitter spite and mocking hate!

This sight such grief exposing,
The love divine disclosing
Of Father, Spirit, Son!
Beyond man's art expressing
Pain radiant with such blessing,
Christ's countenance of loving grace.

It beams with love's clear splendour,
With patience strong and tender
Beneath that crown of thorns
To master all men's scheming,
The cursing and blaspheming,
With pow'r to heal and reconcile.

O sight demanding silence!
In heav'n all bow in rev'rence
Before their thorn-crowned Lord.
In pain God's heart travailing,
Yet by His love prevailing.
Lo! here we see our guilt portrayed.

Well-spring of Joy 65

O Jesus, my dear Master,
I give to You my heart;
You are so scorned, despisèd,
And none would take Your part.

I hardly dare behold You
In torture and deep shame,
Dishonoured by Your subjects,
And yet withholding blame.

It was my pride so sinful
That brought You down so low,
That robbed You of due honour,
And shamed, disgraced You so.

Before all men I humbly
Would lie in spirit now,
With You in love shame bearing,
For You have shown me how.

THE CHAPEL OF FLAGELLATION –
A MESSAGE FOR US

Flagellation – a terrible word! In this chapel at the beginning of the Via Dolorosa we remember how Jesus was scourged. Dreadful pictures come to mind. Bound to a pillar, Jesus was at the mercy of brutal mercenaries, who inflicted deep lashes on His sacred body with their instruments of torture. They probably whipped Jesus until His body was covered with hundreds of bleeding wounds. Suffering inhuman torment, He must have been at the point of collapsing in a pool of His own blood. Whole chunks of flesh must have been torn away by the barbed hooks of the instruments of torture. The words of prophecy in the Psalms were being fulfilled. "I am a worm, and no man!" (Psalm 22 : 6).

Yet this savage act was introduced by Pilate's words, "I find no crime in Him. Take Him and scourge Him." Thus the paradoxical occurred. Jesus was made to suffer this gruesome flogging, because Pilate, the Roman governor, a man well-versed in law, found no crime in Him. What then made Pilate hand Jesus over to such torture? He merely wanted to appease the mob and avoid rousing hostility against himself. At the same time he desired to appear guiltless in his own sight. Not wishing to be held responsible for Jesus' death, he merely delivered Him to be scourged, even though scourging sometimes resulted in the death of the victim. But then it was the fault of the tormentors who had performed their task too violently. Thus Pilate washed his hands publicly to indicate that he was innocent.

Jesus, the Lamb of God, stood in silence before His shearers. Though declared innocent, He was bound to the pillar of scourging. By saying that he found no crime in Him, Pilate unwittingly declared that Jesus was bearing our sins. Therefore, at this place commemorating the Scourging we cannot but say:

> O Jesus, here Thou showest
> What love can bear for me.
> This path of pain Thou goest
> From guilt my soul to free.

111

Thy body now is tortured
With countless bleeding wounds.
Thou didst in love choose freely
To die, for sin atone.

Who then can fail to love Thee,
Thou holy Lamb divine?
Thou noblest of all beings,
Who bore such pain as Thine?
Who else but Thou chose suff'ring,
The cruel scourge's smart
And bleeding wounds for sinners,
Forgiveness to impart?

It is inconceivable that we, mere creatures of God, inflicted such wounds upon Jesus, the Son of God. God had prepared a body for His Son – holy and without blemish – and therefore it should have been sacred to us. Yet we not only dared to lay hands on His body, but we lacerated it beyond recognition. We beat Jesus until His blood flowed and now we murderers may receive healing from His wounds. Who can comprehend such love and forgiveness? The wounds of our Lord have become fountains of life from which salvation now flows to us sinners. In adoration and worship we ponder this amazing mystery here at the site of the Flagellation.

May we take Jesus' words to heart as He entreats us here at this spot, "Do not defend yourself when wounds are inflicted upon you – whether they be wounds of the soul caused by hurtful, unkind words, or wounds of the spirit caused by disgrace and shame, or wounds of the body inflicted by tormentors. Think of My wounds, which proclaim an eternal law of God: streams of life and blessing will flow from wounds and suffering more than from any active form of service – provided, however, that you bear these wounds together with Me and humbly as I did, admitting yourself to be a sinner." Jesus is seeking souls who will bear wounds, for through such souls He establishes His kingdom. Do we bear wounds or do we inflict them upon others? This is the question we are being asked at the site commemorating the Scourging.

Jesus asks us further, "Do you ever consider that I bore lashes because of your sinful, carnal desires? If you are mindful of the pain I suffered, you will hate every sin of the flesh, starting with every lustful glance, for even this is adultery." Out of love for us Jesus let His sacred body be covered with countless wounds, so that our body may be redeemed from its sinful cravings and one day be resurrected in purity, beauty and glory. O that His suffering for us may not be in vain! Let us give Him the response of love by hating sin and being willing to bear wounds – that is His plea to us at this site.

✛

O come, bewail in sorrow
The Scourging of our Lord
Till all the world does wonder,
"Who is so praised, adored?",
Till earth and heaven marvel
How loved our Lord must be,
And man, repenting, worships
The Lamb on bended knee.

PRAYER IN THE CHAPEL OF FLAGELLATION

Dear Lord Jesus,

Because of our sins You were tortured and scourged until blood poured from Your body. I humble myself before You at the thought of Your body covered with bleeding wounds. My heart is filled with deep gratitude, for in Your wounds I find salvation and Your blood brings me redemption from all my carnal desires.

O Lord Jesus, may the image of Your sorely wounded body be deeply impressed upon my heart. May it speak to me more forcefully than every sermon on repentance and show me the terrible power exerted by my sin, which inflicted such wounds upon You.

Lord Jesus, give me a passionate hatred of sin, for it was sin that caused You immeasurable suffering long ago and continues to bring You anguish today. In the power of

113

Your redemption I want to break with sin and deny my longing to indulge myself and gratify my desires. In the power of Your redemption I renounce all sensual cravings.

O Holy Spirit, hear my prayer. Bring about such a transformation in me that my life will testify to the healing power of Jesus' wounds and the saving power of His blood, which cleansed me of all my sins and gave me victory over my bonds. Grant that my life may glorify the power of Jesus' wounds, so that He may receive praise and thanksgiving.

Amen.

Heaven Bows Itself in Wonder

8.7.8.7. D.

Heaven bows itself in won - der;//
Weep, O heavens, don your mourn - ing;//

Angels, awe-struck, veil their sight!//
Darkened be__ the source of light!//

God's own Son is bound for scourging,//Stripped and naked

to the post.// There the cru - el stripes a-

wait-ing / On— the way to shameful death.

Patient as a lamb He suffers,
'Gainst their frenzy, meek and still,
Bows Himself beneath the scourging,
Lets them treat Him as they will,
Hides His face all marred by torment
Of the body, mind and soul.
Yet through every wound inflicted
Pours His love to make us whole.

O most dear and blessèd Saviour,
Can Your heart bear greater strain?
Yet You tread the way still further;
Love still drives despite the pain.
So desiring man's salvation,
You the cruel Cross embrace,
Bleeding from a thousand gashes
As the bitter death You face.

✝

Who can fathom the love of Jesus? For our sakes He took
on human form and let men inflict bleeding wounds upon
Him, so that He might atone for our sins of the flesh, deliver
us from our sinful drives, and gain for us a new and spotless
resurrection body.

116

THE CHAPEL OF CONDEMNATION –
A MESSAGE FOR US

The fact that the Chapel of Condemnation stands next door to the Chapel of Flagellation shows us that the Scourging was not the last phase of Jesus' suffering. By ordering Jesus to be scourged, Pilate committed the first injustice – merely to save himself. The second injustice now followed. In order to maintain his position, to avoid appearing to be Caesar's enemy and not to incur his displeasure, Pilate condemned Jesus to death, and in doing so he became guilty of the most serious crime of all. He delivered the pure and innocent Son of God up to death.

And now at this site the amazing and incomprehensible occurred: the pure, innocent and sinless Lord, who had the power to condemn and destroy His judges instantly, accepted the verdict. Of His own free will He accepted the sentence, and meek as a lamb He let the Cross be placed upon Him – the Cross on which He would suffer the penalty of death.

In deep shame we stand in this chapel. Jesus had to be judged and condemned, because time and again we refuse to accept the judgments that are passed on us, although they are usually just. As human beings we find nothing so hard as to accept reproach. When others draw our attention to what we have done or said wrong or neglected to do, it is a struggle for us to say, "You are right. I'm to blame."

And now Someone stands before the judgment seat on behalf of us all – Jesus Christ. He humbles Himself beneath the verdict, takes up the Cross and walks the path to death. This He does for us, for you and me. We are so quick to censure the words, deeds and conduct of others – and usually wrongly, since we are unable to know their real motives. Yet we resent being censured. Thus it is inevitable that we fail miserably when God lays a cross or a burden upon us. Usually we defend ourselves, because we do not have the attitude of the penitent thief on the cross, "I am receiving the due reward of my deeds. As a sinner I deserve the burden of the cross. I need a cross, so that it will chasten me and thus purify, cleanse and transform me."

Jesus, who had no need of chastening, submitted so readily to the Cross that was laid upon Him at the Condemnation.

He accepted it, as if He really were a criminal, a sinner, who deserved to stoop beneath the heavy weight of the Cross. At this site it is deeply moving to remember how humbly Jesus as the Lamb of God let the Cross be laid upon Himself for our sakes. He took it up for us, because we are not "lambs" but rather "bulls" that rebel against God and man.

Now Jesus is waiting for us to thank Him for His amazing act of love. He is waiting for us to honour the truth from now on instead of living in self-deception; He expects us to accept the reproaches and verdicts of others, for as sinners we are usually at fault even if the other person has not acted quite fairly. Jesus is waiting for us to humble ourselves instead of explaining everything away and excusing ourselves. Let us remember that Jesus, although He was without sin, humbly accepted the unjust death sentence. He let the Cross be placed upon Himself, and now He is waiting for us not only to accept the verdict, but to say when God has prepared a cross for us, "Give me the cross. I will gladly bear it. Out of love and gratitude I want to follow You."

✝

Jesus, whom no one could charge with any sin, humbly accepted the condemnation and permitted the Cross to be placed upon Himself for our sakes. He did this, so that the Cross would no longer bring death but blessing to those who bear it humbly in the knowledge that as sinners we need to be chastened.

PRAYER IN THE CHAPEL
OF CONDEMNATION

Dear Lord Jesus,

I thank You and worship You for letting Yourself be condemned to death for our sakes, as the sinless Son of God. I worship Your love and humility in taking upon Yourself all my sin as if it were Yours, so that I may go free. I worship You for accepting the death sentence and bearing the burden of the Cross. Before such love I can only humble myself and fall down at Your feet.

My Lord Jesus, out of gratitude I will follow You and take up the cross that the Father gives me, and bear it in wholehearted dedication. I long to learn from You how to carry the cross in patience and humility; You bore the Cross innocently, but I deservedly. Help me to humble myself beneath it, for I know that it contains hidden blessing and glory. Lord Jesus, I yearn to be a true follower of Yours, so that You may see in my life the fruit of Your suffering.

Amen.

Meek and Silent Comes the Victim

8. 7. 8. 7. D.

Meek and silent comes the Vic — tim / Sac-ri-

fice to Gol — go — tha; / Here we sin - ners

see the suff'ring / That we caused our God to bear. /

Not one cry and no complain - ing / from His

sacred lips we hear,/ But His face so full of an-guish,/Tortured limbs, wrung heart de-clares.

Yea, the Love of God is silent,
Patient bears this grief and pain.
This was planned for man's redemption;
Calv'ry did God foreordain.
Jesus walks the way of suff'ring;
Home He calls men lovingly,
Till fulfilled the world's salvation,
Sinners from all guilt set free.

Those for whom He took that pathway
See His pain but pass Him by;
Now as then it means but little
That for them He had to die.
So alone He bears their burdens.
Who of us sees there his own?
Who is moved by this, resolving
Every smallest sin to shun?

Well-spring of Joy 68
Can also be sung to the melody,
"Love Divine, All Loves Excelling"

121

THE VIA DOLOROSA

To retrace the steps of Jesus along His path of sorrows to Calvary is our deepest desire when visiting His city. After having stood at the site of the Fortress of Antonia, which is traditionally regarded as the place where Jesus was condemned to death and given the Cross to bear, we continue on our way through the Old City to the Church of the Holy Sepulchre by following those crooked lanes known as the Via Dolorosa (see sketch-map). Of course, the original streets that Jesus trod lie buried beneath many layers of debris as a result of the various destructions of the city. Yet these narrow, partly covered, dark lanes do give the impression that time has stood still.

Part of the Via Dolorosa is the Suq Khan Ez-Zeit, the Bazaar, which is closed to motor traffic. Here the typical oriental life holds sway. Masses of people surge between the open shops lining both sides of the street, while overloaded donkeys jostle their way through the crowds. Strange smells surround us. The cries of the shopkeepers mingle with the clamours for "money" from swarms of children. Probably no chapel could help us to visualize the Crucifixion procession more vividly than this street scene resembling that of the first Good Friday.

Thousands of feet, native and foreign, walk across this street. But is there anyone who hesitates to cross it as casually as he would any other street? Is there anyone who hesitates to go about his business here as he would elsewhere? Considering the hustle and bustle, we realize that it must be a very rare occurrence for anyone to kneel here where Jesus collapsed under the burden of our sin.

Yet once a week, on Friday afternoon, the scene changes, and we can sense what an exceptional street this is. A procession to the fourteen Stations of the Cross is held, a custom that has been gradually established since the time of the Crusaders. Nine of the stations are taken from the Gospels; the other five are based on traditions of varying antiquity. If we come to the courtyard of the El Omariyeh College *(see chapter on The Fortress of Antonia)* on Fridays at 3 p.m., we shall find a few Franciscans surrounded by a group of people. Beginning with the first Station of the Cross, which commemorates the Condemnation of Jesus, the procession — sometimes headed by a few men who take turns in carrying a wooden cross — moves out into the street where the second station (Jesus receives the Cross) is commemorated on the outside wall of the Chapel of Condemnation, which is directly opposite the college.

Then the procession passes under the Ecce Homo Arch. At this point the Via Dolorosa leaves the area of the former Fortress of Antonia, and leads a little way down into the Tyropoeon Valley. Following the procession, we turn left into the street called Al Wad, which comes from the Damascus Gate. At the corner a halt is made at the chapel commemorating Jesus' first fall under the burden of the Cross (third station, Armenian Catholic). How grateful we are for this hour when the usual hustle and bustle of the crowd is interrupted by the pilgrims praying and singing at every station of our Lord's path of sorrows! A few steps farther we come to the place commemorating the fourth station (Jesus meets His mother). Apart from a church in the courtyard, the Armenian Catholics have a chapel by the roadside with a relief on its lintel depicting the scene.

About 20 m. farther the Via Dolorosa branches off to the right from the Al Wad and on the left-hand corner is a Roman Catholic chapel belonging to the Franciscans. Over the entrance is the inscription "Simon Cyrenaeo crux imponitur" (the Cross is laid on Simon of Cyrene, fifth station). The way continues uphill along the steps of a narrow lane spanned by numerous arches and vaultings. Halfway up on the left the procession pauses at a chapel beneath the first large vault for the sixth Station of the Cross, commemorating Veronica's act of compassion (according to tradition she wiped Jesus' face with her veil). This chapel is served by the Little Sisters of Jesus (of Charles de Foucauld), who observe the Greek Catholic rite here.

At the end of this terraced lane, which leads uphill, we come to the busy Bazaar and opposite the junction we find a small Franciscan chapel commemorating Jesus' second fall (seventh station). The eighth and ninth stations can no longer be approached directly, but we shall not miss them if we follow the procession, which turns right into St. Francis' Street just beyond the Franciscan chapel. About 10 or 15 m. farther we see a cross on a high wall with the inscription, "IC XC NIKA" (Jesus Christ is victorious). This is the eighth station and it commemorates Jesus' encounter with the weeping women of Jerusalem.

To reach the ninth station we return to the Bazaar and make our way through the hustling, bargaining crowds in this busy market street. After proceeding about 50 m., we climb a stone stairway on the right, which leads into the courtyard of a Coptic convent where the third fall of our Lord under the Cross is commemorated, although the event is normally remembered at the entrance to the Coptic church.

The Via Dolorosa

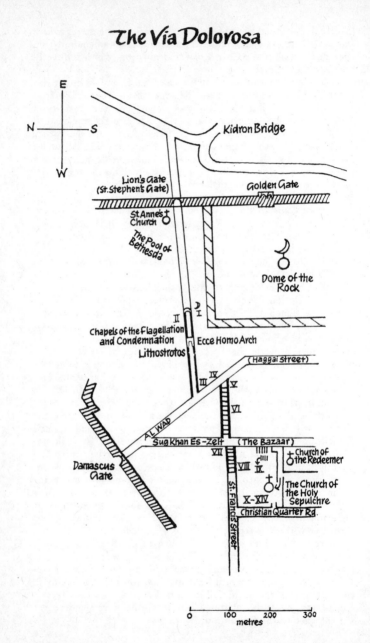

We are now very near the Church of the Holy Sepulchre, but we must first retrace our steps, returning to the Bazaar. At the end of the covered part is the Russian hospice. Here we turn right, passing by the Lutheran Church of the Redeemer, which lies on the left. After a few steps we come to a high wall built across the street. A small door in this wall leads into the courtyard before the Church of the Holy Sepulchre where we find the last five Stations of the Cross *(see chapter on the Church of the Holy Sepulchre)*.

Nowadays it takes approximately a quarter of an hour to follow this way. But who can tell how long it must have taken our Lord Jesus in His weakened condition as He staggered beneath the heavy weight of the Cross? In those days the level of the Tyropoeon Valley was considerably lower and this must have made it even more strenuous for Jesus, since the greater part of the way led steeply uphill to Calvary.

The courtyard of the Moslem college (first station) and the chapel of the third station are open all day.
The chapel of the sixth station can be reached by way of the shop belonging to the Little Sisters of Jesus. (8:30 a.m. till noon; 3 p.m. — 6:30 p.m. Please ring the bell.)
The other chapels are only open during the procession.

FROM THE HOLY BIBLE

So they took Jesus, and he went out, bearing his own cross, to the place called the place of a skull, which is called in Hebrew Golgotha. As they were marching out, they came upon a man of Cyrene, Simon by name; this man they compelled to carry his cross.

And there followed him a great multitude of the people, and of women who bewailed and lamented him. But Jesus turning to them said, "Daughters of Jerusalem, do not weep for me, but weep for yourselves and for your children. For behold, the days are coming when they will say, 'Blessed are the barren, and the wombs that never bore, and the breasts that never gave suck!' "

John 19 : 17; Matthew 27 : 32 and Luke 23 : 27-29

Then Jesus told his disciples, "If any man would come after me, let him deny himself and take up his cross and follow me." Matthew 16 : 24

THE VIA DOLOROSA –
A MESSAGE FOR US

Via Dolorosa – my Saviour's heart is rent.
Via Dolorosa – O raise the great lament!
Tell us of Jesus' suffering
And how He bore the Cross,
Weighed down beneath our sin and guilt,
Until He died for us.

Via Dolorosa, the one true way of sorrows on this earth, for it was trod by the only one who was not a man like us, but the Son of man and the Son of God. He did not tread this way of sorrows as a sinner in need of chastening, but as the pure and sinless Lord, who chose this path freely out of love for us.

Via Dolorosa – a street of sorrows like none other, for here Jesus bore all the grief of mankind in His Cross. Each one of us has a cross to bear, but who bears it like Jesus? He bore the Cross, condemned to death, though He was the very essence of life. He bore the Cross, crowned with thorns and blasphemed by man, though all glory in heaven and on earth was His due. He bore the Cross, bound and bruised, although He alone had a pure and spotless body. He bore the Cross, forsaken by all, since His closest friends, the disciples, had fled, leaving Him to walk this bitter path alone. The greatest disgrace, however, was that a stranger had to be forced to carry His Cross. None of His disciples offered their assistance, although Jesus, like no one else, had lovingly devoted Himself to all men and to His disciples in particular.

Via Dolorosa, the way of sorrows, that heard the deep sighs and lamentation in Jesus' heart and saw Him fall to the ground! Via Dolorosa, a way of sorrows like none other, for what street has ever seen what it saw! Here Jesus walked without complaining, without rebelling against God, without asking a single "why?", without reproaching His tormentors, who had condemned Him to death, in response to all the goodness He had shown. What path of suffering has ever been trod by a person in such humility with but one thought in his heart, "Give me the cross. I will bear it gladly!"? Who has ever walked the path of grief and pain as meekly as Jesus, who did not return insult for insult when, in utter exhaustion, He staggered beneath the weight of the heavy Cross on His way to Calvary? Via Dolorosa – what pathway of sorrows has ever witnessed such mocking cries or seen a person so maltreated? Tormented and cruelly afflicted, the innocent Son of God was led through this street, derided by those to whom He had done good.

Via Dolorosa, where the innocent Lord not only suffered for the sin of a few individuals or a nation but bore the sin of the entire human race upon His shoulders. That was why the Cross was immeasurably heavy; it was so heavy that Jesus was scarcely able to bear it all the way to Calvary. Who has ever borne a cross that caused such agony of soul and spirit as it did here? All the sins of His children, all of God's judgments and punishments that they had rejected now lay on Jesus, who had come to bear the Cross for us all.

Via Dolorosa, O holiest of all streets, which the Holy One of God trod to make atonement for the sons of men! You are worthy to be honoured with voices raised in praise and with humbled hearts full of adoration for Jesus. Here all other voices should fall silent, all other activities cease. In response to the holy act of our Lord and Saviour His children can only show Him due reverence on this street. Should we not humble ourselves here, because He graciously inclined Himself to us? Should we not kneel in the dust in adoration that He walked this path of agony for us? Let us adore Him, for He did not grow weary, but followed this path to the end.

Indeed, the omnipotent God together with all the hosts of heaven is waiting for groups of people who will keep this street holy today for the sake of their Lord's suffering and who will sanctify it anew with tokens of their love and devotion. Our Lord Jesus is waiting here for those who will bear their cross in response to His challenge, "If any man would come after Me, let him take up his cross." He is waiting for us to follow Him and bear our crosses like true disciples – humbly, without complaining, meekly, without rebelling, and lovingly as He did.

PRAYER ON THE VIA DOLOROSA

Dear Lord Jesus,

On Your way of sorrows where You stooped low beneath the burden of the Cross for us, I would humble myself in the dust. O innocent Son of God, You were made to bear the burden, because we who are guilty refuse to bear the cross, which we deserve a hundred times over because of our sin. I beg forgiveness for the many times in my life when I bore my cross unwillingly, complained about it or threw it down.

But here on Your way of sorrows, I believe that You, O Jesus, Cross-bearer for the world, have redeemed me from my reluctance to bear the cross, and granted me a love for it. Every time I begin to feel burdened, or when hardships come into my life and I am tempted to rebel, You will help me to say, "Give me the cross. I will bear it gladly."

As I now think of my cross, I dedicate myself to bear it at all times, saying, "I accept my cross willingly, for it comes from Your hands, and I want to follow You, bearing it lovingly and humbly, out of gratitude for Your suffering." Grant that it may prepare me to be at Your side one day, at Your throne. And grant that as a true cross-bearer I may inspire many others to take up their cross in love, so that You may rejoice and be rewarded for Your bitter suffering on the Via Dolorosa.

Amen.

"COME, TAKE UP YOUR CROSS AND FOLLOW ME!"

Whoever belongs to Jesus cannot but follow the path He took, for love is constrained to accompany Jesus on the way of the cross.

Whoever loves Jesus loves his cross, for the cross is a part of Him.

The cross that weighs you down now has transforming power and will one day lift you up to heaven. Therefore, is it not worthy of all honour and praise?

If you do not want to be a mere spectator who will one day stand outside the kingdom of heaven, carry your cross. The path of the cross-bearer ends at the throne.

Whoever admits that he is a sinner accepts the burden God lays upon him, for he knows that sinners need chastening in order to be purified and transformed into the image of God.

Do not carry your cross as if under compulsion like a slave, but voluntarily as someone who loves Jesus. Then your cross will begin to shine.

If the weight of your cross is great, the hidden blessing will also be great.

If your sole possession in life is a cross, guard it as your most prized possession. Hidden in the cross is all that a human heart can desire – deliverance from the power of sin, and peace and joy.

The more you humble yourself under the burden God has laid upon you, the greater and more wondrous will be the glory that your cross will bring – in this life and in eternity.

✝

Via Dolorosa, O path of grief unknown,
Via Dolorosa, He bore His Cross alone.
Via Dolorosa, where deaf'ning tumults are,
Via Dolorosa, O path from God so far.
Via Dolorosa, where stiff-necked pride is found,
Via Dolorosa, He comes bowed to the ground.
Via Dolorosa, who knows the grief He bears?
Via Dolorosa, 'tis love alone that cares.
Via Dolorosa, God bears anew for us
The burden of the Cross.
Who shares His grief today?

> How He longs for a soul
> That will humble himself as He did
> And bear the cross out of love!
> Who will that soul be? O who?

J Kiss Thy Cross

4. 7. 4. 7. 4. 6.

J kiss Thy cross; / Thy hands outstretched in blessing / Didst give it me; / And J, Thy love con — fess - ing, / Accept it then, / A greeting, Lord, from Thee.

130

I kiss Thy cross;
To me it hath been given
By love alone,
That I may reap in heaven
Harvest of joy
Whose seed with tears was sown.

I kiss Thy cross,
For bravely Thou didst bear it.
One day above
I shall be asked, "Didst share it?
Didst follow Me
Abiding close in love?"

I kiss Thy cross;
I know its special blessing;
For there's enshrined
A treasure past all guessing.
Each in his cross
Thy gift of love will find.

So will I trust,
Thy cross in love embracing,
O dearest Lord,
Upon Thy torment gazing;
Thou rescued us
From fear of suffering.

So shall I sing
And praise the wondrous blessing
Within the cross –
The glory everlasting
That You prepare
For those who tread this path.

Jesus Bears the Heavy Crossbeam

8.7. 8.7. D.

Jesus bears the heavy crossbeam/To the hill of Golgo-tha./ Here we see such pain and suff'ring/That outstrips man's reas'ning far. / for 'tis God who bears that crossbeam,/Which

to crim-i—nals belongs./ Yet no voice for Him was

pleading /From amongst those jostling throngs.

Jesus, now the Burden-bearer,
Standing in the sinner's place,
In Your mercy for us sinners
Man's dilemma You embrace.
But You still must bear our crosses,
For we push them all away.
Yet You bore Your Cross that henceforth
We might carry ours each day.

Lord, through Zion's streets so narrow,
Stagg'ring 'neath the weighty Cross,
Deeply to that Cross committed,
Saving man at bitter cost,
Steadily You still go onward
To Your goal, Mount Golgotha,
Where You give Yourself as Victim
On the Cross they lifted there.

Lord, for love of us, all bearing,
Lord, for love of us, will die,
Lord, for love of us, now hearing
Words of scorn and blasphemy,
Willing for our sake You carry
Cross of shame to Calvary,
For Your love saw not the anguish,
But our chains and misery.

Jesus, Jesus, You have carried
All this poor world's guilty load.
Man of Sorrows, yet a Sovereign,
You have sin and Satan smote;
You for us have won the vict'ry
On the Cross of Calvary.
We will praise You, Lord, for ever.
Lo! from sin You set us free.

THE CHURCH OF THE HOLY SEPULCHRE

In order to have sufficient time to visit Calvary and the Holy Sepulchre, these most significant holy places, it is best to take a new day. The Church of the Holy Sepulchre can be reached by way of the Via Dolorosa *(see chapter on the Via Dolorosa)* or by starting from the Damascus Gate in the northern city wall. A few steps within the gate we descend a terraced street and 50 m. later we come to the Bazaar, which branches off to the right. The last part of the Bazaar as well as the short street with its entrance to the courtyard of the Church of the Holy Sepulchre will already be familiar to us from the Friday procession along the Via Dolorosa. Today we pass through the small doorway in the wall and enter the paved court before the Church of the Holy Sepulchre. Various chapels and a monastery surround the courtyard. Next to the bell tower is the main entrance to the church.

At first we are somewhat bewildered by the interior of the church. Many chapels and churches in a variety of architectural styles seem to have been built into one another. However, we are chiefly concerned about visiting the two focal points — the site of the Crucifixion and the Tomb, where Jesus was laid. Immediately inside the entrance a steep, narrow flight of steps on the right leads up to Calvary. The original Rock of Calvary has been entirely covered with marble and surrounded by walls and altars; the platform itself is only partly built on the actual rock — the rest is supported by a man-made substructure. (Later when we come to the Chapel of Adam beneath Calvary, we can see a little of the original rock, which has been exposed here, even showing the fissure in it.) On the right-hand side of Calvary on the floor there is a mosaic commemorating the tenth station, Jesus is stripped of His garments (Roman Catholic). The altar behind it has a large fresco depicting the eleventh station, Jesus is nailed to the Cross (Roman Catholic). Turning to the left altar at Calvary we find the site where the Cross was erected (twelfth station, Greek Orthodox). Frequently pilgrims come here and kneel down, many stooping beneath the altar where it is possible to touch the actual Rock of Calvary. This is said to be the spot where the Cross was rammed into the rock. Between the two large altars is a small one, dedicated to the Mother of Sorrows commemorating the thirteenth station, Jesus' body is taken from the Cross (Roman Catholic).

Much though we long to tarry here in complete silence, it is somewhat difficult, for usually there is a noisy coming and going of people speaking in all languages. Nevertheless, we feel moved to spend time here in prayer. At Calvary, more than at any other holy place, we yearn to bring praise and thanksgiving to our Lord, who was crucified for us.

As we descend the stairs, we come to the Stone of the Anointing, where the embalming of Jesus' body is commemorated (opposite the main entrance). To the left is the fourteenth station, a small edifice containing the Holy Sepulchre. Like a "church within a church" it consists of a small vestibule called the Chapel of the Angel and the Holy Sepulchre itself. In order to have a closer look inside, we must wait a while, for there are always crowds pressing forward. Eventually, like Peter on that first Easter morning, we are able to pass through the low, narrow entrance, which leads from the Chapel of the Angel into the Sepulchre. Its walls are covered with white marble and a raised marble slab marks the burial place of Christ. Nothing can be seen of the original rock — and yet, we are standing at the site of our Lord's Resurrection.

THE HISTORICAL ASPECT

At first we may be surprised to find the site of the Crucifixion and the Holy Sepulchre under one roof and in the centre of the city of Jerusalem. But according to excavations it is almost certain that the area where the Church of the Holy Sepulchre now stands lay outside the city wall at the time of Jesus. Not until ca. A.D. 40 was this area enclosed within the city by a new wall. In the mid-nineteenth century remains of the old city wall were found east and south of the Church of the Holy Sepulchre, and when the Russian pilgrims' hospice was built, the threshold of a city gate was discovered.

Calvary must have lain not far beyond this gate. It was not a hill, as we usually assume, but merely a rocky outcrop. At the foot of this protruding rock the rolling grounds were interspersed with gardens and rock-hewn tombs, no doubt Joseph of Arimathea's family sepulchre as well as his own new tomb among them (John 19 : 41). The burial chambers that can still be seen in the Church of the Holy Sepulchre date from Jesus' time and are named after Joseph of Arimathea. These rock-hewn tombs are the strongest proof of the authenticity of the site, for according to Jewish law burial places must always be located away from places of residence.

The Rock of Calvary was probably not so common as a site of execution. Otherwise a respected member of the council like Joseph of Arimathea would not have had a garden laid out here containing his tomb. Perhaps the name "the place of a skull" was derived from the appearance of the rock. This site was probably chosen for the Crucifixion, since it lay just outside the city wall where the sentence could be carried out swiftly before the Sabbath began.

After Jesus had been taken down from the Cross, He was laid in the nearby grave belonging to Joseph, and some of the details supplied by the Gospels are still recognizable in the Church of the Holy Sepulchre. It was a rock-hewn tomb, which, unlike most graves, was intended to hold only one body; according to John 20 : 1-10 it probably consisted of an outer chamber as well as the actual tomb chamber. The opening into the latter was so low that the disciples had to stoop in order to look in (Luke 24 : 12). The burial place of Christ must have lain to the right of the entrance to the tomb chamber, for it was here that the women saw the seated angel (Mark 16 : 5). Most likely it was a trough-like cavity, for Peter could see the "napkin" only when he had looked into the hollowed-out slab of rock (John 20 : 7). A large stone closed the outermost entrance, but on the morning of the Resurrection it was found rolled away.

This site of the Crucifixion and Resurrection of Jesus was buried beneath rubble in A.D. 135 by the Emperor Hadrian after he had suppressed the last Jewish revolt, which was led by Bar Kochba. A pagan Roman temple was then erected upon it. In his passionate hatred Hadrian wished to root out every remembrance of the Jewish religion as well as of Christ and everything that testified to Him, but in his zeal he actually preserved these holy places, for the temples that were built over them served as a special mark of identification. Thus in A.D. 326 the Emperor Constantine arranged a search for these sites and had the Roman works removed. His mother Helena herself supervised the undertakings. The entire Christian population of Jerusalem and thousands of Roman soldiers from the garrison, assisted eagerly and within a few months Hadrian's marble buildings were disassembled. To their great joy the Rock of Calvary and the Holy Sepulchre were discovered, intact, as they are described in the Gospels. In the process other rock tombs were also laid bare. This labour of love has preserved the site of Calvary and the Holy Sepulchre for us after they had been buried for almost two hundred years.

The Emperor Constantine then had a vast basilica erected over this holy place. Part of this basilica was the Rotunda, with the empty Tomb in the centre. The rock surrounding the Tomb was cut away, leaving only a stone block containing the Tomb. Over it a magnificent cupola was erected on pillars.

The actual basilica with its five naves was called the Martyrion (Witness) and joined to the Rotunda, called the Anastasis (Resurrection), by a pillared courtyard. Out in the open, in the southwest corner of this courtyard was the bare Rock of Calvary, which had been sculptured into a cubic block. Five metres in height, it was crowned by a platform on which the crosses had stood. Constantine's basilica was completed in 336, but it was destroyed by the Persians in 614. After it was reconstructed, Caliph Hakim demolished it completely in 1009, save for the crypt of Helena beneath the central nave of the basilica and the adjoining grotto, in which the Cross was said to have been found. The Holy Sepulchre itself suffered damage several times during these destructions. Rebuilding of the basilica began in 1048. The Tomb was reconstructed on the rocky foundations; likewise the Rotunda, a chapel over Calvary and several other chapels were restored. In this condition the grounds came into the hands of the Crusaders, who enclosed the scattered sanctuaries in a vast unified edifice. A large dome covered the Tomb and a smaller one the Greek Choir (Katholikon). The building was completed in 1149.

After driving out the Crusaders in 1187, the Sultan permitted the Christians to continue using the church, but on the condition that the Moslems be given custody of the entrance. This office was handed down from generation to generation and the same family holds the key to the Church of the Holy Sepulchre to this day. In 1342 the Sultan gave the Franciscans the right of administration in the church. In this position the Franciscans suffered much persecution throughout the centuries. Over the course of time the Moslem rulers divided the rights within the Church of the Holy Sepulchre between Roman Catholics, Greek Orthodox, Armenian Orthodox, Copts, Syrians and Abyssinians, but the Abyssinians have since withdrawn their right.

The Crusader Church was frequently damaged and restored, but it never lost its basic form. In 1808 the Rotunda of the Holy Sepulchre was almost completely destroyed by a disastrous fire. Later it was rebuilt by the Greeks. Hardly fifty years had passed when the cupola of the Rotunda began to give way. After the earthquakes of 1927 and 1937 the main dome was in danger of collapsing, but the various communities concerned could not come to an agreement about the restoration. Consequently, in 1938 the British Mandatory Power was obliged to support the building with steel scaffolding both inside and outside.

For many years the church had an unworthy appearance, its splendour marred by unsightly building alterations of past centuries. Indeed, it could have been called the most wretched church in the world, "without form or comeliness" — a distressing reflection of the present sufferings of Him who wrought His work of redemption for us at this spot. Not until 1961 did the restoration work finally commence.

All the different developments of the basilica have left their imprint on Calvary and the Holy Sepulchre also. The Rock of Calvary, the attested historic site of the Crucifixion, is unrecognizable at first sight. Owing to the various destructions the Tomb has retained only fragments of the original rock. But the foundations have remained and the size of the Holy Sepulchre most likely tallies with that of the Tomb found by Constantine. Up to the seventh century pilgrim reports mention the stone that was rolled in front of the Tomb's entrance, but this stone was probably dashed to pieces during the destruction by the Persians. A fragment built into the wall of the Chapel of the Angel is pointed out as being a portion of this broken stone. Through the centuries the exterior shape of the Rotunda has often changed, once having the appearance of a pyramid, and at one point boasting a tower. It was given its present form, however, by the Greeks, who rebuilt it in 1810.

In spite of all the various developments we can be thankful that the authenticity of the site of Calvary and the Holy Sepulchre is better attested than that of almost any other site of Jesus' earthly life. And scholars from different branches of Christianity maintain that these sites most certainly did witness the events of Good Friday and the joy of Easter morn.

The Church of the Holy Sepulchre is usually open from 4 a.m. — 7 p.m.

CALVARY

FROM THE HOLY BIBLE

So they took Jesus, and led him away to the place called the place of a skull, which is called in Hebrew Golgotha. There they crucified him, and with him two others, one on either side, and Jesus between them. And Jesus said, "Father, forgive them; for they know not what they do."

One of the criminals who were hanged railed at him, saying, "Are you not the Christ? Save yourself and us!" But the other rebuked him, saying, "Do you not fear God, since you are under the same sentence of condemnation? And we indeed justly; for we are receiving the due reward of our deeds; but this man has done nothing wrong." And he said, "Jesus, remember me when you come in your kingly power." And he said to him, "Truly, I say to you, today you will be with me in Paradise."

Standing by the cross of Jesus were his mother, and his mother's sister, Mary the wife of Clopas, and Mary Magdalene. When Jesus saw his mother, and the disciple whom he loved standing near, he said to his mother, "Woman, behold, your son!" Then he said to the disciple, "Behold, your mother!"

And there was darkness over the whole land, while the sun's light failed. And Jesus cried with a loud voice, "My God, my God, why hast thou forsaken me?"

After this Jesus, knowing that all was now finished, said (to fulfil the scripture), "I thirst." When Jesus had received the vinegar, he said, crying with a loud voice, "It is finished! Father, into thy hands I commit my spirit!" And he bowed his head and gave up his spirit.

And behold, the curtain of the temple was torn in two, from top to bottom; and the earth shook, and the rocks were split.

Now when the centurion saw what had taken place, he praised God, and said, "Certainly, this man was innocent!" And all the multitudes returned home beating their breasts.

cf. Matthew 27, Luke 23, John 19

✝

O unfathomable depths of mercy!
For us God bears such suffering,
For us and for our sins!
O Lamb of God, we kneel here
Beneath Thy Cross and worship Thee,
Our grievous sins lamenting.

CALVARY – A MESSAGE FOR US

Calvary! Close to the city of God, the city of the great
King, and yet outside the gate. Calvary! A place of disgrace
to which Jesus was led like a criminal to suffer the cruel
death of crucifixion.

Calvary! Like no other place on this earth it speaks of
immeasurable suffering and anguish, of excruciating pain.
Calvary! This was the place man had appointed for the
Son of God, who came to earth as Saviour and Redeemer
for mankind. Calvary! The place for criminals – the only
place man considered fitting for the Son of God. The world
had no other room for Him than here at Calvary, the place
of a skull, the place of death.

Calvary! What did it see? A wooden Cross lay on the
ground as may well have happened before, waiting for a
guilty man condemned to death to be stretched out upon it.
But this time it was the pure and holy Lamb of God, who
voluntarily chose the terrible Cross as His deathbed. Jesus
surrendered Himself of His own free will, allowing the sons
of men to pierce His hands and feet with nails, driven in
by cruel hammer blows. The sound of these blows must
have penetrated all the heavens and the angels must have
prostrated themselves, weeping that their Lord, the Son of
the living God, had to suffer such abysmal agony because
of the sins of mankind.

Calvary! A Cross was lifted upright and then rammed
into the ground, trembling beneath the weight of its burden,
which was heavier than the entire earth, for this Cross bore
the Creator of the universe, who had taken upon Himself
the sins of mankind. The Cross towered up into the sky,
as if it sought to thrust open the gates of heaven, for the
sins of the world had been taken away on the cursed wood

and paradise was now opened. The foot of the Cross was driven deep into the ground, as if it sought to penetrate the depths of hell and thrust open the kingdom of death, for upon the Cross was He who would deliver all those who had been languishing in the kingdom of death. And the arms of the Cross were outstretched in all-embracing love to receive the world and to call man back home to the Father.

Calvary! Truly, it was Love eternal that hung on the Cross here and, dying, called mankind and all creation back to God with the words, "I thirst! I thirst that they may all come home." Love eternal called men back home to God with the words of forgiveness spoken to His tormentors. "Father, forgive them; for they know not what they do!" Love eternal expressed Himself in the words, "Behold your mother" as He gave a home and a mother to His beloved disciple, who was lonely and bereft; at the same time He entrusted His mother with a new maternal commission. What amazing love! In the hour of utmost personal grief and agony, He remembered the sorrows of others!

The cry, "My God, my God, why hast thou forsaken me?" reveals the deep anguish of soul that Jesus suffered being utterly abandoned and repudiated by God for man's sake. But even so Jesus said, "My God" and with this word "My" He embraced God in love. Indeed, His cry, "Father, into thy hands I commit my spirit" showed how true and sincere His love was, for He continued to trust the Father in the darkest night of abandonment.

Then Jesus uttered those most powerful words of love, "It is finished!" The pathway of suffering for the redemption of all mankind had been followed to the end. The act of love had been accomplished. Love had triumphed. Jesus, Love eternal, did not become embittered, but endured all things, continuing to love when there was nothing left to love. He did not avoid any suffering or torment, but chose to lay down His life for the sake of His enemies.

This overwhelming, immeasurable love of Jesus corresponded to the abysmal depths of pain that He underwent. He was immersed in an ocean of suffering that no man could ever have endured, since no man's love could ever equal the love of Jesus. This suffering was greater than any human suffering; though innocent, the Son of God as the Son of man was made to suffer the utmost agony in body, soul and spirit without any relief. But at the same time He suffered as God and thus His suffering was twofold, for what must it have meant for God to be forsaken by God! Only the Son of God could have known this suffering. He endured inner conflict in double measure. Not only was He rejected as a man, but He was repudiated as the Son of God. He died, spurned by His people, abandoned by His disciples and faced with what seemed to be the ruin of His life-work. No human tongue can declare the agony He endured in His soul, since none can fathom the depths of His unrequited and scorned love.

In addition, He had to suffer immeasurable physical torment, for what death could be more gruesome than that of crucifixion, when the body is put under extreme tension and racked with pain as the limbs are pulled apart? Usually the victim was driven insane by the agony. The full weight of the body was borne by the arms, which threatened to be torn asunder, and the strained muscles were contorted with cramp. The severest pain, however, was caused by the nailing of the hands when usually a main nerve was pierced by the nails, so that the entire body would continually throb with searing pain. In the end the agonizing spasms would spread throughout the suspended body, and the victim would die of suffocation while fully conscious.

Thus Jesus, the Son of God, died on the Cross at Calvary. And to this day Calvary speaks of the power of the infinite love of Jesus, which embraces the whole world. Calvary tells us of a love that knows no bounds, that embraces even its enemies and tormentors, a love that is stronger than the agony of death. Calvary tells us that here Jesus' heart broke out of love for us and that He freely gave Himself to the most horrible death for our sake. Calvary declares to us, "See how much God loves the sons of men and every created being! See how much He loves you!"

Calvary tells of the triumph of love. It proclaims that love is greater than all things and has even overcome the kingdom of death and hell. Calvary declares that when love enters suffering, it bears redeeming power. Thus the cursed wood has become the symbol of redemption, for on it hung Love eternal, who loved even unto death. Calvary proclaims a redemption that has no bounds, that will embrace all creation and the whole universe, and that will bring about complete transformation according to Jesus' words, "Behold, I make all things new!"

Thus at Calvary we can only kneel in adoration, and praise the far-reaching effects of the redemption that has been wrought for us sinners along paths of untold suffering. We cannot but express our gratitude for this redemption and choose His path of love – love that does not shirk suffering, love that spends itself in sacrifices and even prays for its enemies. Jesus longs to see in us the fruit of His sacrifice. He longs for members of His Body to be united with Him, the Head, to be imbued with His Spirit, and to follow the path of sacrificial love, thus helping to save and deliver souls, so that His kingdom of love will soon dawn.

PRAYER AT CALVARY

Dear Lord Jesus,

At this holy place where You laid down Your life for the sake of us sinners, I humble myself in awe, and praise Your amazing love for us. I worship You, O innocent Lamb of God, slain upon the Cross for our sakes. It is we and our sins that were responsible for the agony You suffered when You were nailed to the Cross and crucified. And yet in love You forgave us all our sins through Your unspeakable suffering. On the Cross You thought of us, Your tormentors, with such love, pronouncing the words of forgiveness to us. How shall I ever comprehend this amazing love! Beloved Lord Jesus, accept my overflowing thanks.

Before the visible and invisible world I want to praise You here for what You have done. I praise Your love, which proved itself in suffering, reaching down into the deepest depths and embracing one and all. I praise Your blood that was shed for me. It brings me deliverance from all my sins and redeems me, that I may be a new creation, a child of God. Here at Calvary I worship You for ransoming me from hell and the power of sin. I have but one plea: grant that my life may truly testify that You are the Redeemer of the sons of men, bound in sin.

Amen.

THE HOLY SEPULCHRE

FROM THE HOLY BIBLE

Now in the place where he was crucified there was a garden, and in the garden a new tomb where no one had ever been laid. So because of the Jewish day of Preparation, as the tomb was close at hand, they laid Jesus there.　John 19 : 41 f.

Now after the sabbath, toward the dawn of the first day of the week, Mary Magdalene and the other Mary went to see the sepulchre. And behold, there was a great earthquake; for an angel of the Lord descended from heaven and came and rolled back the stone, and sat upon it. His appearance was like lightning, and his raiment white as snow. And for fear of him the guards trembled and became like dead men. But the angel said to the women, "Do not be afraid; for I know that you seek Jesus who was crucified. He is not here; for he has risen, as he said. Come, see the place where he lay."　Matthew 28 : 1-6

THE HOLY SEPULCHRE –
A MESSAGE FOR US

The Tomb of Jesus and Calvary, the site of His Crucifixion, both under one roof – how can that be? Do we not feel that Calvary ought to be far away from the site of the Resurrection? Calvary witnessed the deepest suffering of all, for there Jesus' pathway seemed to end in an abyss of meaninglessness and His life-work appeared to be in vain. Calvary was the place where mockery and scorn prevailed, where Jesus was silenced and thrust out, where He was killed ten times over, figuratively speaking, to make sure that He would never live again. Calvary, a name that inspires the utmost dread and horror in every person on this earth who realizes what took place here – and close beside it the Tomb of Jesus, speaking of resurrection, joy and victory. How can they be so close together?

God in His wisdom planned that the tomb of Joseph of Arimathea should lie very near to Calvary, so that their physical proximity might help us to see their spiritual relationship. Thus the Tomb next to Calvary testifies that there is no defeat, when suffered in dedication to God and faith in Him, that does not contain the seeds of victory. Here Jesus, the crucified Lord, rose again and triumphed over all His enemies.

Even the soldiers who were placed before the Tomb to guard the corpse to ensure that He would remain there and exert no more influence fell to the ground as though dead at His Resurrection. Jesus Christ, who was nailed to the Cross, so that He could not move a single limb, whose heart stood still at the hour of His death, whose body was a stiff corpse when it was removed from the Cross – He is alive! He moves His limbs and steps out of the grave. He rises in triumph, destroying the power of Death and breaking out of the tomb of rock. The stone must yield as Jesus demonstrates His divine omnipotence. Before, He was powerless and at the mercy of His enemies, but now He has risen in the almighty power and glory of God, having defeated the greatest and mightiest foe of man and of God Himself – Death!

Thus the message of the empty Tomb beside the Cross of Calvary applies to us too: there is no destruction that will not be followed by resurrection, if a work is done to the glorification of God. From every cross that seems to ruin our lives or our ministry new life will blossom. All suffering, no matter how grievous or abysmal, all depths of sorrow in spiritual night, when borne in union with Jesus, will end in the radiant joy and glory of the Easter sun. This we shall experience as a foreshadowing here on earth and in fullness in eternity when "death shall be no more, neither shall there be mourning nor crying nor pain any more" (Revelation 21 : 4).

Everyone who visits the empty Tomb can hear its testimony. Jesus is alive! Christ is victorious! To Him is given all power in heaven and on earth! Jesus has conquered every power of death! Jesus is Victor over all His enemies! Jesus has indeed trodden sin beneath His feet, for lo, He is risen! The sins of the world, which He bore on the Cross, could not bind Him. Instead He triumphed over them, for He is alive! The empty Tomb proclaims that Jesus has bruised the head of the serpent, which bruised His heel. Jesus has destroyed the power of Satan. Henceforth no one can be held in bondage by Satan if he reckons with the risen Lord, for lo, Christ is Victor!

The empty Tomb waits for us to sing hymns of victory in honour of the risen Lord. In our struggles against sin and all oppressive powers and in every hopeless situation the empty Tomb challenges us to have faith in Him who is mightier than all these forces. Jesus Christ will break all fetters, for everything must yield before Him, the Prince of Victory!

Who can ever render Jesus enough praise and thanksgiving for His victory! At the site where He rose from the dead, Jesus is waiting for souls to worship Him for the miracle of the Resurrection, to acclaim Him as Victor and to believe in His victory for their own lives.

PRAYER AT THE HOLY SEPULCHRE

Our Lord Jesus,
We bring You our thanksgiving here at this site. The grave could not hold You, O Lamb of God that was slain, since You have paid the ransom to hell. You have overcome the powers of death and hell, and broken out of the Tomb, releasing us from the prison of our sin.

I praise Your triumphant victory. O risen Lord, Prince of Victory, You will grant us victory in our battle against sin. I claim Your victory in my life, since You have won this victory for me as well.

Thanks, praise and worship be unto You, O Lord, for rising again in glory, after having suffered death for us. I thank You, for with the Resurrection You have given me the blessed hope that as a member of Your Body I too may rise in glory one day and abide in Your kingdom for all eternity. Hallelujah!   Amen.

✝

From the night of deepest suffering
Joy divine is now upwelling;
Jesus triumphs o'er the grave.
Praise the Lamb, our Saviour glorious,
Who in dying was victorious!
Love in suff'ring vanquished the foe.

LITANY OF VICTORY

Jesus, Thou hast broken Satan's power, for Thou art risen. Hallelujah!

Jesus, Thou hast overcome as the Lion of Judah, for Thou art risen. Hallelujah!

Jesus, Prince of Victory, all Thine enemies must lie at Thy feet, for Thou art risen. Hallelujah!

Jesus, Thou hast overcome Death, that we may rise in glory, for Thou art risen. Hallelujah!

Jesus, Thou hast vanquished the powers of hell and sin – in my life too – for Thou art risen. Hallelujah!

Jesus, Thou hast broken asunder all bonds – in my life too – for Thou art risen. Hallelujah!

Jesus, mighty Redeemer, Thy redemption availeth for me, for Thou art risen. Hallelujah!

Jesus, the grave could not hold Thee, nor can the grave of my sin hold me, for I am a member of Thy Body. Thou art risen. Hallelujah!

Jesus, as the victorious Lamb of God, Thou hast taken away the sins of the world, for Thou art risen. Hallelujah!

Jesus, in Thy hands Thou holdest the keys of the kingdom of hell and death. Thou art alive from eternity to eternity, for Thou art risen. Hallelujah!

Jesus, Thou art Lord, and all power in heaven and on earth hath been given to Thee, for Thou art risen. Hallelujah!

Jesus, seated at the right hand of Majesty, Thou wilt establish Thine eternal kingdom above all the kingdoms of the world, for Thou art risen. Hallelujah!

He Burst Out from the Grave's Dark Night

8. 8. 7. 8. 8. 7. 7.

He burst out from the grave's dark night,/ Our Easter

Sun with gladsome light/ Of Jacob's line our

Saviour!/ The soldiers fall to earth aghast!/

The Cross's pain at length is past,/ for Christ, the

149

Lord, is ris — en./For Christ indeed is ris — en.

Yes, he whom Easter joy sets free
His heart cries out his Lord to see,
Though Satan loud may threaten.
My thankful heart the Victor knows,
Hails Jesus, Lord of all His foes,
For Jesus is the Victor!
For Christ, our Lord, is risen!

The Prince of Jacob, full of might,
Brings life to us in sin's dark night;
Now death's long rule is broken.
The morn with Easter praises rings;
New life in dead, cold hearts now springs.
They throb with joyful worship,
For Christ, the Lord, is risen.

Those who today are swept along
By Easter joy to praise and song
Will laugh at Satan's threat'ning.
Oh! praise, my soul, I know the Lord!
His name by me be aye adored!
O sing, "He is the Victor!"
For Christ indeed is risen!

MOUNT ZION

(site of the Upper Room, also known as the Cenacle)

How often we meet the name of Zion in prayers, hymns and psalms! And now we have actually come to Mount Zion, although this is not the original Zion, the City of David. His city, which lay to the south of the old city wall on Mount Ophel, the eastern hill, is no longer in existence. But the new Mount Zion, situated on the western hill (south of the Tower of David), is the scene of two of the most significant events in the New Testament. Here, in one room, both the institution of the Lord's Supper and the outpouring of the Holy Spirit on Pentecost are commemorated.

Taking the road outside the city wall from the Jaffa Gate to the Zion Gate, or passing through the Zion Gate itself, or coming from the Dung Gate, we reach Mount Zion.

As we enter a courtyard, coming from the Zion Gate, we find a door on the left giving access to a stairway that leads to the Upper Room or Cenacle. This plain Gothic room, where no sign indicating its significance can be found, lies directly above a Jewish shrine, the Tomb of David. Although we can hear the sound of singing and praying from below, silence must reign here. Yet how we long to give thanks to Jesus at this site for giving us Himself with the institution of Holy Communion! And how we yearn to praise the Holy Spirit here!

Then we climb up to the observation platform, whose approach is opposite the entrance to the Tomb of David. A winding staircase leads to the roof and soon we are standing beneath the steel blue sky, whence came the "rush of a mighty wind" long ago. Here we have a panoramic view of the Mount of Olives and the city of Jerusalem.

THE HISTORICAL ASPECT

The Gospels tell us nothing of the location of the house where Jesus celebrated the Last Supper with His disciples; they only say that a man carrying a jar of water would show the way. In Mark 14 : 14 and Luke 22 : 11, the Gospel writers call the place a "katalyma", the usual word for "guest room". But the following verses (Mark 14 : 15 and Luke 22 : 12) disclose that the disciples would be shown to a specific room, an "anagaion", that is, an "upper room". The words "upper room" indicate that it was most likely an additional storey, and thus we can assume that Jesus held the Passover in the house of a wealthy man. However, the Gospels give us no clue to its whereabouts in the city and no Early Christian tradition concerning this place has survived.

In contrast, for the site of the outpouring of the Holy Spirit on the day of Pentecost there is an ancient tradition, confirmed by reliable sources, stating that it was a room on Mount Zion. And it was this tradition that gave Mount Zion its name. Because the Early Christians, who called themselves the New Testament "Zion", had their first meeting place here, the name "Zion" was transferred from its original place, the City of David on Mount Ophel, to its present location. At this meeting place of the Early Christians the first church, "the mother of all churches", was built. It evidently survived the destruction of Jerusalem in A.D. 70, for the western quarter was outside the scene of the military operations. Bishop Epiphanius, born in Judea in 315, wrote how the Emperor Hadrian made an inspection tour of Jerusalem in 130 and found everything razed "except for a few houses and a certain small church of the Christians, which stood on Mount Zion in that place where the disciples, returning after the Ascension, went up to the Upper Room (hyperoon)." This report shows that in those days Zion was considered to be the home of the disciples after the Ascension as well as the place where the Holy Spirit descended at Pentecost. According to the description of the nun Etheria, who witnessed the Easter liturgy on Mount Zion in 385, the Upper Room was also regarded as the place where the risen Lord appeared to the disciples (Luke 24 : 36-49; John 20 : 19-29) and as the disciples' meeting place after Jesus' death.

However, this "certain small church of the Christians", which was built at the site of the Upper Room, did not yet commemorate the institution of the Lord's Supper. In the English version of the New Testament accounts the term "upper room" is used to refer to the site of the Last Supper and the outpouring of the Holy Spirit, whereas the Greek text uses two different terms. The "hyperoon" of Bishop Epiphanius' account is also used by Luke in Acts 1 : 13 to describe the centre of the Early Christians, but in his Gospel he uses "anagaion" for the room of the Last Supper (Luke 22 : 12). As early as the year 400 the tradition arose in Syria that both "upper rooms" were one and the same place. This was due to the Syrian translation, which like the English uses the same word for the two different Greek words ("anagaion" in Luke 22 : 12 and "hyperoon" in Acts 1 : 13). In Jerusalem itself between 450 and 500 the supposition was made that the events of the Last Supper and Pentecost took place in the same room, as indicated by the liturgies of that period.

Even so the commemoration of the Last Supper in the church on Mount Zion was slow in receiving acceptance. Several pilgrim reports from the sixth century mention other traditions for the place of the Last Supper, such as the Cave of Betrayal. Yet it is probably not far-fetched to assume that after Easter the disciples gathered in the same room where the Last Supper was held. And although there is no definite tradition to support this view, the Upper Room is surely a suitable place to commemorate the institution of the Lord's Supper.

In about 340 a large basilica, the "Hagia Sion" (Holy Zion) was erected over that "certain small church of the Christians", but in 614 it was destroyed by the Persians, sharing the fate of almost all the other churches. It was later rebuilt only to be destroyed again; during the time of the Crusaders it was rebuilt once more. From that time onwards the church on Mount Zion also commemorated the death of the Virgin Mary, and a special chapel within the church building probably marked the site. Today the nearby Church of the Dormition (taken from the Latin *dormitio* – to sleep) perpetuates this memory. The reports, however, do not make it altogether clear whether the Upper Room was inside the church on Mount Zion or an adjoining building.

The badly damaged church of the Crusaders was acquired in 1333 by the King of Naples and handed over to the Franciscans, who restored the room of the Last Supper (the chapel of the Cenacle), giving it its present appearance. Throughout the centuries this site changed hands several times, and it even served as a mosque. Since 1948 the building has been open to visitors. However, Christian worship services in the Cenacle are only permitted on Maundy Thursday and Pentecost.

In the ninth or tenth century tradition transferred the veneration of the Tomb of David to Mount Zion. This has resulted in the Jewish shrine directly below the Cenacle in the same building, which is now under Israeli administration.

THE LAST SUPPER

FROM THE HOLY BIBLE

Jesus said to Peter and John, "Behold, when you have entered the city, a man carrying a jar of water will meet you; follow him into the house which he enters, and tell the householder, 'The Teacher says to you, Where is the guest room, where I am to eat the passover with my disciples?' And he will show you a large upper room furnished; there make ready." And they went, and found it as he had told them; and they prepared the passover.

When it was evening, he sat at table with the twelve disciples. And he said to them, "I have earnestly desired to eat this passover with you before I suffer; for I tell you I shall never eat it again until it is fulfilled in the kingdom of God." And as they were eating, he said, "Truly, I say to you, one of you will betray me." And they were very sorrowful, and began to say to him one after another, "Is it I, Lord?" Jesus answered, "It is he to whom I shall give this morsel when I have dipped it." So when he had dipped the morsel, he gave it to Judas, the son of Simon Iscariot. Then after the morsel, Satan entered into him, and he immediately went out; and it was night.

Now as they were eating, Jesus took bread, and blessed, and broke it, and gave it to the disciples and said, "Take, eat; this is my body." And he took a cup, and when he had given thanks he gave it to them, saying, "Drink of it, all of you; for this is my blood of the new covenant, which is poured out for many for the forgiveness of sins."

cf. Matthew 26, Luke 22, John 13

THE UPPER ROOM –
A MESSAGE FOR US

In the Upper Room we remember how Jesus came together with His disciples to celebrate the last Passover with them before beginning His way to the Cross on Calvary. Here Jesus held His farewell discourses, which were filled with a wonderful radiance. Only such a Master could have uttered these words on the eve before His death as a legacy to us.

In these words of farewell we are once more given a glimpse of who Jesus is and of the supreme and noble gift He has given as a lasting possession to those whom He loves.

Is it not deeply moving to see that in this hour when Jesus prepares to undergo the most agonizing death, He does not speak of Himself? Instead He is full of loving concern for His disciples. Although Jesus is aware that night has come and with it the dominion of darkness, although He knows that one of His disciples will betray Him, that the rest will forsake Him and that Peter will deny Him, He speaks words of love and gratitude to them. Although He knows that within the next hours they will bring Him grief upon grief, He thanks them for having continued with Him in His trials. He makes them the supreme promise that He will prepare a place for them with His Father in heaven (Luke 22 : 28 f.). And He promises them even more. He will come again and make His dwelling with them. He will send them the Comforter, the Holy Spirit. And just as they share His suffering now, they will share His glory for all eternity.

Such words can only come from a heart brimming over with love for those who wound and desert Him, for those who betray Him. Here it becomes evident that Jesus looks with eyes of divine love upon sinful beings, engulfed in darkness. Although He is aware of how disgracefully His disciples will behave, Jesus in His majesty sees beyond all the sin and suffering with the eyes of faith, as Love who triumphs over sin. Divine love believes and hopes all things for sinful man, and thus when Jesus looks at those who cause Him immeasurable anguish, He can already see what He intends to achieve in their lives and what will become of them. Indeed, Jesus' loving gaze reaches into eternity, into the Kingdom of God, where His own, redeemed by His love, will abide for evermore.

How fitting that these parting words of our Lord should be spoken during the Last Supper, which He held with His disciples! Yet what pain must have seared His heart during this feast! He celebrates this meal with them, since He wishes to institute the New Covenant, the covenant of love, which would be sealed by His death. And in the very moment that Jesus offers His heart and life as the basis of this covenant, one of the Twelve, who were closest to His heart, leaves the feast to betray his Master. Even then the love of Jesus, which is true, divine love, does not cease. Thus this meal is a true expression of love.

It is almost beyond human comprehension that our Lord Jesus, who knows all things and can see into the hearts of His disciples, then says in this hour when He is about to be betrayed, "I have earnestly desired to eat this passover with you." God in His love yearns to have communion with men, even if they sin against Him. Our natural human reaction would be to avoid those who wrong us and to keep our distance, whereas Jesus longs to be with the disciples and to celebrate the feast with them. Thus the Upper Room has witnessed a love that cannot be found anywhere else in this world. It is the love of Jesus. He came from heaven in order to regain for us true, divine life, which is love. By His very life He demonstrated what genuine love is; it is not embittered, it forgives, it lays down its life for its enemies and in the face of their sins believes in the victorious power of redemption.

Should we not, therefore, believe that in Holy Communion Jesus, who is eternal Love, gives Himself to us and lets us partake of His nature? Has He not said, "He who eats my flesh and drinks my blood has eternal life" (John 6 : 54)? Thus Holy Communion has a deep significance for us and we can never praise God enough for this gift. Let us then follow the invitation to come and draw from His inexhaustible riches to our hearts' content. Our body, soul and spirit receive all the strength and renewal they need through this gift of Jesus, for in the Lord's Supper we are united with Jesus Himself and drawn into the fellowship of His love and suffering.

At this place, which perpetuates the memory of the Last Supper, we cannot but worship the amazing love of Jesus. Let us respond to the love with which He made the covenant of love in the Breaking of Bread. May our response be an act of committal to follow His example by loving our brethren and laying down our lives for them. In Holy Communion Jesus wishes to give us the love that will enable us to do so.

PRAYER IN THE UPPER ROOM

Our Lord Jesus,

We thank You for saying to us as You did to the disciples long ago, "I have earnestly desired to eat this passover with you!" We worship You for Your love, which yearns to be united with us, sinful though we are. We thank You that in Holy Communion You come to us, granting us this union and letting us partake of eternal, divine life. We worship You, for in Your love You not only bestow many gifts upon us, but grant us Yourself with Your precious body and blood, that we may receive the forgiveness of our sins and partake of Your divine nature.

Dear Lord Jesus, I will heed Your loving invitation and give the response of my love by hastening joyfully to You, that I may be united with You. O hear my prayer and fill me with Your love as I partake of Holy Communion.

Amen.

+

The Lord's Supper — a feast of joy for sinners who receive forgiveness of their sins, a meal of love in which God unites Himself with human souls, and therefore a true agape, born out of the fellowship of love with God. A blessed meal that lets us have a taste of heaven in the presence of God, in love and joy!

Feast of Love

7.7.7.8.8.7.

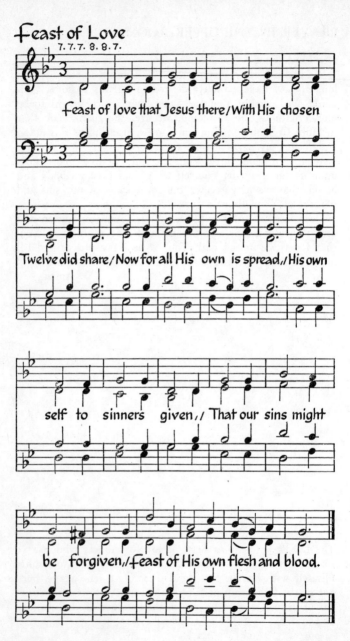

Feast of love that Jesus there / With His chosen
Twelve did share / Now for all His own is spread, / His own
self to sinners given, / / That our sins might
be forgiven, / / Feast of His own flesh and blood.

Feast of Jesus, who once gave
His own life our souls to save
In entire self-sacrifice,
Now in bread and wine He proffers
Life divine, Himself He offers,
Holy myst'ry of His love!

Feast of Jesus, holy food,
Cov'nant of His sacred blood,
Reuniting God and man.
Here we find our fullest union,
Love itself's own sweet communion
For the body and the soul.

Feast of Jesus, for us spread,
Lord, Your body is the bread,
Which makes wholly new our lives;
And the wine, Lord, which You furnish
Is Your blood, us to replenish
With the very life divine.

Feast of Jesus, feast most blest,
Grace of graces holiest!
We receive our Lord Himself,
That we in His Passion sharing,
For our cross may be preparing.
God be thanked eternally!

Well-spring of Joy 49

THE DAY OF PENTECOST

FROM THE HOLY BIBLE

On the evening of that day, the first day of the week, the doors being shut where the disciples were, for fear of the Jews, Jesus came and stood among them and said to them, "Peace be with you" ... Eight days later, his disciples were again in the house, and Thomas was with them. The doors were shut, but Jesus came and stood among them, and said, "Peace be with you."   John 20 : 19, 26

And while staying with his disciples, Jesus charged them not to depart from Jerusalem, but to wait for the promise of the Father. He said, "Before many days you shall be baptized with the Holy Spirit." And when he had said this, as they were looking on, he was lifted up.

Then they returned to Jerusalem and when they had entered, they went up to the upper room, where they were staying. With one accord they devoted themselves to prayer, together with the women and Mary the mother of Jesus, and with his brothers.   cf. Acts 1 : 4-9, 12-14

When the day of Pentecost had come, they were all together in one place. And suddenly a sound came from heaven like the rush of a mighty wind, and it filled all the house where they were sitting. And there appeared to them tongues as of fire, distributed and resting on each one of them. And they were all filled with the Holy Spirit.   Acts 2 : 1-4 a

Sacred Upper Room Is This

7. 7. 6. 7. 7. 6. 7. 7. 6.

Sacred Upper Room is this, / full of joy and
from this day for ev-ermore / God's own Spir- it

holy bliss,/ Where the fire de—scend—ed./
we a—dore./ Prais—es have a—scend—ed./

from His flesh He fashioned here/ His own Church,

His bride so dear,/ God's own ho—ly tem—ple.

Myst'ry great that holy morn,
Church of God, Christ's bride, was born,
Heavenly creation!
God's creative work we see,
By His breath it came to be,
Called of God and chosen!
Holy Ghost, Thou camest down,
Thou of all God's gifts the crown.
For Thy deeds we praise Thee.

The Upper Room   November 12, 1959

THE UPPER ROOM – A MESSAGE FOR US

The Upper Room where we commemorate the Lord's Supper reminds us of yet another mighty event in God's plan of salvation – the outpouring of the Holy Spirit. To this day we are filled with awe and wonder as we contemplate this tremendous miracle, hitherto unknown and surpassing all human understanding.

Like the rush of a mighty wind the Holy Spirit, the third Person of the Godhead, comes down to earth, to a specific place – the Upper Room on Mount Zion. He seeks out specific people, the disciples, a handful of miserable failures, who had lost faith and deserted their Lord during His Passion. Indeed, the Holy Spirit comes especially to the disciples, who are so poor and needy, for in them He can demonstrate His power as Creator Spirit. He brings dead hearts to life. He imbues despondent and fearful hearts with courage and power to witness. He accomplishes great transformations in the hearts of men.

In Acts 4 : 31 we read that when the company of believers were assembled in prayer the place was shaken. But what must it have been like when the Holy Spirit Himself descended and poured out the fullness of grace upon the gathering in the Upper Room! In tongues of fire He descended upon the heads of the disciples, imparting to them fervent love and the courage to suffer, setting them wholly on fire for God and His kingdom. Is it surprising then that the disciples appeared to be intoxicated with the Holy Spirit? The mighty, rushing wind of the Holy Spirit seized them so powerfully that they probably rejoiced and wept at the same time. And being filled with the fullness of God, they were moved to speak in other tongues.

Something of the very nature of God was imparted to their hearts by the Holy Spirit. They were set ablaze with the love of God, a consuming ardour that could no longer be expressed in the tongues of men. Fire was cast into their hearts by the Holy Spirit, setting them aflame with a fervent love for God, which constrained them to tell everyone about Jesus, regardless of the cost.

Can we imagine the joy of that hour when the miracle of Pentecost occurred? Truly, it was a blessed Pentecost when the fire of love blazed brightly, kindling not only love for

God, but also love for the brethren – love that seeks to hold all things in common. Constrained by the love of God, which the Holy Spirit had imparted, this small group of people now became of one heart and soul. Who can refrain from worshipping the Holy Spirit, the third Person of the Godhead, who performs such mighty deeds?

The Holy Spirit manifested Himself as the Creator Spirit, who called into being here the Church of God, which exists to this very day. Surely, we must love, thank and honour Him today for what He has done. Today as yesterday He is the same Creator Spirit, zealous to establish the Kingdom of God in our midst.

Today the Holy Spirit still comes down upon wretched, needy souls if with one accord they devote themselves to prayer, claiming in faith God's promises for the Spirit's coming. Today He grants people a second birth through His life-giving power. Today He transforms people and pours into their hearts the ardour of divine love. As the Spirit of joy He fills the hearts of men today with joy, laughter and singing. Today He unites divided members of the Body of Christ in the love of God. Today He bestows His blessings and gifts as they are defined in the Bible – the gifts of knowledge, faith, wisdom, prophecy, speaking in other tongues and working miracles. Even though we resist and grieve Him so much, He continues to work tirelessly in our hard hearts to remould us into the image of God. Now He is also waiting today for us to say, "I believe in the Holy Spirit", and to reach out for Him with believing, imploring hearts, for Jesus has said, "If I go, I will send him [the Holy Spirit] to you" (John 16 : 7).

Today, when Jesus' second coming is on the threshold, surely He yearns all the more to grant the members of His Body a new experience of Pentecost. Here in the Upper Room on the day of Pentecost the body of believers was born to be His bride. And surely He will now complete His bride in number and lead her on to maturity through the creative power of His Holy Spirit. Indeed, Jesus longs to find His bride "adorned" when He comes again, so that He can gather her to Himself for the Marriage Feast. All those who are willing to be transformed into the image of Jesus will be prepared by the Holy Spirit, that they may attain the supreme goal.

The disciples gather behind closed doors,
United in the Upper Room.
They pray and watch and wait and pray –
Will Jesus' promise be fulfilled?

Expectantly they wait and yearn
For things unspeakable and great.
Their souls are lifted heavenwards,
That God may touch them with His light.
They pray and wait and watch and pray:
Will Jesus' words come true – today?

Another day ... Again they wait
United in the Upper Room
When suddenly the Spirit comes!
Like rustling wings, a mighty wind
Fills all the room while tongues of fire
Descend and set their hearts ablaze.

O blessèd Pentecost that brought
Fulfilment of the prophecy!
Baptized with fire and power divine,
The hearts of the disciples now
Are seized with a triumphant joy.
Aglow with ardour, faith and strength,
No longer bereft, they rejoice
That Jesus, their belovèd Lord,
Comes to them in the Holy Ghost,
Comes to them in omnipotence!

They praise and sing, courageously
Proclaiming now that Jesus Christ
Has filled them with such happiness.
The Upper Room vibrates, and thousands hear
The Spirit speaking to their souls.
Repentance wells up in their hearts;
Now weeping, laughing – fearlessly,
With joy they own Him as their Lord.

Pentecost, O blessèd day!
A thousand voices praise aloud:
Our sins have been forgiven!
Born of the Spirit, given new life,
We sing and rejoice.
The Holy Spirit came indeed,
Descending like a mighty wind
With ardour and tongues of fire!

PRAYER IN THE UPPER ROOM

O Holy Spirit,

We thank You for descending here like the rush of a mighty wind, and for giving birth to the Church, the Body of Christ. We thank You that at this place You set the disciples afire with love and bestowed upon them an abundance of spiritual gifts. And we praise Your mighty power, for You turned cowards into fiery witnesses and martyrs. We thank You for the miracle of Pentecost when You demonstrated Your power as the Creator Spirit to call into existence the things that do not exist – the New Testament Church, the mystic Body of Christ, imbued with the power of love, prayer and sacrifice and endowed with the unmerited favours of God and the gifts of the Spirit.

Here, at this site, as I consider the blessings and spiritual gifts I lack, I declare that I believe in You, O Holy Spirit, and in Your creative power. In my life too You will call the things into existence that do not exist and supply all that I need in the way of courage to witness, ardent love and sacrificial spirit. I trust that You will grant me Your blessings.

O Holy Spirit, I thank You for working untiringly in my hard heart, that I may be transformed into the image of Jesus, the image of His love. Therefore, I pray, kindle in me a love for all brothers and sisters in the Lord, including those in other denominations and branches of Christianity, for then the world will see by the love we have for each other that Jesus, the Head of the Body, is Love eternal.

Amen.

LITANY OF ADORATION
TO THE HOLY SPIRIT

O Holy Spirit, be praised and adored!
O fiery Flame of God Most High, You descend upon us sinners to kindle us with an ardent love for God.

O Holy Spirit, be praised and adored!
Spirit of life, You infuse life into dead bones and as the Breath of God You breathe upon our dead hearts to bring them to life, so that we may praise our Saviour and Redeemer.

O Holy Spirit, be praised and adored!
Spirit of power and might, You cast down all that is lofty and arrogant, and humble the proud, so that God, and God alone, is exalted.

O Holy Spirit, be praised and adored!
Spirit divine issuing from God, You penetrate the depths of the Godhead and reveal these mysteries to those who love Him.

O Holy Spirit, be praised and adored!
Spirit of joy, You comfort the sad and make troubled hearts rejoice and fill them with the radiance of God.

O Holy Spirit, be praised and adored!
Spirit of truth, like a sword You pierce and divide us to the joint and marrow, judging the thoughts of the heart and bringing hidden things to light.

O Holy Spirit, be praised and adored!
As the bright Light of God You shine forth in the darkness, imparting light to us, so that we can see the path of God and not go astray.

O Holy Spirit, be praised and adored!
Creator Spirit, You grant new birth to the sons of men and transform sinners into God's children.

O Holy Spirit, be praised and adored!
Spirit of God, You accomplish Your work in us sinful sons of men, moulding us into the image of God, that we may reflect His divine glory.

O Holy Spirit, be praised and adored!
Like a mighty wind You rush through heaven and earth, filling the Body of Christ with the spirit of adoration and thanksgiving.

O Holy Spirit, be praised and adored!
Eternal Spirit, who is and was from the beginning, You are coequal with the Father and the Son and with the Father and the Son You are one as the eternal Godhead. Glory be to You!

✝

To the Upper Room Descending

8.8.7.D.

To the Up – per Room descending,// full of pow'r and grace un-ending,// Comes the ho-ly Dove divine,// Cleaves the air with

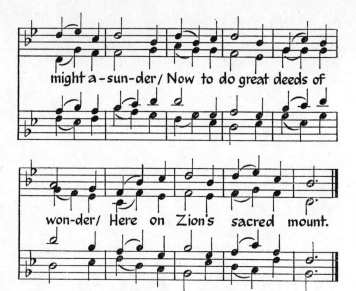

might a-sun-der/ Now to do great deeds of
won-der/ Here on Zion's sacred mount.

Hear that mighty tempest blowing!
Yes, it is the Spirit showing
Witness of His mighty power.
Now Christ's people raise their voices;
Fervently each heart rejoices,
Kindled by the tongues of fire.

Wondrously illuminated,
By the love of God elated,
Praise they now what He has done.
Fire of love their hearts inflaming,
All the praise of Christ proclaiming;
With new tongues they laud His name.

Hour of grace and exultation!
Place of loving visitation
When God came to dwell with men!
Let the Spirit's praise be chanted
For His grace so freely granted
To the whole of Christendom.

Well-spring of Joy 108, The Upper Room, Nov. 12, 1959

At Pentecost the Holy Spirit lavishly poured out His gifts. And today He is still the same Spirit, who longs to bestow on us the fullness of His blessings. Yet who will come begging to Him with empty hands? Only those who suffer because of their poverty will be richly blessed by Him.

✝

We must heed the gentlest admonishment of the Holy Spirit, for no one is so sensitive as the Holy Spirit, who withdraws from us when we grieve Him.

✝

In view of your poverty and the chaos in your soul, say, "I believe in the Holy Ghost, the Lord and Giver of life" – and by your faith you will experience His wonder-working power in your life.

BETHPHAGE

How often have we heard the story of Jesus' entry into Jerusalem! Each time, as we may recall, a place was mentioned where a donkey stood ready for our Lord. And now our way takes us to the modern-day Bethphage, which is marked by a Franciscan monastery and church, lying in a hollow on the eastern slope of the Mount of Olives.

Bethphage can be reached via the Jericho motor road. Halfway to Bethany, a road branches off to the left to Bethphage and the Mount of Olives. But since we wish to have an impression of the way from Jerusalem to Bethany via Bethphage, which Jesus must have taken scores of times, we choose a different route and go by foot. From the middle summit of the Mount of Olives it is only a 15 minutes' walk to the church of Bethphage. Following the narrow road eastwards, we pass the Carmelite convent and the Pater Noster Church on our right. On the left lies the property of the Russian Orthodox Mount of Olives convent. In the east we can see the Mountains of Moab rising above the hills of the Judean Desert and in the south the conical mountain known as the Herodium. Looking down into the valley on our right, we can make out the course of the Jericho motor road to Bethany as well as one of the new roads to Bethlehem, which passes by the Mount of Evil Counsel.

A few houses of the Mount of Olives village Et-Tur reach down the slope. Soon we come to the extensive Franciscan grounds, which are surrounded by walls and cypress trees. As we tarry in the church, our thoughts are turned to Palm Sunday. From here Jesus set out for Jerusalem, which He would enter uncrowned and misunderstood — on His way to Calvary.

The church will be opened upon request.

THE HISTORICAL ASPECT

The Biblical Bethphage, whose name probably means "house of unripe, juiceless figs", is described in the Gospels as lying on the eastern slope of the Mount of Olives in the vicinity of Bethany, with which it is usually coupled. But the exact location can no longer be ascertained. It must have lain "opposite" (Luke 19 : 30), that is, somewhat to the north of the spot where the disciples brought the donkey and where Jesus mounted it. And the place now called Bethphage is regarded by an ancient tradition to be the site of the mounting.

We can easily imagine that Jesus, coming from Bethany, would have mounted the donkey at the place where the present Bethphage church stands. The path leading up from Bethany was a poor one, cumbersome for both the rider and his mount. But here in the hollow of Bethphage the path grew smoother, so that the procession may well have started at this point.

There was a church here as far back as the fourth century. According to the report of the nun Etheria, it also commemorated Jesus' encounter with Martha and Mary as they hastened to Him when He came to raise Lazarus from the dead. Up to the seventh century this church is mentioned a number of times; later it was probably destroyed. However, the memory of the place remained. The report of the Russian Abbot Daniel in 1106, at the beginning of the Crusader period, makes it clear that Jesus' encounter with Martha and Mary as well as the mounting of the donkey were commemorated at the same spot.

During the time of the Crusaders all memory of the meeting with Martha and Mary vanished, and only Palm Sunday was commemorated in the church, which they rebuilt. The German pilgrim, Theoderich, relates in 1172 that he was shown the stone "on which Jesus put his foot to mount the donkey". This stone with its paintings and inscriptions was discovered in 1877. In 1880 the Franciscans acquired the land and the stone, which they placed in the church they erected in 1883. While the church was being built, they discovered the remains of the medieval church. The paintings on the block, which they arranged to have restored and completed in 1950, depict the bringing of the donkey, the entry into Jerusalem and the raising of Lazarus.

FROM THE HOLY BIBLE

Rejoice greatly, O daughter of Zion! Shout aloud, O daughter of Jerusalem! Lo, your king comes to you; triumphant and victorious is he, humble and riding on an ass, on a colt the foal of an ass.   Zechariah 9 : 9

And when they drew near to Jerusalem and came to Bethphage, to the Mount of Olives, then Jesus sent two disciples, saying to them, "Go into the village opposite you, and im-

171

mediately you will find an ass tied, and a colt with her; untie them and bring them to me. If any one says anything to you, you shall say, 'The Lord has need of them,' and he will send them immediately." This took place to fulfil what was spoken by the prophet.

The disciples went and did as Jesus had directed them; they brought the ass and the colt, and put their garments on them, and he sat thereon. Most of the crowd spread their garments on the road, and others cut branches from the trees and spread them on the road. And the crowds that went before him and that followed him shouted, "Hosanna to the Son of David! Blessed be he who comes in the name of the Lord!"

And when he drew near and saw the city he wept over it.

Matthew 21 : 1-4, 6-9   Luke 19 : 41

Then I saw heaven opened, and behold, a white horse! He who sat upon it is called Faithful and True, and in righteousness he judges and makes war. And the armies of heaven followed him on white horses.   cf. Revelation 19 : 11, 14

BETHPHAGE – A MESSAGE FOR US

Bethphage! A site that will never be forgotten, for this is where Jesus' royal procession began. From here Jesus was to enter His royal city as the Son of David. However, the triumphal entry ended in the Crowning with Thorns and death on the Cross at Calvary.

Bethphage! Once an ass and her foal stood tethered here – their Creator needed them; indeed, they had been chosen to serve Him for His royal entry into Jerusalem. This colt, the foal of an ass, was deemed worthy to bear the noblest burden of all, the Creator of the world, God Himself – a privilege granted to none other. On this momentous occasion mute creation was employed in God's service as seldom before in history.

Bethphage! A place where Jesus, who had veiled His power, who had become a Servant of all, nevertheless revealed Himself as Lord. In His sovereignty He could utter the words, "If any one says anything to you, you shall say, 'The Lord has need of them,' and he will send them immediately."

Bethphage! A place that also speaks of the extreme poverty

of Jesus. Here He asked for a donkey, since He did not possess one. Yet did not every second man in the Orient own one? Though Lord and Maker of all creatures, Jesus was obliged to borrow a mount for His royal entry into His city.

Bethphage! Our hearts are stirred at the sound of its name, for Bethphage speaks to us of the obedience of the Son of God. Why did He mount the donkey when He knew that His entry into Jerusalem was utterly pointless? He would never be acknowledged as King, but rather be put to death on the Cross like a criminal. Was it not an act of folly to undertake this royal procession, which would end in a shameful death on the Cross? How senseless it was to let Himself be hailed as King by those who would kill Him but a few days later! However, in obedience to the Word of God and "that the scripture might be fulfilled" Jesus mounted the donkey here in Bethphage in order to enter Jerusalem.

Bethphage! This place testifies that all God's promises and prophecies are "yea and amen". Here the words were fulfilled, "Tell the daughter of Zion, behold, your king is coming to you, humble, and mounted on an ass, and on a colt, the foal of an ass." How literally, how tangibly God fulfils His promises! He does not make His word come true merely in the figurative sense. This became evident here in Bethphage. God is Lord and He Himself accomplishes His purposes through His personal involvement. Jesus, the Son of God, who should have been received as King, entered His city meek and lowly, riding on a donkey, in order to give Himself as an offering and to be slain as the Lamb of God.

Bethphage! What feelings must have been stirred in our Lord Jesus as He mounted the donkey amid the jubilant shouts of His disciples and of the throng that gathered round Him! His heart must have been heavy-laden with sorrow. He knew that even His disciples were not loyal subjects and that their rejoicing was not genuine. They did not wish to serve Jesus as the King of lowliness, but sought in Him a king who would match their earthly conceptions. They coveted high positions for themselves. They strove for their own honour and refused to heed their Master's words and do His bidding. Jesus alone was humble. Though He was their Creator and King, He rode on a donkey, whereas the disciples, who were merely created beings and sinners, were high and mighty. Seldom had there been such a contrast between self-exaltation and lowliness. In that hour a wide rift separated the disciples from Jesus – their hearts were not moved by that which moved Him. Whereas Jesus' heart was weighed down in sorrow, their hearts were elated in joy. How grieved Jesus must have been, for nothing is so wounding as sham affection or mock homage when people are unwilling to prove their love with utter devotion or to pay due reverence with submissiveness! And a little while later as Jesus descended the Mount of Olives on the donkey, He broke out in tears at the sight of His city Jerusalem, where even greater grief and pain awaited Him.

Bethphage of old was the starting point for that sad entry of Jesus into His city on Palm Sunday. Bethphage of today waits for us to prepare Him a different entry into His city, one worthy of Him, when He comes again as King of kings. To judge by the signs of the times prophesied by Jesus for the close of the age, His second coming is not far off. Thus Jesus entreats us to prepare ourselves, so that on that day He will truly be acclaimed as King and accompanied by a host of subjects who have learnt to let Him rule over their lives in every sphere, who have learnt to humble themselves under His will and leadings and to do His bidding. Then indeed Jesus will be followed by a train of souls, who, having been redeemed by Him, reflect His image, which He revealed to us in Bethphage – the image of humility, meekness and obedience. As the "pioneer of our salvation", who has forged the way before us, He waits for such followers today.

PRAYER IN BETHPHAGE

Dear Lord Jesus,

We humble ourselves in shame. Although You alone are the High and Lofty One, You began Your kingly reign in such humility, meekness and obedience, riding on a borrowed donkey. You sought to win our hearts with Your humble love, that we might willingly accept Your rule. But tears and sorrow marked Your entry, because we are so proud and rebellious at heart and refuse to submit to Your dominion.

O Lord Jesus, how meek You are! May Your tears bring me to repentance, that I may cast myself at Your feet in true humility. Lord, You are King, and from now on I place my whole life under Your rule. Do with me as You please. Lead me as You will. Send me whatever You wish. I want to obey Your word. Grant me this attitude as I live in expectation of Your return, and help me to prepare myself for this day, so that I may receive You as King in sincerity.

Rouse the faithful and Your chosen people to prepare themselves in this way, so that Your sorrow will then be turned into joy and You will be hailed with true hosannas.

Amen.

Upon a Donkey's Colt He Rode

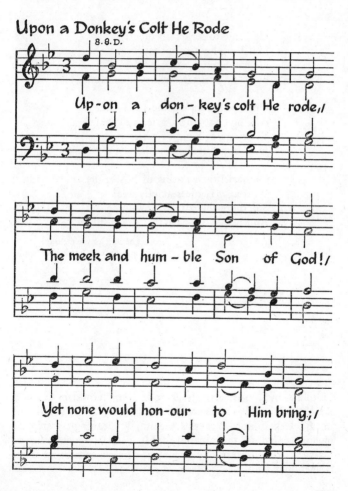

Up-on a don-key's colt He rode,/
The meek and hum-ble Son of God!/
Yet none would hon-our to Him bring;/

None humbly loved this hum-ble King.

He came to serve, obediently
Fulfilling holy prophecy.
He came unto Jerusalem,
But they prepared a Cross for Him.

Once veiled in lowliness He came,
A King of sorrows, grief and shame.
Yet soon, as King of majesty,
He'll come again in radiancy.

Oh hark! the praising of His bride,
Who now rejoices at His side!
She chose the path of lowliness
And helped prepare this day of bliss.

Can also be sung to the melody,
"All People That on Earth Do Dwell"

✝

Humbly and obediently Jesus rode into Jerusalem upon a
donkey, although He knew that this royal entry would end
in the Crucifixion. Yet this seemingly meaningless step of
obedience led to the greatest deed of all – redemption at
Calvary. To this very day such steps of obedience bring forth
tremendous fruit.

BETHANY

This place, which so often drew Jesus, will also draw us, for it treasures many memories of His words and deeds. The tomb of Lazarus and the nearby Franciscan church offer an opportunity to contemplate the events of long ago. Today Bethany is a Moslem village, known as El-Azariyeh (Lazarium). It lies within easy reach, about 3 km. from Jerusalem on the Jericho motor road.

But now that we are in Bethphage, we proceed by foot, taking a rough and stony path to the right of the Franciscan property. This path, which leads down to the valley in a southeasterly direction, is most probably the one that connected the Mount of Olives with Bethany in Jesus' day. Before us lies Bethany surrounded by the hills of the nearby Judean Desert. From afar we can locate the site of Lazarus' tomb, for close to it are the dome and tower of the Franciscan church and a minaret. A short way uphill from Lazarus' tomb lies a new Greek Orthodox church. The path leads straight to the entrance of the tomb and about 15 to 20 m. farther down the hill is the Franciscan church. If we come by the road and take a left-hand turn where it curves sharply to the right within the village, we reach the church first and then the tomb.

We must descend 24 narrow stone steps down into the tomb; it is no longer at ground level in the garden as it was in Jesus' day, but rather 5 m. beneath the surface. First we find ourselves in the antechamber where Jesus' weeping is commemorated. A few steps below is the actual tomb, which resembles the Tomb of Christ, measuring 2 m. × 2 m. The three niches indicate that the tomb was intended for three bodies. On the rock wall is a plaque that reminds us of Jesus' mighty victory over Death. Later we shall be seeking out the nearby Franciscan church in order to contemplate all that Bethany has to say to us.

THE HISTORICAL ASPECT

According to John 11 : 18 the Bethany of Jesus' day was situated "about two miles" from Jerusalem. Lying at the foot of the Mount of Olives in the southeast, it must have been even more of an idyllic spot than it is now — the last bit of green before we reach the barren hills of the Judean Desert. Excavations between 1951 and 1953 revealed that ancient Bethany was situated somewhat northwest of the present-day El-Azariyeh, in other words, closer to Bethphage. This appears to verify the authenticity of the tomb now shown as that of Lazarus, for Jewish custom required that tombs be situated outside places of residence.

The raising of Lazarus from the dead not only excited the village, but roused the hostility of the Pharisees and chief priests (John 11 : 46 ff.). This may well account for the fact that the tomb of Lazarus was deeply impressed upon the memory of the Early Christians of Jerusalem. Thus an early tradition associated with this tomb was perpetuated by a three-naved church, facing eastwards, which was built over the tomb in the fourth century. The church was later destroyed by an earthquake and rebuilt in the fifth century. It was frequently damaged and many alterations were undertaken; in the twelfth century it was attached to the neighbouring church of a Benedictine convent. The tomb could then be approached from the crypt of this second church. In the sixteenth century the latter was converted into a mosque and the Moslems bricked up the original entrance to the tomb. The Franciscans obtained permission to make a new entrance from the street. Thus in the sixteenth century, or seventeenth century according to other sources, they carved out of the rock the narrow, steep steps leading down into the tomb.

The tomb of Lazarus is still in Moslem hands and the minaret of the mosque rises behind it in place of the former Christian church. However, at the end of the nineteenth century the Franciscans were able to acquire houses lying to the east of the tomb and they started excavations on this site in 1949, laying bare the remaining walls of the different building periods of the Lazarus Church. In 1952—54 a new, circular church with three altars was erected over the eastern half of the twelfth century church. It commemorates the raising of Lazarus and also the anointing of Jesus by Mary.

From early times tradition sought to identify the house of Mary and Martha besides the place commemorating the raising of Lazarus. In addition, several sites were regarded as the house of Simon the leper in which the anointing took place. But there is no clear and authenticated tradition concerning these houses. In the time of the Crusaders it was assumed that the site of the house of Simon was marked by the Lazarus Church and that of the house of Mary and Martha by the neighbouring Benedictine convent church. However, it is unlikely that either house stood so near to the tomb, since, as mentioned above, tombs had to be situated away from places of residence.

According to the report of the Franciscan, Odoricus, in about

1320, the house of Martha lay a double stone's throw away outside Bethany. This may refer to what are known as the "houses of Mary and Martha", which lie about 500 m. away from the tomb, east of Bethany, right and left of the road to Jericho. Today these sites lie in the grounds of the Russian and Greek Orthodox — the latter possessing a church. Both properties are connected with the names of Mary and Martha. Ancient pilgrim narratives mention what might have been two separate houses belonging to the sisters or possibly their tombs, over which churches and convents were later erected. Excavations have shown that the earliest church dates from Byzantine times.

FROM THE HOLY BIBLE

Now as Jesus and his disciples went on their way, he entered a village; and a woman named Martha received him into her house. And she had a sister called Mary, who sat at the Lord's feet and listened to his teaching. But Martha was distracted with much serving. The Lord said to her, "Martha, Martha, you are anxious and troubled about many things; one thing is needful. Mary has chosen the good portion, which shall not be taken away from her."   cf. Luke 10 : 38-42

Six days before the Passover, Jesus came to Bethany, where Lazarus was, whom Jesus had raised from the dead. There in the house of Simon the leper they made him a supper and Martha served. Mary then took a pound of costly ointment of pure nard and anointed the feet of Jesus and wiped his feet with her hair; and the house was filled with the fragance of the ointment. But there were some who said to themselves indignantly, "Why was the ointment thus wasted?" But Jesus said, "You always have the poor with you, and whenever you will, you can do good to them; but you will not always have me. She has done what she could; she has anointed my body beforehand for burying. And truly, I say to you, wherever the gospel is preached in the whole world, what she has done will be told in memory of her."
                    cf. John 12 : 1-8 and Mark 14 : 3-9

BETHANY – A MESSAGE FOR US

Jerusalem, the city of God, in which God and thus the Son of God should have taken delight, had become for Jesus the city of His sufferings. The Temple, the house of God, of which Jesus had once said, "I must be in my Father's house", had been turned into a den of thieves. What immeasurable grief for Jesus! And when He nevertheless felt compelled to proclaim His message in Jerusalem under the contemptuous eyes of the Pharisees, who constantly sought to waylay Him, He would often long to retire somewhere else at the end of His day's work – to a place where He would find people who would accept His message. And that place was Bethany.

After only one year of public ministry Jesus could no longer risk spending the night in the city of Jerusalem owing to the plots of His enemies. Very likely He then made Bethany His habitual residence whenever He came to Jerusalem. What must it have meant for Jesus to have a home here where He was always welcome! Did He not sometimes have to search like a beggar for a place to lay down His head as He Himself said? But here in Bethany was a home where He was greeted with loving words in contrast to the angry heckling and disputing of the Pharisees, which He probably had to suffer up to the moment He left the city.

Thus Bethany was a place for which Jesus had a special affection – and what must that have meant! Even today the name of Bethany has a sweet sound to it, conveying love and warmth, speaking of close friends and attentiveness. In Jerusalem Jesus was always wished away by the Pharisees, but here in Bethany Mary, Martha and Lazarus received Him with great joy and a loving heart. Here His physical needs were also attended to, for He could rest and partake of the food and drink Martha prepared for Him. Here were people who had an open heart for His sufferings and hardships.

Here Jesus could speak to Mary of His innermost concerns, since her greatest desire was to listen to what He had to say. His words were more precious to her than gold. She simply had to listen to Him and when she did so, she forgot all else. From His words she discerned that which moved His heart and learnt of His desires and concerns for His people, His disciples and the whole world. Indeed, she could perceive what caused Him joy or grief and thus she realized when the hour of His deep affliction had come and consoled Him by anointing Him for His burial with precious spikenard. This was an expression of her love for Jesus. The disciples, however, neglected to show Him kindness in His hour of grief and even begrudged Him this mark of affection, as Judas did.

How precious the love that Jesus experienced in this home must have been to Him! Of all His many followers, very few sought Him for Himself, very few were genuinely interested in Him. The majority came to Him, as He sorrowfully said, because they ate their fill of the loaves (John 6 : 26) or because they had been healed. Jesus, however, desires love that seeks not His gifts but Himself. Whoever loves Jesus in this way will be loved by Him in return and Jesus will reveal Himself to such a soul. This became evident in Bethany. Mary, Martha and Lazarus loved Jesus with a pure love, and therefore Jesus was able to open His heart to them. Indeed, He loved them in return, as the Gospel of John mentions several times. He loved them as His true friends. Thus Bethany speaks to us of the most precious secret, of Jesus' love for those who open their hearts and homes to Him in love.

And today Jesus is seeking a "Bethany" in our midst, a place He can enter at any time, knowing that He is always expected, that here are souls who are not taken up with other matters, letting their career or work, people or things fully occupy them. He seeks a "Bethany" where the innermost chamber of the heart is reserved for Him, even as we go about our daily work; He seeks a place where He can dwell and speak at all times and where His voice and His deepest concerns will be heard. Today Jesus is looking for true friends like those in Bethany, friends who He knows consider nothing more important than Him and His visit. He seeks those whose hearts ever yearn for Him in great love and who therefore always have time for Him first and foremost.

Indeed, Jesus is seeking a "Bethany" today. He is seeking homes with people who, like Mary, will love Him with a heartfelt, tender and yet so fervent love, giving everything for His visit and yearning to show Him kindness. Jesus seeks the quiet and contemplative, the "Mary-like souls", who, as far as their profession and other commitments allow them, lay all else aside, heeding the call to come apart for times of quiet and seclusion in which they are available for Him alone. Bethany has gone down in history, because people who truly loved Jesus and were wholly at His disposal lived there. Who would not yearn for his home or the room where he spends much time in prayer to become a "Bethany" for Jesus, a place where He would be loved much and therefore a place where He would often come to visit and grant His love in return as He did long ago to Mary, Martha and Lazarus?

PRAYER IN BETHANY

Dear Lord Jesus,

You are seeking people like Lazarus, Mary and Martha, who will be Your friends. Grant that I may love You with all my heart and abide by Your word, so that, sinful as I am, I may have the tremendous privilege of being called Your friend.

Lord Jesus, I entreat You. Teach me to love You with a fervent love, that my heart may become Your dwelling place like the house of Mary and Martha, and that Your promise will be fulfilled in my life, for You have said that You dwell with those who love You and keep Your commandments. Cleanse my heart's chamber of all thoughts and feelings that would prevent You from entering. Cleanse me of all preoccupation with work, people and things that would leave no room for You. You shall be my first Love; I will ever hearken to Your words.

I give myself wholly to You. The first and best time of the day, the week, the year shall be Yours. I will seek more time in stillness and solitude, that I may draw near to Your heart and I will show You love and kindness as Mary did. From now on I will live first and foremost for You, my Lord Jesus, and not for earthly, transient things. By Your grace and the redeeming power of Your blood help me to keep this pledge.

Amen.

CONVERSATION WITH JESUS IN BETHANY

"Give Me more time, more room in your life and in return
I shall give you My love, in which all wealth is hidden."

"Lord Jesus, I desire You, and You alone, for what
could be more wonderful than being with You?"

"Be prepared for Me at all times, that when I come to visit
you, the chamber of your heart will be quiet and still."

"Nothing and no one can make a person happier than
You can, O Jesus. And therefore my heart is only at
peace when it is wholly surrendered to You."

✝

Today as long ago in Bethany Jesus in His love is seeking
lodging in our midst, a place where He is lovingly expected
and ever welcome. But most hearts He finds occupied by
people, work and the things of this world. And thus He
pleads, "Remove the things that fill Your heart and receive
Me lovingly."

I Come to Live within You

7. 7. 8. D.

"I come to live with-in you." / God's Son, the Lord
Christ Je - sus, / Says this to ev'ry Christian soul. /

"Prepare for Me a lodg-ing / With ardent love and long-ing, / That I may with your soul u-nite."

"Make ready your heart's chamber;
Put far all earthly clamour.
Silence all worldly longings now.
Upon you take My quietness,
Eternity's own stillness,
And My approaching footsteps hear."

"Give up your will entirely;
Surrender all completely.
To Me and to My will be giv'n.
Then can I make My dwelling,
Within your heart now reigning,
One then with you in love and pain."

What then could be more glorious
Or sweeter than Your presence
Within my heart, O Jesus Christ?
Now all within is silence,
That You may deign to enter
My soul, and make it ever Yours.

Well-spring of Joy 226

THE TOMB OF LAZARUS

FROM THE HOLY BIBLE

Now a certain man was ill, Lazarus of Bethany, the village of Mary and her sister Martha. So the sisters sent to Jesus, saying, "Lord, he whom you love is ill." But when Jesus heard it he stayed two days longer in the place where he was. Then after this he said to the disciples, "Our friend Lazarus has fallen asleep, but I go to awake him out of sleep."

Now when Jesus came, he found that Lazarus had already been in the tomb four days. Bethany was near Jerusalem, about two miles off. When Martha heard that Jesus was coming, she went and met him and said, "Lord, if you had been here, my brother would not have died. And even now I know that whatever you ask from God, God will give you." Then Mary fell at his feet, saying to him, "Lord, if you had been here, my brother would not have died." When Jesus saw her weeping, and the Jews who came with her also weeping, he was deeply moved in spirit and troubled, and he wept.

Then he came to the tomb; it was a cave, and a stone lay upon it. Jesus said, "Take away the stone." Martha, the sister of the dead man, said to him, "Lord, by this time there will be an odor." Jesus said to her, "Did I not tell you that if you would believe you would see the glory of God?" So they took away the stone. And Jesus lifted up his eyes and said, "Father, I thank thee that thou hast heard me. I knew that thou hearest me always, but I have said this on account of the people standing by, that they may believe that thou didst send me."

When he had said this, he cried with a loud voice, "Lazarus, come out." The dead man came out, his hands and feet bound with bandages, and his face wrapped with a cloth. Jesus said to them, "Unbind him, and let him go." Many of the Jews therefore, who had come with Mary and had seen what he did, believed in him.   cf. John 11

THE TOMB OF LAZARUS –
A MESSAGE FOR US

What a sweet sound the name of Bethany has when it speaks of the warmth and affection between Jesus and His three friends there! Yet Bethany also tells us how Jesus tests those whom He loves, how He tries His chosen ones in the "furnace of affliction". It tells us how He leads them along dark avenues of faith in order to refine their faith like gold in the furnace, how He lets them face impossible situations and even Death himself, so that they may experience the glory of God through their faith.

For this reason Jesus permitted Lazarus to die. He did not come to help Mary and Martha in their deep anxiety and distress. They had to endure those days of utter darkness, when Jesus did not seem to be concerned about them, despite their request for His assistance. But He delayed, so that in the end He might display His great power and glory all the more. He let Death strike, so that as "the resurrection and the life" He might demonstrate His victory over Death. Bethany witnessed an event that scarcely any one of His people had ever witnessed. Lazarus, whose body was already decaying, had to step out of the tomb at a word from Jesus. The power of Death was broken and Lazarus was alive!

Thus Bethany has a two-fold message for us. Through the lives of Mary and Martha we are challenged to love Jesus and give Him room in our hearts and homes as the most beloved Guest. But we are also called to prove our love in hours of utter darkness when Jesus seems far away and does not answer our pleas at first. Bethany bids us to put our faith in Jesus at such times in the conviction that we shall then see the glory of God as He has promised.

The Foe You Have Defeated

7. 6. 7. 6. D.

The foe You have defeated,/ O dearest Lamb of God!/

Thus we will ever praise You,/ O Victor on the Cross./

The enemy's dread power/ Before You, Lord, must flee;/

You conquered hell and Sa-tan/ To set his prisoners free.

O King of kings, we laud You
And praise You as is right,
Because You have defeated
The devil with Your might.
Now we can be victorious,
If we in Christ believe,
And if we fight faith-battles,
His vict'ry we'll receive.

So from our hearts we thank You,
O Christ, the Lamb of God,
Who bore for us such anguish
Upon that Cross of wood.
For there You conquered Satan
And vict'ry won for all;
So evermore Your praises
Must reach the realms of hell.

Of Jacob's tribe the Hero,
Be evermore adored!
May the whole world accept You
As Lamb of God and Lord.
Around Your throne for ever
Sweet songs of joy we'll raise.
For then all grief and sorrow
Shall end in ceaseless praise.

Can also be sung to the melody,
"Stand Up, Stand Up for Jesus"

PRAYER AT THE TOMB OF LAZARUS

Dear Lord Jesus,

I worship You and Your great love. You only led Mary
and Martha through such abysmal darkness so as to reveal
to them the brightness and radiance of Your glory all the
more.

I thank You for leading me too along dark avenues, that
I may learn to keep faith and one day inherit the crown of
life. Teach me to understand that every act of faith is rewarded and we shall see that which we have believed – often

in this life, but most certainly above. Teach me to believe that suffering is always followed by joy, because Your paths are always paths of love and they never end in weeping, but in laughter and blessedness. Teach me the kind of faith that stands the test by firmly expecting Your aid and the revelation of Your power and glory in every difficulty and hardship.

Jesus, I am reckoning with Your words, "Be it unto you according to your faith", and I am waiting for the moment when my faith will be rewarded and I shall see that which I have believed.

Amen.

+

The glory of God will be seen by those who in situations of utmost distress and hopelessness put their faith in Jesus in the assurance that He is greater than every hardship. Today as long ago Jesus displays His omnipotence and majesty most gloriously in our darkest moments of utter helplessness.

THE MOUNT OF TEMPTATION

The Mount of Temptation near Jericho lies approximately 37 km. away from Jerusalem. Starting out from the Old City bus station, we follow the Jericho Road and cross the Kidron Valley bridge. Our way takes us past Gethsemane and on to Bethany. The road then serpentines down through the Judean Desert into the Jordan Valley. We descend more than 1,000 m., since it is the most low-lying valley in the whole world.

A short distance beyond Bethany we pass by a spring known as the Fountain of the Apostles. Our way now takes us mostly through rolling countryside with rock-strewn hills, which are barren all year round apart from a few weeks in the spring when they are covered with patches of green grass. Isolated flocks of sheep graze on the slopes and Bedouin tents can be seen occasionally, but there has never been a settlement here. For the first few kilometres we sometimes see thinly-planted pine groves but soon we are surrounded by the numerous white sand-hills of a striking desert landscape.

In the distance we can discern the outlines of a building. Halfway to Jericho we pass by the ruins known as the Good Samaritan Inn. Today a police check-post is located at the site. In the courtyard of the ruins we can still see the foundations of a building proven to have stood there in the time of Jesus. Thus Jesus embedded His parable of the Good Samaritan in this sinister stretch of countryside where an inn was located. On a neighbouring hill are the remains of a Crusader castle.

A few kilometres farther on, the old Roman road branches off the asphalt one, later leading alongside the desert gorge, Wadi el-Kelt. Our Lord Jesus must have walked along this ancient Roman road in the burning heat every time He went to Jericho. Today, however, the road is not much used except by the natives and their flocks. It approaches modern Jericho from the west, whereas the motor road first swerves southeast, later approaching the city from the south.

Shortly after the old Roman road has branched off, we come across a notice announcing that we have reached sea level. With sweeping curves our road continues downhill into the valley. As we now drive through the wide Jordan Valley, we notice the sudden change of scenery from a mountainous to a flat desert landscape. The area seems to be devoid of all life. The last stretch of the road to Jericho offers us a panoramic view of the surrounding mountain chain against which the steep Mount of Temptation with its flat summit stands out prominently.

Before entering the city, our road meets up again with the ancient Roman road and the Wadi el-Kelt, which opens up into the plain at this point. Modern Jericho is a fertile oasis with luxuriant plant growth. We pass by plantations of bananas, pomegranites and oranges with their overpowering scent, interspersed with many palm trees and colourful shrubs. Leaving the city in a northwesterly direction, we head straight for the Mount of Temptation. Just before the road ends, we see, about 50 m. to the right, ancient Jericho and the Fountain of Elisha at the foot of the mound (2 Kings 2 : 19-22). The history of the town since ancient times has been revealed as a result of recent excavations that unearthed ruins from the topmost wall, dating from ca. 1700 B.C., to the earliest remains on bedrock, dating from ca. 7000 B.C., among them the ruins of Joshua's Jericho.

Now we are at the foot of the Mount of Temptation, in an area of desolate gorges where a deathly hush reigns. This landscape helps us to visualize the setting for Jesus' Temptation. A stony footpath winds its way in serpentines up to the top, leading past stone-strewn slopes and bizarre overhanging rock formations, honeycombed with caves. Halfway up the mountain, after about 25 minutes' walk, we come to a Greek Orthodox monastery that appears to be hanging over the precipice. Inside we find the traditional Grotto of Temptation, now a small chapel. Having obtained permission from the Greek Orthodox Patriarchate in Jerusalem, we may pass through the monastery and climb to the top of the mountain. When we reach the plateau, we find lying at our feet many disc-shaped stones, resembling oriental loaves of bread. From the summit we have a sweeping view far into the Jordan Valley. Mountains tower up on all sides. The ridge of the Mount of Olives is outlined on the western horizon. Looking eastwards, we can see the Mountains of Moab beyond the River Jordan and Mount Nebo. Immediately below us lies modern Jericho with its lush and brightly-coloured tropical gardens. A panoramic view that truly must have given Jesus an impression of "the kingdoms of the world and the glory of them". As we can see with our own eyes, the region offers the external conditions that the Enemy must have used to tempt Jesus. No doubt this accounts for the tradition that regards this mountain as the Mount of Temptation.

THE HISTORICAL ASPECT

Neither the Gospels nor any archaeological finds can help us to determine the exact spot where Jesus underwent the temptations. All we are told is that "Jesus was led up by the Spirit into the wilderness to be tempted by the devil" (Matthew 4 : 1). It must have been a time of solitary wandering through deep wadies and over barren heights. Only in later tradition are further details given. These usually refer to the mountain near Jericho called the Mount of Temptation as the place where Jesus was tempted by the devil after forty days of fasting. In 1102 the English pilgrim Saewulf remarked that he found this tradition very much alive among all the Christian inhabitants of the land.

The eastern slope of the Mount of Temptation is honeycombed with 30 to 40 caves, some natural, some man-made. As far back as the fourth century they were occupied by hermits. The southern slope is also rich in caves. The grotto that tradition designates as the place where Jesus sheltered during the forty days was turned into a chapel, probably in the sixth century. In the twelfth century at the time of the Crusaders it belonged to the Canons of the Holy Sepulchre, who decorated the walls with frescos depicting the Temptation of Christ. At the beginning of the twentieth century these were still visible. The chapel remained desolate from the thirteenth century until 1874 when the Greek Orthodox monks took it over. Their monastery, which they built into the cliff, stands to this day.

According to tradition the summit of the mountain was the site of the third temptation when Satan offered Jesus all the kingdoms of the world. A fortress of the Maccabees stood here in about 130 B.C. Hermits dwelt at this site in Early Christian times and the remains of a Byzantine chapel have been found. No doubt the Crusaders also had a church here. Rebuilding was commenced by Greek Orthodox monks before the First World War, but the project was discontinued.

FROM THE HOLY BIBLE

And Jesus, full of the Holy Spirit, returned from the Jordan, and was led by the Spirit for forty days in the wilderness, tempted by the devil. And he ate nothing in those days; and when they were ended, he was hungry. The devil said to him, "If you are the Son of God, command these stones to become loaves of bread." But he answered, "It is written, 'Man shall not live by bread alone, but by every word that proceeds from the mouth of God.'"

Then the devil took him to the holy city, and set him on the pinnacle of the temple, and said to him, "If you are the Son of God, throw yourself down; for it is written, 'He will give his angels charge of you,' and 'On their hands they will bear you up, lest you strike your foot against a stone.'" Jesus said to him, "Again it is written, 'You shall not tempt the Lord your God.'"

And the devil took him up, and showed him all the kingdoms of the world in a moment of time, and said to him, "To you I will give all this authority and their glory. If you, then, will worship me, it shall all be yours." Then Jesus said to him, "Begone, Satan! for it is written, 'You shall worship the Lord your God and him only shall you serve.'"

And when the devil had ended every temptation, he departed from him until an opportune time. And behold, angels came and ministered to him.   cf. Matthew 4 and Luke 4

Because he himself has suffered and been tempted, he is able to help those who are tempted.   Hebrews 2 : 18

For we have not a high priest who is unable to sympathize with our weaknesses, but one who in every respect has been tempted as we are, yet without sinning.   Hebrews 4 : 15

Always choose to lose your life. Jesus shows us that this is the way to be victorious over temptation.

THE MOUNT OF TEMPTATION – A MESSAGE FOR US

The Tempter never finds a situation more suited to his purposes than when a person is in distress. Every time a person suffers want in one respect or another, whether it be of the body, soul or spirit, the Enemy is presented with an opportunity to attack. And a place where all these needs become especially apparent is the desert, for here man has to suffer untold wants in every sphere of life. The desert is a place of dire poverty and extreme loneliness, a place fraught with distress, fear and danger.

Thus when Jesus withdrew for forty days of fasting into such a wilderness, traditionally where the Mount of Temptation is located, the Tempter's hour had come. He made full use of the occasion, staking everything on an attempt to defeat Jesus. Hardship and want drive us to seize the hand that offers help, irrespective of whose hand it is. Satan knew that Jesus, having taken on human flesh and blood, was subject to temptation "in every respect as we are". Thus Jesus too may have felt the longing to extricate Himself from distress.

He was hungry, and hunger is painful. Having a human body like ours, the Lord surely must have longed to satisfy His hunger. Would He not also need new strength for the ministry that lay ahead of Him? Why else should these loaf-like stones be lying at His feet? Could He not turn them into bread? Was He not the Son of the living God, who had been sent into this world?

And in His soul would He not have been repeatedly assailed by an agonizing inner conflict? "What proof is there that I am the Son of God? Am I not a human being living among other human beings, the poor son of a carpenter? Am I not one among many?" Now a hand is outstretched, offering to help Jesus out of this plight. Satan leads Jesus in spirit to Jerusalem and invites Him to leap off the Temple Pinnacle. The Tempter dares Him to prove Himself to be the Son of God, who has all the powers of the universe at His disposal. Satan may have spoken very persuasively. "Believe me, your might will be demonstrated and no harm will befall you. You will feel like the Son of God again and the people will also regard you as such. Behold, I will strengthen you."

Jesus had come to earth in order to bring the Kingdom of God to men. Thirty years had already elapsed. He had done His work as a carpenter. But where was the Kingdom of God that He was to establish? Now Satan offered Him a way out of this conflict. The kingdoms of this world in all their glory, so temptingly arrayed before Him, could have come under His dominion in a single moment. All the inner conflict and anguish of waiting for His commission to materialize would be over in a flash. He could then rule the kingdoms of the world according to His divine precepts and thus establish His kingdom of love and peace.

How easy it would have been for Jesus to grasp the outstretched hand of Satan! It would have brought Him relief from His dire physical need when He was in a state of extreme hunger. It would have delivered Him from the severe trials of soul and spirit. What a temptation for Jesus, who was born in the likeness of men!

But Jesus did not take the hand held out to Him. He consented to the hardship in which He found Himself. He had the courage to remain in these circumstances and to persevere in suffering. He was willing to wait, however long it might be, till God's hour came when God Himself would deliver Him. Jesus was reckoning with the truth that powerlessness, humiliation and obscurity were the very factors that would bring about the Kingdom of God and He consented to follow such paths of complete self-denial. With this act of committal He victoriously stood the test in temptation.

And now Jesus challenges us for our times of temptation, "Follow Me. Do not grasp the outstretched hand of the Tempter, even if you desperately seek release from hardship of body, soul or spirit." Do not listen to Satan, who promises to give you the desires of your heart – money, possessions, privileges, rights, honours and friendship – through people or circumstances. He offers a solution by swift and dubious means. No matter how reasonable his arguments seem, do not be deceived! It is Satan's hand that offers you such an easy way out of your plight; he promises to fulfil your wishes much faster than if you had to wait for God's intervention. Beware of Satan's hand! It seems so harmless but entices you to make a hasty and fatal move. Give God your consent to hold out in your distressing circumstances in the firm belief that God, who is your Father, already has advice and help in store for His child. And when His moment has come, He will grant His aid, though not until He has purified us like gold in the fire and made us glorious. This is the rich fruit yielded by times of temptation.

Therefore, in every temptation it is vital that we give God our consent to our plight, thus commending ourselves into the Father's hands. Then Satan's attempts will be foiled and we shall emerge as victors from the hour of trial and temptation. Satan will be forced to flee and the angels of God will minister to us too. In His own time God as a true Father will shower us with His gifts and make us happy, for He truly delights in doing good to His children.

I Sing, I Sing, God Adoring

8.8.5.5.

I sing, I sing, God a-dor-ing,/
My praise to heaven up-soar-ing./
May my psalmo-dy/ Give pleasure to Thee.

I'll sing of God's will in sadness,
How its fulfilment brings gladness
To those who obey
And follow God's way.

I'll sing in hours of temptation –
The wondrous help and salvation
Through Jesus we gain,
The Lamb that was slain.

I'll sing of God's grace and mercy,
The aid His love ever brings me.
Supplies He indeed
His child's ev'ry need.

I'll sing in pain and in sorrow,
In grief and fear of the morrow.
Thy praise will remain
My constant refrain.

Well-spring of Joy 198

+

PRAYER ON THE MOUNT OF TEMPTATION

My Lord Jesus,

You were tempted in all respects as we are, yet without sinning. I thank You for not succumbing to the Enemy but overcoming him. Teach me, I pray, to confront the Enemy in my times of temptation the way You did, so that I may be victorious.

Give me the strength to refuse Satan's hand when he offers to produce the things that I desire. Help me to be willing to abide in distressing situations, as You did, and to wait until You, Lord, prepare a way out for me.

My Father, I will trust You, for You know Your child's needs and You will grant me the things that I really do need and that will serve to my highest good. This I will hold up before the Enemy in every temptation. Then You will give him the word of command and he will depart.

Amen.

SPIRITUAL WEAPONS FOR TIMES
OF TEMPTATION

In times of temptation our best aid in refusing Satan's hand, which offers us an easy way out, is to confront him by saying the royal words, "I will not shirk suffering. Suffering brings glory."

The Tempter's method is to offer immediate assistance and instant transformation of the depressing situation. You will drive him away with the words, "I can wait for God's hour. His help never comes too late."

When we are consumed by a desire, the Enemy finds it easy to trap us. But he is put to flight when he sees that we are determined to surrender the object of our desire to God in the knowledge that the Father cares for us better than anyone else and always supplies our needs at the right time.

Temptations are necessary, for we shall not obtain the crown of victory unless we have struggled against temptations. Therefore, be willing to enter combat, that is, be prepared to let it cost you tears and wounds. Only he who fights the battle will be able to overcome Satan in the power of Jesus.

THE PLACE OF BAPTISM
BY THE RIVER JORDAN*

Returning from the Mount of Temptation, we pass through the lively market place of modern Jericho on the way to the eastern city limits. The outskirts of the city are surrounded by plantations, but soon the landscape reverts to the flat, sandy desert, which is seldom broken by a bit of green. We can trace the course of the River Jordan in the distance because of the dense vegetation along its shores.

Near Jericho the Jordan Valley is about 20 km. wide and lies almost 400 m. below sea level — an inland depression such as is found scarcely anywhere else, probably resulting from gigantic volcanic eruptions in prehistoric times. The sun is scorching in this basin, where the hot air is entrapped. Even the wind is burning hot in the Jordan Valley. As we follow the road to the river with the sun beating down upon us and see the long distances, we suddenly realize what is implied by that brief sentence in the Bible's account of Jesus' life, "Then Jesus came from Galilee to the Jordan" (Matthew 3 : 13). What physical strain this must have cost Jesus, who went everywhere by foot!

About 8 km. from modern Jericho we come to a square, walled-in, fortress-like building, which is the Greek Orthodox Monastery of St. John the Baptist (also called Prodromos = the Precursor). Here begins a short stretch of rolling desert landscape with fissured marly hills and immediately beyond that are the broad green banks of the Jordan, densely covered with reeds and tamarisks. The road leads past the Franciscan property to what is considered to be the site of the Bethabara Ford. On the other side of the river, on the eastern bank, is the traditional Place of Baptism. The Franciscans have erected a small chapel on the western side, directly on the bank. Here the river is only about 10 m. wide and serpentines with strong currents to the Dead Sea.

THE HISTORICAL ASPECT

The place where John preached and baptized was in the desert along the lower reaches of the Jordan. The words of the prophet

* At present this site is out of bounds for military reasons.

199

about the voice crying in the wilderness (Isaiah 40 : 3) and the Baptist's symbolic life of penance drove him into the desert, and his office as baptist led him to seek the waters of a river. Here he found both. But where exactly was the spot where he ministered? And where was it that Jesus let Himself be immersed in the waters of the Jordan?

The Gospel of John describes this place as "Bethabara beyond the Jordan, where John was baptizing" (John 1 : 28 A.V.). Some manuscripts read "Bethany" instead, not to be confused with the Bethany of Lazarus. Perhaps Bethany was a place a little way off the Jordan, a place where John might have lived and performed his ministry, whereas Bethabara might have been the actual place of baptizing, located on the banks of the River Jordan. Judging by the reports of the Christian scholar Origen in ca. 230 and the historian Eusebius in ca. 300, Bethabara on the Jordan must still have been well-known in the third century. But where exactly was the site of Bethabara, the "house of the ford"?

It is certain that John was dependent upon a ford in order to baptize. Since there were paths leading to the ford, it was accessible to the crowds that flocked to hear his preaching. And only at a ford was he able to immerse those who came to be baptized, for elsewhere the banks were too steep and the current too swift. But there were several fords "opposite" Jericho. Which one of them was Bethabara?

In 333 the Pilgrim of Bordeaux gives the answer in his account when he describes the route from the Dead Sea to Bethabara. "It is five miles from there [the Dead Sea] to the part of the Jordan where our Lord was baptized by John. From a hill offshore at this point Elijah ascended to heaven." And from the Dead Sea to the Greek Orthodox Monastery of St. John the Baptist on the west bank of the River Jordan it is a distance of 5 Roman miles (7,400 metres). The Place of Baptism is pointed out today near this monastery. The Pilgrim of Bordeaux indicates that the Place of Baptism was in this district, but on the east bank. The hill of Elijah's ascension, which he mentions as a further mark of identification and describes as lying farther inland on the east bank, can still be seen there today.

If Bethabara, and thus the Place of Baptism, lay at this point on the River Jordan, it was certainly a highly significant site in the history of God's people. From the accounts of the pilgrim nun Etheria (385) and the details supplied by the Church Father Jerome (400) the traditions connected with this particular ford become evident. It was here that the Israelites under Joshua went dry-shod over the Jordan (Joshua 3 : 16 f.). Here the water parted when Elijah crossed over with Elisha before his ascension. And the same happened when Elisha returned alone (2 Kings 2 : 8-14).

Thus for the Jews this was not one ford among many, but rather a unique and unforgettable place, because their forefathers crossed the river here. The site of Elijah's ascension in the vicinity also contributed to its significance. The Baptist must have chosen this ford, since it was well-known because of Elijah, in whose power and spirit he had come to minister. Thus the people from all Judea would flock here.

When in early times the Christians identified this site as the place where John baptized and thus the site of Jesus' Baptism, they had certainly chosen historical soil. However, the fact that buildings were set up to commemorate the Baptism is not mentioned until ca. 530 when the pilgrim Theodosius made his report. At that time a marble pillar marked the exact spot of Jesus' Baptism on the east bank and a church built in honour of John the Baptist probably stood at the site of the present Monastery of St. John the Baptist on the west bank.

In later centuries tradition temporarily transferred the place of Jesus' Baptism to the west bank, presumably because the east bank was more difficult to reach. But the actual spot continued to be pointed out as lying "beyond the Jordan". In recent times there was a tendency to regard the Ford of the Partridge, located farther south, as the place where Jesus was baptized, because it is more shallow. If today the steep banks by the Monastery of St. John the Baptist make it hard to visualize the Place of Baptism, this can no doubt be attributed to the fact that the river bed has shifted its position several times, as has been observed. Thus we cannot determine exactly where the Bethabara of the Baptist lay or what it looked like. But it is highly probable that the Baptism of Jesus took place in this district.

The Greek Orthodox, Syrians, Copts and Abyssinians also have sites along the bank of the Jordan south of the Franciscan Place of Baptism to commemorate this event.

FROM THE HOLY BIBLE

In those days came John the Baptist, preaching in the wilderness of Judea, "Repent, for the kingdom of heaven is at hand." Then went out to him Jerusalem and all Judea and all the region about the Jordan, and they were baptized by him in the river Jordan, confessing their sins. And the multitudes asked him, "What then shall we do?"

Then Jesus came from Galilee to the Jordan to John, to be baptized by him. And when Jesus was baptized, he went up immediately from the water, and behold, the heavens were opened and he saw the Spirit of God descending like a dove, and alighting on him; and lo, a voice from heaven, saying, "This is my beloved Son, with whom I am well pleased."

The next day John saw Jesus coming toward him, and said, "Behold, the Lamb of God, who takes away the sin of the world!"

This took place in Bethany* beyond the Jordan, where John was baptizing.   cf. Matthew 3, Luke 3 and John 1

THE PLACE OF BAPTISM
BY THE RIVER JORDAN – A MESSAGE FOR US

What mighty waves of contrition and repentance must have swept across the people at the time of Jesus! From all Judea they gathered in crowds to receive the baptism of repentance. In the scorching heat of the wilderness they walked to the tropical Jordan Valley. Their willingness to make this journey indicated their willingness to repent. From Jerusalem, for instance, it was a whole day's journey to Jericho with a 1,000 m. drop in height, and then there was the stretch from Jericho through the hot Jordan Valley to the ford where John was baptizing.

One cry filled the hearts of the people who gathered here – the cry for forgiveness of their sins. That is why they flocked in such crowds to the River Jordan for baptism. And Jesus too was drawn to the Jordan before beginning His ministry. This was inevitable. Had He not come to make sinners whole? He yearned to be with these people, for the Saviour belongs to sinners. And how Jesus' heart must have rejoiced to find that John was actually preparing the way for Him! Here at the River Jordan Jesus saw crowds of people who not only confessed their sins in deep repentance, but asked, "What shall we do?" These were people who made a radical break with sin – they no longer wished to continue in their former way of life. They were determined to make amends wherever they had sinned and to walk in the opposite direction, living in obedience to God and His commandments, as John the Baptist had instructed them to do.

And now Jesus drew near to the throng at the River

---

* Bethabara in the A.V.

Jordan. Had the moment arrived for Him to reveal Himself as the Saviour, who had left the throne of God to come to them and to grant them forgiveness of their sins in His mercy? Would He now manifest Himself as their Lord and God and exercise His royal authority to forgive sins? No, He came in such humility, His power veiled, that none could recognize Him. Later He would come to sinners and sit with them, but here at the River Jordan He even entered the waters to be baptized like the sinners who needed to do so to receive forgiveness of their sins. Truly, even then in the River Jordan it was possible to see the Lamb of God, who a few years later would hang upon the Cross, having taken upon Himself all our iniquities and been made sin for us. Only because the Lamb of God let Himself be baptized for the sins of mankind, thus prefiguring His act of redemption, could the waters of the Jordan wash away men's sins.

What joy must have filled the hearts of those whose sins had been forgiven! On their homeward journey from the River Jordan they must have paid even less attention to the heat and strain than when they had come. They had but one desire now – to put into practice what they were told at the River Jordan and thereby seal the forgiveness they had received.

But at that time the people who by the River Jordan were granted a foretaste of the fruit of Jesus' act of redemption did not grasp what had actually taken place for them and what was yet to come. Today, now that the Lamb of God, the Saviour of sinners, has been manifested on the Cross for all the world to see, the River Jordan proclaims even more powerfully the blessedness of repentance. Thus God longs for those who come here to bring Him their sins, mindful that Jesus entered these waters for the sake of man. Of the many pilgrims who visit the Jordan who will thank Jesus for taking away our sins and who will ask, "What shall we do? How can we mend our ways? How can we lead a new life to Your glory?" Jesus is seeking such souls.

Today the Place of Baptism at the River Jordan is waiting to see people going away with uplifted hearts – with even greater joy and happiness than the people of long ago, for the oft-repeated words of John the Baptist have been fulfilled in their lives, "Repent, for the kingdom of heaven is at hand." Jesus has made repentance the gateway to the kingdom of heaven. Those who repent will experience the kingdom of heaven here on earth; they will taste its joy, peace and love. And then they will be able to let this kingdom of love and joy shine forth into our dark world. What a blessed message resounds to this very day from the shores of the River Jordan, "The kingdom of heaven is at hand!" Whoever receives Jesus with a truly penitent heart will also receive the kingdom of heaven, and the kingdom of heaven will become a reality in his life.

✝

Deeper, deeper, ever deeper
I would humble myself beneath my sins,
For Jesus, my Lord, did humble Himself.
Here in the River Jordan
He came to be baptized
Amid the throng of sinners.
And now He yearns for us to turn
To Him in penitence.

PRAYER AT THE PLACE OF BAPTISM

Dear Lord Jesus,

We thank You that Your Holy Spirit is able to make us willing to hear that which we so dislike by nature – judgment pronounced on our sins. If this miracle could take place in the time of John the Baptist when the crowds flocked to the shores of the Jordan, undergoing all the hardships of the journey only to hear their verdict, I believe that You can do the same for me today. You can make me covet the very thing I naturally avoid, but which actually serves to my highest good.

Therefore, I pray, grant me also such an eagerness to be shown my sins and to confess them, that I heed no humiliation or pain, because Your word of forgiveness is so precious to me. May Jordan's call to repentance never depart from my heart, and help me to make a radical break with sin whenever You show me that there must be a change in my life. I believe that in this way You will enable me to lead a new life and grant me an experience of the kingdom of heaven, so that I shall be able to radiate the love and joy of Your kingdom.   Amen.

O Holy Ghost, Descend Today

8.8.7.D

O Ho - ly Ghost, descend today! / On Jor-dan's banks I humbly pray / For Your great gift, repent - ance. / Here my Lord showed such humbleness- / The Lamb of God made man - i - fest, / Who bore my sins and bur-dens.

Give me a heart that weeps and mourns,
Acknowledging my countless sins
To God and man most humbly,
That ever hastens to the Cross,
Receiving by the Saviour's grace
His blessèd gift, forgiveness.

Give me a heart that sings with praise
Of how He grants such joy and grace
To sinners through forgiveness.
Graciously come anew each day,
Spirit of penitence, I pray;
Quicken my heart and spirit!

✝

Here by the River Jordan
Where once the Lord was baptized
Is there a single soul today
Who weeps in penitence?
Though many come to see this place,
They go away, unmoved.
And yet the Son of God looks down
With yearning from above.
He waits and waits again to find
Souls here at Jordan's banks
Whose contrite tears make known their grief,
Their heartfelt penitence.

THE TREASURE IN REPENTANCE

Repent! Turn from your old ways – and heaven will dawn in your life.

Do you long for a new life, filled with victorious power and a fiery love for God and your fellow men? The gateway to this new life is repentance!

Nothing can bring us more joy than repentance, for to repent is to turn from our former life and ways, which brought us only misery and the judgment of God, and to begin a new life with God and for Him, which makes us free and happy.

Repentance means a change of heart. The Holy Spirit will effect such a change in our attitude, filling us with good and divine thoughts if we ask Him to do so.

A life devoid of daily contrition and repentance leaves us spiritually dead. Only a stream of ever new contrition and repentance imparts spiritual life to us, fills us with love for Jesus and our fellow men, and grants us abundant joy.

Love for Jesus is born out of contrition and repentance. If you yearn to love Jesus more fully, ask Him for more repentance.

BETHLEHEM
THE CHURCH OF THE NATIVITY

Since childhood the name of Bethlehem will have been familiar and especially dear to us, for it unfolds the mystery and miracle of the holy night. Thus with great joy we set out for the Bethlehem of today, following the same ancient road that the Wise Men took when they sought the Babe after their visit to Jerusalem.

Bethlehem lies only about 8 km. south of Jerusalem. Starting out from the Jaffa Gate, or from the Old City bus station near the Damascus Gate, we take the Hebron Road to Bethlehem. We drive along the outside of the western city wall, pass Mount Zion and cross the Valley of Hinnom. From there we drive through the eastern outskirts of the New City. Soon after passing the kibbutz Ramat Rachel on our left, we come to the Mar Elias Monastery where we meet the road that for almost 20 years (1948—1967) was the only route from Jerusalem to Bethlehem.

In the distance we can pick out Bethlehem with its light-coloured houses and numerous towers, spread out over two hills in terraces. The dark, rich soil on the slopes is strewn with many stones and the young shoots are a bright green. The valleys and hillsides are clad with olive groves, fig trees and vineyards. This obvious fertility explains why this town on the edge of the Judean Desert was called Bethlehem ("house of bread"). It was here that Ruth once gleaned in the fields and found favour with Boaz. Here David kept his father's flocks of sheep before he became king.

Of all the hills surrounding Bethlehem the most conspicuous one is the cone-shaped mountain called the Herodium. Half of it was artificially built up by Herod for the site of his fortress and tomb.

On the outskirts of Bethlehem lies Rachel's Tomb to the right of the road. Tradition says that this is the spot where Rachel wept for her children (Genesis 35 : 16-20). And the Evangelist Matthew sees the weeping of the Bethlehem mothers over Herod's massacre of the Innocents as the fulfilment of the prophet's words, "Rachel is weeping for her children" (Jeremiah 31 : 15; Matthew 2 : 18). For centuries the Bedouins of the neighbouring desert in the east have buried their children round this tomb.

Behind Rachel's Tomb we take Manger Street, which forks off from Hebron Road to the left. It makes a detour round the town centre and heads eastwards, bringing us to the large square in front of the Church of the Nativity, which can be recognized immediately by its ancient, fortress-like walls. Here in a grotto we find the historic site of the greatest miracle of all — God became man.

THE HISTORICAL ASPECT

As early as the mid second century the philosopher and martyr Justin, a native of Palestine, testified that the Saviour was born in a cave near Bethlehem. The Roman Emperor Hadrian (117—138), who erected a pagan temple on Calvary, also tried to obliterate all memory of the Christian tradition associated with the site of the Nativity, by planting a grove in honour of the god Adonis, the paramour of Venus. But his attempt had precisely the opposite effect; the grove served to preserve the knowledge of the exact site. The Christian scholar Origen, who lived in Palestine about the middle of the third century, wrote that the Nativity Grotto in Bethlehem was known to everyone.

The Emperor Constantine erected a magnificent basilica over the Nativity Grotto in 325, even more magnificent than his other edifices, the Eleona Basilica on the Mount of Olives and the Church of the Holy Sepulchre. Although these last two churches were repeatedly destroyed, the Church of the Nativity has been preserved to this day as the world's oldest church still in use. In 529 the Samaritans damaged it badly during their insurrection, but it was restored in the same century under the Emperor Justinian. In 614 when the Persians invaded the Holy Land, they destroyed most of the churches, but spared the Church of the Nativity, since they recognized their own national costumes in the mosaic of the pediment depicting the Nativity scene with the Magi. This church also escaped destruction in later centuries.

Here, at Christmas in the year 1100 Baldwin of Flanders, the leader of the Crusader Army, was crowned King of the Latin Kingdom of Jerusalem. After the Crusaders had been driven out, the Church of the Nativity came under the guardianship of the Franciscans, though they were deprived of most of their rights later during the Turkish rule. Since 1757 the church has been in the possession of the Greek Orthodox.

In the course of time the three large portals of the basilica were bricked up so as to prevent people from entering the church on horseback. Only a small doorway was left in one of the portals. If we wish to enter the church, we must stoop, a truly appropriate reminder of the humility of God, born here as a human Child.

209

Passing through the narthex, we come to the wide nave of the church with its four rows of pillars. The actual Grotto of the Nativity is beneath the High Altar. A flight of stairs on either side of the great choir leads down to the grotto. In a niche at the front of the spacious grotto we find the traditional spot where Jesus was born as Saviour of the world. A silver star in the marble pavement beneath the altar bears the inscription, "Hic de Virgine Maria Jesus Christus natus est" (Here Jesus Christ was born of the Virgin Mary). The niche is under Greek Orthodox care. Of the fifteen lamps burning day and night round the star, six belong to the Greeks, five to the Armenians, four to the Roman Catholics.

In another niche, three steps lower, the manger is shown — originally a fodder trough hewn out of rock. The manger grotto is very small. It provided room for only a few cattle, which the shepherds could keep an eye on from the actual cave higher up whenever they sheltered here. When Mary and Joseph lodged in this cave, the upper cave would have been the dwelling and the place of the birth, and the lower one would have provided a sheltered spot for the Child in the manger. Pilgrim reports have described how people in loving devotion plated the manger with silver and gold. Today it is covered with marble. This spot is in the hands of the Franciscans and likewise the altar opposite, which commemorates the adoration of the Wise Men.

The entire Nativity Grotto is furnished with amianthus curtains and partly covered by white marble; in addition, the natural ceiling has been replaced by a sturdy barrel vault. Consequently, little of the cave's original appearance remains. But we forget the externals, for are we not standing at the very place where our Lord was born? Here we cannot but bring Him our adoration and sing our Christmas carols in praise.

There are other grottos in the vicinity that we shall also wish to visit. As a rule we cannot reach them directly from the Grotto of the Nativity, but must enter the Franciscan church, St. Catharine's, which adjoins the Church of the Nativity on the north. We leave the Church of the Nativity via the left nave and pass through the cloister of the Franciscan monastery; then we come to the right nave of St. Catharine's, from where we descend to the grottos. First we come to St. Joseph's Grotto, where he is said to have heard the angel's message, "Rise, take the child and his mother, and flee to Egypt." Nearby is a crypt dedicated to the Holy Innocents (Matthew 2 : 16 f.). A man-made tunnel connects this grotto with a number of other caves where during the fourth and fifth centuries well-known people, such as the Church Father Jerome and his pupil Eusebius of Cremona, St. Paula and her daughter Eustochium lived and were buried. Jerome founded a monastery next door to the basilica and in one of these caves he produced the Vulgate, the first Latin translation of the Bible.

After visiting the Church of the Nativity, we are indeed grateful that the site of the birth of our Lord Jesus Christ has been preserved for us as an historically undisputed place, and that the church with the grotto has been spared destruction during the wars throughout the centuries.

The Church of the Nativity is open all day.

About 400 m. southeast of the Church of the Nativity we find the Milk Grotto (Franciscan). According to tradition Mary hid here with the Child before the flight to Egypt. Open 7:30 a.m. — 11:40 a.m. and 2:30 p.m. — 5:45 p.m.

The Lutheran Christmas Church in Bethlehem is a Protestant place of worship commemorating our Lord's birth. It was built some decades ago and lies to the west, about 10 minutes' walk from the entrance of the Church of the Nativity.

FROM THE HOLY BIBLE

But you, O Bethlehem Ephrathah, who are little to be among the clans of Judah, from you shall come forth for me one who is to be ruler in Israel, whose origin is from of old, from ancient days. Micha 5 : 2

In those days a decree went out from Caesar Augustus that all the world should be enrolled. And all went to be enrolled, each to his own city. And Joseph also went up from Galilee, from the city of Nazareth, to Judea, to the city of David, which is called Bethlehem, because he was of the house and lineage of David, to be enrolled with Mary, his betrothed, who was with child. And while they were there, the time came for her to be delivered. And she gave birth to her first-born son and wrapped him in swaddling cloths, and laid him in a manger, because there was no place for them in the inn. Luke 2 : 1-7

✝

O Bethlehem – what a privilege to behold thee,
Thou city favoured above a thousand others!
Here I humble myself in the dust,
For thou dost hold the world's greatest treasure.
In thee, O Bethlehem, God came to dwell;
For us He took on human flesh.

O Bethlehem, to whom didst thou give lodging? –
The Son of God, who left His throne above
And came to earth to bring us to the Father.
But only those who come like little children,
Who humbly bring their sins and guilt to Him
Will find the blessing of the Holy Child.

+

BETHLEHEM – A MESSAGE FOR US

Bethlehem! What place on earth has such a lovely sound to it, although it tells us of a dark cave and a rock-hewn manger? Here lay the most beautiful Child ever born, a Child such as the world has never seen, nor ever will see, for this was not a sinful child, but a Child from heaven, the Father's belovèd Son, who entered human form. Full of awe and wonder the cherubim and seraphim must have brought Him adoration as they beheld Him. Was He not their Lord and Creator, whom they had honoured and glorified unceasingly in all the heavenly spheres? And had not the Father said, "Let all God's angels worship him" (Hebrews 1 : 6)?

And now in His inconceivable humility this Lord and Maker lay as a tiny, helpless, newborn human Baby before those who came to the manger. As adults they seemed to be high above Him. Who can fathom heaven's adoration and amazement to see the almighty God so divested of His power and glory? How could the mighty princes of the angelic hosts comprehend such self-abasement of their God? And what feelings must have stirred in the Father's heart when He beheld His only-begotten Son, His very image of divine splendour and dignity, lying here as a human Child, a helpless Infant, shorn of all divine majesty and glory? God the Father saw His Son humbled to the deepest depths, for the

Child Jesus was housed in a cave like the poorest of the poor, His bed a cattle trough.

How could this be? Would not the angels and the cherubim have asked how God the Father could allow such a thing to happen? Then the heavenly host, hearing the wonderful tidings from the Father's heart, will have whispered in awe, "God so loved the world – loved it so very much – that He gave His only-begotten Son that whoever believes in Him should not perish but have everlasting life." The angelic hosts, the cherubim and seraphim will have worshipped this amazing love of God for His children, a love that continues to embrace the world in spite of all its wickedness and rebellion against Him. Because God so loved the world, He took upon Himself human flesh and blood and was born as a poor, helpless Babe in His desire to draw very close to His children.

Now the heavenly hosts and mankind were shown what incurs the pleasure of the Most High, the omnipotent God. He delights in those who let themselves be made poor, small and lowly. And when the Child grew to manhood, His disciples heard from His lips the momentous words, "Unless you turn and become like children – small, dependent and humble – you will never enter the kingdom of heaven." The kingdom of heaven belongs to those who are like children.

Indeed, God humbled Himself and came to us in Bethlehem as a poor, tiny Child, lying helpless in the manger. But that is precisely how He won everyone's heart. Likewise God loves those who follow Jesus' example and abase themselves, making no demands, becoming as small and natural as a child. He rejoices over such disciples. Thus the heavenly hosts yearn that all who come to the manger and who believe in the miracle of Christmas have the mind and attitude of Christ Jesus. All heaven longs that we, as grown men, renounce our intellectual pride, our prejudice and opinionatedness, that we empty ourselves of all arrogance, self-confidence and presumptuousness, and gladly become small and humble.

God became man and went the way of self-abasement, so that we, set free from our pride, could once more become children of God the Father in the truest sense of the word. If we bear this mark of the kingdom of heaven – that is, if we have implicit trust in God and are utterly dependent upon Him as little ones, if we are selfless and brimming over with childlike joy – the light that shone from Bethlehem's manger will radiate from us too. And the Child in the manger with His radiant joy will be brought to many others through us. This is Bethlehem's challenging message for us today.

✝

The high and lofty God
Humbled Himself so deeply,
Laying aside His mighty power
And all of heaven's glory.
O man, should this not challenge you
To choose abasement too?

✝

O dearest Jesus, little Child,
I come to sing Thy praise
Here in the place where Thou wast born,
This poor and dismal cave.
Accept my humble song, O Lord,
And may it soothe Thee well,
That Thy heart will no more be sad
That Thou on earth must dwell.

O dearest Jesus, little Child,
Who should not bow his head,
Kneeling to praise and worship Thee
Beside Thy manger bed?
From Thy dark cave a light doth shine
Throughout the universe.
In heaven's wondrous radiance
Thou dost the world immerse.

O dearest Jesus, little Child,
Who should not be Thy friend?
Who should not bring to Thee his gifts,
On Thee his treasures spend?
O dearest Jesus, little Child,
How poor and small Thou art!
I now would bring Thee many gifts
That will delight Thy heart.

Who is as small as Thee, my Lord?
Therefore, I ask of Thee,
Work in my heart until I too
May small and childlike be.
That I may then, O dearest Child,
Of use and service be
And as the least of brothers serve
The people next to me.

O dearest Jesus, little Child,
Who should not bring Thee joy?
Who should not want to make Thee glad,
Thou poor, small, baby Boy?
We thank Thee, Lord, that Thou didst come
Into earth's woe and night,
Descending for our sakes, that we
In Thee might see the light.

O look upon us and forgive
The evil we have done.
We wait for Thee and know that Thou
For sinners' sake didst come.
Beside Thy manger bed we sing
And praise exultantly,
"My Saviour, my Redeemer! Christ
Indeed was born for me!"

O dearest Jesus, little Child,
We will not stop to rest
Till all mankind doth worship Thee
And Thou art praised and blessed.
For all mankind Thou didst descend
And open heaven's door.
Heaven is ours! We sing with joy,
Worshipping Thee, O Lord.

The Nativity Grotto in Bethlehem, February 16, 1961. Can
be sung to the melody, "It Came upon the Midnight Clear"

✝

To be loved by Love eternal and to love Him in return is
the secret of the kingdom of heaven. If you become like little
children, you will discover this secret and enter the kingdom
of heaven.

O Child of Peerless Beauty

7. 6. 7. 6. D.

O Child of peerless beauty,/ Whom angels magnify,/

You radiate the glory/ That comes from God Most High!/

O Child, O clearest image/ Of God's most tender love,/

That sinners dare to praise You,/ Whom angels laud above!

The wonder of Your coming
No man can fully know,
For God Himself lives in You,
From heav'n You came below.
What man had lost You brought him:
The bliss of heav'nly love.
For us the way is opened
Back to our home above.

A shaft of heav'nly sunlight
In You mankind has blessed;
The love of God the Father
In You has man caressed.
The world can now find healing;
From heaven falls the dew.
In Your dear human features
The face of God men view.

Since You to us descended,
No more seems heaven far;
You bring it close for all men,
O radiant Morning Star!
With You love made its entrance,
Among us to abide.
O rapture for all sinners;
Their thirst is satisfied!

We are belovèd children;
Our sorrow turns to mirth.
The Father's heart is open
To all the sons of earth.
O Child, You make us children
In God's great family,
To love and be belovèd
And serve You joyfully.

Well-spring of Joy 27

PRAYER AT THE MANGER

Our dear Lord Jesus,

Though Lord of all things, You let Yourself be laid as a Babe in the manger. How small and lowly You became! In deep awe and gratitude we worship You for choosing lowliness.

At Your manger I kneel in shame before You. O Son of the Most High, whose throne is in heaven, You emptied Yourself and descended so low. Yet I, a sinner, who deserve to be humiliated, time and again cling to my self-importance, prestige and pride, although in truth I deserve no honour at all.

O little Child Jesus, I bring You now my arrogant nature and all my sinful pride and lay them in Your manger. O Son of God, who became a Child for me, You have redeemed me from my self-importance, my presumptuousness and sophistication. I believe that You will make me a true child again – small, humble, undemanding and natural.

Here at the manger I dedicate myself to You and out of love and gratitude I give You my consent to every way You choose to make me humble and lowly. O Child, make me like You, no matter what the cost. You have said that the kingdom of heaven belongs to children. And I pray that this promise will come true for me.

Amen.

THE SHEPHERDS' FIELD

Not only the Nativity Grotto and the manger are inseparable from the events of the Holy Night, but also the shepherds' fields where for the first time the "Gloria in excelsis" resounded. Thus we now turn eastwards from the Church of the Nativity to the fields where the heavenly host appeared to the shepherds as they were keeping their watch. From the square in front of the Church of the Nativity it is about 20 to 30 m. to the motor road leading to the shepherds' fields. After descending a steep hill, we notice on our left the olive groves in the valley. Looking across the fertile fields and the barren hills to the north and east, we can see the Dead Sea.

From here we also have a view of the three different enclosed fields where the appearance of the angels to the shepherds is commemorated. To the left on a slope we can discern the dome of the Angel's Chapel in the Franciscan Shepherds' Field. Straight ahead is the dark green grove of the Y.M.C.A.'s Shepherds' Field. In the valley on the right lies the walled-in property of the Greek Orthodox, known as the Convent of the Shepherds.

As we descend the hill, this view is lost to sight. Soon after we have passed the last houses of Bethlehem, we arrive at the shepherd village of Beit Sahur, which is about 2 km. in length. In order to reach the shepherds' fields, we follow the main road to the end of the village. Directly after the church and the boys' seminary of the Greek Catholic Patriarchate there is a signpost at the fork in the road. The street on the right leads to the Greek Orthodox Shepherds' Field; the one on the left, to the Franciscan Shepherds' Field and to the one belonging to the Y.M.C.A. First let us go to the Franciscan field, turning left at the fork. After about 500 m. we take the road to the north, following a signpost, which says that we have only 300 m. to go before we reach the Franciscan Shepherds' Field. The Franciscans built a chapel here on a hill in 1954 beside a large shepherds' cave, which had previously served as the sanctuary. Excavations in the nineteenth century revealed the remains of an ancient church and monastery on the slope of this property. Some of the ruins date from the fourth century and others from the sixth century. But

219

the buildings must have been destroyed in very early times, perhaps by the Persians in 614.

From the Franciscan Shepherds' Field we take the main road again, heading eastwards. About 600 m. later on the left we reach the Shepherds' Field acquired by the American Y.M.C.A. several years ago. Here is another ancient cave similar to many in the neighbourhood that may have served as a shelter for shepherds.

In order to reach the Greek Orthodox Shepherds' Field, we take the main road again, going back towards Beit Sahur. Some distance after the fork to the Franciscan Shepherds' Field, we find a street forking off to the left. A signpost points the way to the Greek Orthodox Shepherds' Field. After 200 m. we come to the entrance gate in the wall surrounding the olive garden. Inside we find the ruins of a monastery known as the Convent of the Shepherds as well as a grotto. Reports from early times mention that this is where the angels appeared to the shepherds.

From all three shepherds' fields, but especially from the Franciscan one, we have a delightful view of Bethlehem lying high up on the hill with the Church of the Nativity. We can easily picture the shepherds hastening joyfully to the Grotto of the Nativity after they had heard the angels' tidings. And as if we had been there, we too are moved to raise our voices in song, rejoicing over the miracle of that holy night.

The fact that there is no definite tradition about the exact site of the Shepherds' Field does not disturb us. Here more than anywhere else should it not be easy for us to feel free of the conflicting opinions? All three fields lie close together and surely we do not wish to limit the heavenly host to a few square yards. In any event, all the traditions agree that the heavenly host appeared in this area east of Bethlehem, and therefore all three fields must have seen the open heavens that night and heard the message that fills our hearts with such joy, "Unto you the Saviour has been born this day!"

The Franciscan and the Y.M.C.A. Shepherds' Field can be visited all day; the guardians will allow anyone to enter upon request. The Greek Orthodox Shepherds' Field is also always open, but the grotto only occasionally.

FROM THE HOLY BIBLE

And in that region there were shepherds out in the field, keeping watch over their flock by night. And an angel of the Lord appeared to them, and the glory of the Lord shone around them, and they were filled with fear. And the angel said to them, "Be not afraid; for behold, I bring you good news of a great joy which will come to all the people; for to you is born this day in the city of David a Savior, who is Christ the Lord. And this will be a sign for you: you will find a babe wrapped in swaddling cloths and lying in a manger.

And suddenly there was with the angel a multitude of the heavenly host praising God and saying, "Glory to God in the highest, and on earth peace among men with whom he is pleased!"

When the angels went away from them into heaven, the shepherds said to one another, "Let us go over to Bethlehem and see this thing that has happened, which the Lord has made known to us." And they went with haste, and found Mary and Joseph, and the babe lying in a manger.

And when they saw it they made known the saying which had been told them concerning this child; and all who heard it wondered at what the shepherds told them. But Mary kept all these things, pondering them in her heart. And the shepherds returned, glorifying and praising God for all they had heard and seen, as it had been told them.

Luke 2 : 8-20

✝

O blessèd Shepherds' Field,
Who can know what thou hast seen?
Who can fathom what once happened here,
O land, chosen by God?

O blessèd Shepherds' Field
Near the little town of Bethlehem,
To thee God sent His hosts of angels!
Heaven came and touched the earth,
Bringing wondrous, blessèd news
To thee from God on high.

Awaken, put forth thy green shoots,
O field, honoured by God!
And come ye poor and lowly;
Rejoice today as long ago
On this blessèd Shepherds' Field!

THE SHEPHERDS' FIELD – A MESSAGE FOR US

What a holy night that must have been for the shepherds who were out in the field, keeping watch over their flock! A night when the heavens were opened and a light shone with unexcelled brilliance in the depths of darkness! The voice of the angel of God rang out from heaven and a vast host of angels were gathered about him. Mighty anthems filled the air, resounding over the shepherds' fields of Bethlehem, "Glory to God in the highest!" and the wonderful tidings of great joy were delivered, "Unto you the Saviour has been born this day!" What rejoicing must have broken out on these fields as the glad tidings were brought to the shepherds – tidings for all the people, indeed for the whole world!

In those days shepherds were more or less ranked with publicans and sinners. Yet they were the ones who received the amazing news. They must have been scarcely able to grasp it. From heaven the angels of God were sent to them of all men. They were to behold the Saviour of the world. And where were they to find Him? In a manger, in a cave! Again they must have been filled with astonishment, for such was their own dwelling. They lived in poverty, not dwelling in proper houses, but sheltering in caves, as shepherds do to this very day in the region of Bethlehem. Even now their newborn babies are often laid in such a stone manger, which would normally serve as a feeding trough for animals.

Would not these poor, despised shepherds have been filled with adoration to see that God, who had taken on human form, had laid aside all glory and humbled Himself so deeply? They were such sinners that they were of no account among their people. Yet it was to them that God chose to draw near, so very near. How God must have loved these shepherd folk to become one of them, manifesting Himself in their lowly estate and dwelling, and choosing to visit them above all others!

What a happy throng that must have been, setting out from the Shepherds' Field to seek the grotto where Jesus was born! Probably never again during Jesus' earthly life was He met by such a joyful crowd! We read that the shepherds "went with haste". They did not walk at a comfortable, leisurely pace, but must have leapt to their feet and rushed up the hill to the cave in joyful expectation, their hearts brimming over with jubilation. The dogs were barking and perhaps some of the sheep followed at a distance. One and all must have been gripped by the tremendous joy. Everyone hastened to see what had happened and to greet the little Child. The shepherds may have even raced one another to reach the Babe in the manger, all of them eager to be the first to see Him and bring Him their salutation and worship.

Are we too gripped by this joy when we visit the Shepherds' Field today? Whoever sees himself, like the shepherds, as a wretched sinner, will gladly welcome the good news proclaimed here long ago, for this is a blessed message, relevant to this day. Those who feel their lack and recognize their sins know their need of a Saviour. And what could be more joyful for those who groan and languish in the chains of sin than the tidings, "Christ the Saviour is born!"

On that holiest of nights God in His amazing love graciously descended to earth. And wretched sinners, humble shepherds, were privileged to witness this event. The almighty God manifested Himself first to them and invited them to come to the place where He entered this world. And His promise still holds true today: He will look graciously upon all who have a broken and contrite heart and will make His dwelling with them. Joy and exultation will fill their hearts, for whenever they weep over their sins, heaven will open up for them and proclaim the glad tidings as of old, "Unto you is born the Saviour!" Turn your eyes upon the Child in the manger, the Saviour of the world, and as you behold and worship Him, you will be transformed into His image.

> Rejoice! The manger holds a Child.
> Who can in grief repine?
> He's come to take away our sin,
> Light in our hearts to shine.

PRAYER IN THE SHEPHERDS' FIELD

Dear Lord Jesus,

You know that we all thirst for happiness. I thank You for the tremendous joy that You brought with You when You came into this world as our Saviour and the Fount of all joy. I thank You for proclaiming these glad tidings long ago through Your angels to the shepherds in the field, who were imprisoned in darkness and sin. I pray now, let me too be so gripped by this overwhelming joy that others can see it in me and that my life will be a genuine testimony to Your redemption.

Here in the Shepherds' Field, I ask You, dear Lord Jesus, make me poor in myself and in need of Your grace just as the shepherds were. Grant me a broken and contrite heart over my sin, that I may comprehend that the Saviour has been born for me and may rejoice at these glad tidings. Let me seek You as the shepherds did, always hastening to You the moment I become painfully aware of my sin.

I thank You for the assurance that You will then grant me forgiveness and abundant joy. You will make me so radiant with this joy that others too will come to believe that You are the true Saviour and Fount of all joy.   Amen.

WHAT DID THE HOLY NIGHT BRING US?

A Child – the Father's only Son,
Who left His glory and His throne.

A Child so lowly, meek and small,
And yet the Ruler over all.

A Child – the radiant Morning Star
That shines in darkness near and far.

A Child who has victorious might
And puts the Enemy to flight.

A Child whose name is "Wonderful" –
Such wondrous things He's done for all.

A Child who frees from chains of sin,
Makes all things new, without, within.

A Child – the Fount of joy and cheer;
To those in sorrow He draws near.

This Child, so humble, small and meek
Brings heaven down to all who seek.
Yes, truly He brings heaven near,
For no one can with Him compare!

O Belovèd, Little Child

O belovèd, lit-tle Child,/ Who sings Your ba-by songs?/ Sings of the Father,/ Of Holy Spir-it,/ And bright an-gel-ic throngs?

O belovèd, little Child,
Who saw Your lowly birth?
Shepherds and children,
Donkey and oxen –
These welcomed You to earth.

O belovèd, little Child,
Now will I take Your part,
Songs ever singing,
Sweet music bringing,
The love of all my heart.

O belovèd, little Child,
Let me Your minstrel be,
Of heaven singing,
With joybells ringing,
Praise my King's majesty.

O belovèd, little Child,
Let me with You remain.
In all You suffer
Hear, Lord, my offer;
Take me to share Your pain.

O belovèd, little Child,
I praise You, Lord, most dear,
Sent from the Father,
Sent from the Spirit,
Bringing us heaven here.

Always I must love You, Lord.
How could we ever part?
Jesus, my Treasure,
Joy beyond measure,
Great gift from God's own heart.

Well-spring of Joy 24

The Shepherds Did Hasten
6.5.D.

The shep-herds did has — ten;/ We speed the same way,/ for none who seeks Jesus/ His quest should delay.

We hasten at Christmas
The manger to find,
The Babe doth expect us;
His welcome is kind.

He seeth our longing;
It brings Him delight.
He longs to enrich us
On this holy night.

The shepherds were joyful;
I share in their bliss.
The sight of Christ's manger
Draws my heart to His.

The shepherds adored Him
On reverent knee.
I kneel at the manger;
The Child smiles at me.

227

The wise men came off'ring
Their gifts rich and rare;
But my gift is greater,
My self offered there.

The Babe blessed their giving
With riches more true;
His love will enrich us,
Create us anew.

My sins do I give Him
And all I possess;
His love is my portion,
My true blessedness.

Well-spring of Joy 17

✛

O dearest, dearest little Jesus,
How I thank Thee for Thy goodness
That I may belong to Thee alone!
Make me like Thee, small and lowly,
That within Thy heart so holy
I may dwell, with Thee for ever one.

EIN KEREM

Let us go "into the hill country" and visit the place that is closely associated with the events related in the first chapter of the Gospel of Luke. Here in Ein Kerem, situated in the Judean hills, on the western outskirts of Jerusalem, we think of Mary's encounter with Elizabeth and the birth of John the Baptist.

With Ein Kerem as our destination we leave Jerusalem in the west, taking the Jaffa Road. Near the large building of the Nation's Hall (Hebrew *Binyanei Ha'ooma*) the road to Ein Kerem veers to the left, branching off the main road to Tel-Aviv. Our road passes through new residential quarters and leads past Mount Herzl on the right. The tomb of the renowned Zionist leader, Theodore Herzl, stands on the summit of the mount, surrounded by gardens and nearby is the Military Cemetery. A little later the road divides into three. The road bearing slightly to the left is one of the routes leading to the high-lying Hadassah Hospital, the Hebrew University Medical Centre. The road forking off to the right leads to the monument and memorial of Yad Vashem. We continue along the middle road another 3 km. down into the valley of Ein Kerem. For the greater part of this last stretch we have a delightful view of the village, but especially of the high-lying grounds of the Convent of the Sisters of Zion and the surrounding hills.

Ein Kerem lies in dreamy loveliness, nestled on the slopes of the ancient terraced hillsides, which are covered with olive groves and clusters of dark green, slender cypress trees. The towers of the various churches and convents rise into the sky. The terraced slopes lead us to assume that there were vineyards (Hebrew *Kerem*) here in the past. The ancient village fountain with its spring (Hebrew *Ein*) discloses the full meaning of the name — "the spring of the vineyard".

Near the village centre, shortly before the main road bends to the right, a narrow lane forks off to the right, leading to the Franciscan Church of St. John the Baptist, which lies a little way uphill. We enter the church and descend a small stairway in the left nave, which brings us to a grotto, where the natural rock ceiling of an ancient cave dwelling is recognizable. Here the birth of John the Baptist is commemorated.

229

On the hill opposite, to the south, is the Franciscan Church of the Visitation. In the valley, which separates the church from the village, lies the ancient village fountain (The Spring of the Vineyard or Fountain of the Virgin) with its pleasant-tasting spring water. From here we follow a broad stone stairway, which leads uphill, passing by the Russian Orthodox Gorny Convent. After 10 to 15 minutes' walk we come to the lovely, ornate, wrought-iron gateway of the Franciscan grounds with the Church of the Visitation, which consists of an upper and lower church. A well in the grotto of the lower church confirms the belief that dwellings existed in the region in Jesus' day. On a long wall in the outer court of the church we find colourful ceramic plaques inscribed with the Magnificat in many languages. These plaques, which remind us of the Visitation when Mary broke forth in praise, challenge us to bring God our canticle of praise too.

The view to the north helps us to imagine the loneliness of the way the Mother Mary must have taken when she came from Nazareth to the Judean hill country. On our way back as we climb down into the valley, we are once more greeted by the sight of the Church of St. John the Baptist. The loveliness of this village, embedded in the Judean hills, makes a deep impression upon us.

Times of opening:

Church of St. John the Baptist (Franciscan)

March 2 — September 30	October 1 — March 1
weekdays: 8 a.m. — 11:45 a.m.	weekdays: 8:30 a.m. — 11:45 a.m.
2:30 p.m. — 6 p.m.	2:30 p.m. — 5 p.m.

Sundays: 9 a.m. — 4 p.m.

Church of the Visitation (Franciscan)
9 a.m. till noon
3 p.m. — 6 p.m.

THE HISTORICAL ASPECT

Neither the Bible nor tradition indicates the exact spot where Mary met Elizabeth or where John the Baptist was born. But the Greek term used by Luke for the hill country of Judea to which Mary hastened (Luke 1 : 39) is suggestive of the mountainous district near Jerusalem. The same term is used again in verse 65, which says that when the tongue of Zechariah was loosed after his son was named, the news spread "through all the hill country of Judea". Other descriptions from that period use the same term for this district near Jerusalem. Moreover, the place must have been within easy reach of Jerusalem, because Zechariah was a priest in the Temple. Thus the location of the picturesque village of Ein Kerem, west of the city, corresponds to the account in Luke's Gospel. Since there was no tradition from the first centuries, several other places were suggested for the commemoration of the Visitation and the birth of John the Baptist, but only in Ein Kerem has the memory of these events been kept alive.

The history of Ein Kerem goes back as far as Old Testament times. Graves and various finds prove that it was also inhabited in Jesus' day. The first testimony pointing to Ein Kerem as the site of these Biblical events appears in the writings of the pilgrim Theodosius in about 530. He wrote, "It is five miles from Jerusalem to the place where St. Elizabeth, the mother of St. John the Baptist, dwelt." Though he does not mention the name, we may conclude from the given distance as well as later references that Ein Kerem is the place meant. The name Ein Kerem is first mentioned in ca. 638 in the Georgian calendar of Jerusalem, which lists all the stations where the Georgians celebrated their festivals, including the Church of St. Elizabeth (now called the Church of the Visitation) in Ein Kerem.

At that time Ein Kerem perpetuated only the memory of a legendary story relating Elizabeth's escape from the Herodian slaughter of the Innocents when a rock is said to have opened to receive her and the infant John. Until the early ninth century it had been assumed that John the Baptist was born in Jerusalem and this event was commemorated in a church there. Only later did the tradition arise that Zechariah lived in Ein Kerem.

Not until 940 is there any mention of a church dedicated to Zechariah here. In this church, later called the Church of St. John the Baptist, the birth of John the Baptist and the Benedictus of his father Zechariah were commemorated. The Church of the Visitation, however, which had originally been associated only with the legendary escape of Elizabeth, later also commemorated the Gospel story of the Visitation and the Magnificat, Mary's canticle of praise. It was assumed that Zechariah had a summer dwelling in addition to a proper residence according to Jewish custom. And over the course of the years tradition maintained that it was in this summer dwelling that Elizabeth "hid herself", as the Gospels relate, when she knew that she was with child.

Thus this could well be the site where the Visitation took place. Mary may first have sought the residence of her kinsman Zechariah and then hearing that Elizabeth had retired to the summer dwelling, she would have gone there. Upon Mary's arrival, Elizabeth greeted her as the mother of her Saviour. Then from Mary's lips poured forth the words of the Magnificat, which is commemorated here.

At one time the Benedictus was also commemorated here — probably while the Moslems were in possession of the Church of

St. John. But now St. John's has resumed this tradition, since both the circumcision and the naming of the child after eight days would most likely have taken place in the same house as the birth.

The two-storey Church of the Visitation, which originated from a fifth-century shrine, has belonged to the Franciscans since 1679. They have repeatedly restored it and a few decades ago they rebuilt the Upper Church. They are also the guardians of the Church of St. John the Baptist, the ruins of which they acquired in 1621. And at the end of the seventeenth century they were able to reconstruct this edifice.

THE CHURCH OF THE VISITATION

FROM THE HOLY BIBLE

The angel said, "Behold, your kinswoman Elizabeth in her old age has also conceived a son; and this is the sixth month with her who was called barren. For with God nothing will be impossible."   cf. Luke 1 : 36 f.

In those days Mary arose and went with haste into the hill country, to a city of Judah, and she entered the house of Zechariah and greeted Elizabeth. And when Elizabeth heard the greeting of Mary, the babe leaped in her womb; and Elizabeth was filled with the Holy Spirit and she exclaimed with a loud cry, "Blessed are you among women, and blessed is the fruit of your womb! And why is this granted me, that the mother of my Lord should come to me? Blessed is she who believed that there would be a fulfilment of what was spoken to her from the Lord."

And Mary said, "My soul magnifies the Lord, and my spirit rejoices in God my Savior, for he has regarded the low estate of his handmaiden ..."

And Mary remained with her about three months, and returned to her home.   cf. Luke 1 : 39-56

THE MAGNIFICAT

"My soul magnifies the Lord,
and my spirit rejoices in God my Savior,
for he has regarded the low estate of his handmaiden.

For behold, henceforth all generations will call me blessed;
for he who is mighty has done great things for me,
and holy is his name.

And his mercy is on those who fear him
from generation to generation.

He has shown strength with his arm,
he has scattered the proud in the imagination of their hearts,

233

he has put down the mighty from their thrones,
and exalted those of low degree;

he has filled the hungry with good things,
and the rich he has sent empty away.

He has helped his servant Israel,
in remembrance of his mercy,

as he spoke to our fathers,
to Abraham and to his posterity for ever."

Luke 1 : 46-55

THE PLACE OF THE VISITATION –
A MESSAGE FOR US

Ein Kerem – the place of visitation! The place of visitation for Zechariah. Here he had to suffer for nine months the consequences of his unbelief after he had been struck dumb instantly for doubting the revelation of the living God.

Ein Kerem – the place of visitation for Elizabeth. Though advanced in years, she conceived a child by a miracle of God – a child of grace, who would be called John.

Ein Kerem – the place of visitation. Here the Mother Mary was visited with such grace and blessings that the Magnificat, that glorious song of praise, poured forth from her lips – a canticle of jubilation and thanksgiving to her God. What was it that made her rejoice? The most wonderful anthems of praise are raised by those who experience divine comfort, help and intervention like a bright light from God shining into their night of deepest suffering, trials and temptations. Then the soul soars like a lark towards the sun, singing its sweet song of praise and thanksgiving. And indeed, the Mother Mary had walked along dark paths fraught with inner conflict, engulfed in spiritual night, up to the moment she reached the house of Zechariah and Elizabeth where she experienced the encouraging visitation of God.

As Mary hurried to Elizabeth, the flowers and blades of grass must have bowed low before this pure maiden, who bore such a precious treasure within her. How her soul must have rejoiced to know that she had been chosen to bring mankind the Son of God, the Saviour! Yet what trepidation must have filled her at the thought of the disgrace she would have to bear! She was to return to Nazareth and that meant exposing herself to shame and humiliation. Joseph was sure to break their betrothal. How would she be able to bear it? And according to law, she would be stoned to death. Would her faith be strong enough for her to believe in a miracle of God that would prevent the people from stoning her? The voice of the Tempter must have been harassing her, "Weren't you mistaken? Was it really the voice of God speaking to you through the angel? Is this really God's leading?"

The nearer Mary drew to the house of Zechariah, the more persistent this voice must have grown. "What will my kinswoman Elizabeth say when I tell her what has happened to me? Will she believe that the child I am expecting is the Son of God, or will she treat me with contempt? Then at last Mary reached the house, her heart full of trepidation.

Yet behold, God was gracious to her. Through all these inner struggles God drew Mary closer to Himself. In leading her to Elizabeth, He brought her to His very heart. In His love He desired to show her kindness, to reveal to her His eternal purposes for her life and to confirm them. And when Mary crossed the threshold, the incomprehensible occurred. Elizabeth, who could have known nothing of the revelation Mary had received, greeted her with the same words as the angel, "Blessed are you among women." Elizabeth bowed low before the younger woman and honoured her as the mother of the Son of God, saying, "Why is this granted me, that the mother of my Lord should come to me?"

What could have been more wonderful for Mary? God's confirmation of His leading for her through this totally unexpected salutation from Elizabeth delivered her from all inner conflict, fears and anxieties. The fact that Elizabeth addressed her as the mother of her Lord gave Mary a confirmation that it was God who had given the prophecy. It was His Son, the Messiah, that she had been chosen to bear! And therefore God would wonderfully bring her through all the hardships with her people and with Joseph that she would have to face. This God would do, just as surely as He had performed the miracle that she had conceived a child through the Holy Spirit and that He had disclosed this to Elizabeth.

A divine visitation in Elizabeth's house! Once again Mary was able to comprehend her election and the favour bestowed on her. Her eyes were opened to see the great and wonderful purpose of God for her life: she was privileged to bring the Son of God to the world. All her doubts, fears and inner conflicts must have been lifted from her. She had stepped out of the night into the light of day, the brilliant sunlight. The heavens were opened anew to her and she might even have seen the angels descending and worshipping Jesus, the Son of God, to whom she would give birth. Mary could not but break out in exultation and rejoicing, in praise of God for the great things He had done and would continue to do for her, a lowly maiden, who a few moments ago had been envisioning utter degradation and humiliation in the sight of Joseph and all her countrymen.

Indeed, after enduring all those inner conflicts, after undergoing the shame and humiliation in advance, she could scarcely comprehend this divine Visitation. God had looked upon this deeply humiliated maiden and exalted her highly. He had honoured her with the amazing election to be the mother of the Son of God.

Ein Kerem, the place of the Visitation, has a message for us also, for God is the same yesterday and today. When we are in the midst of inner conflict and spiritual night, He visits us and draws us to Himself, giving us encouragement. Ein Kerem tells us that after periods of darkness, God lets His light shine forth. Ein Kerem helps us to see that God is a merciful Father, who lovingly thinks of us, who always provides a way out of our troubles, and whose wise plans always work out for the best.

Thus Ein Kerem, which once heard Mary's canticle of praise, seeks to draw the same response from our hearts. It longs to hear songs of worship raised ever anew in the night of suffering, anthems praising this God, who does such marvellous things for wretched, sinful beings, if they, like Mary, will let themselves be humbled.

But Ein Kerem waits for even more. It yearns to see souls in whom Jesus can be born today – souls who by faith in the love of God consent to His word and divine will when He leads them along hard paths of suffering. God is waiting here for such people. They will be able to bring Jesus today to a world that has strayed from God.

✝

Only if we walk paths of faith and brave the night, can we experience the aid and miracles of God, which in turn will fill us with the joy and exultation of a magnificat.

✝

No hymn, no magnificat has a purer note than that which springs from a humbled heart. No canticle of praise sounds sweeter to the Lord than that which is raised in times of dire distress and along pathways fraught with trials and temptations.

✝

PRAYER IN THE CHURCH OF THE VISITATION

Our dear Father,

We thank You for Your bountiful goodness. Here at the place of the Visitation You granted the Mother Mary a strengthening of her faith and inner encouragement in all her trials and temptations. In the life of Mary You show us that such dark paths end in a joyful magnificat, if we follow them by faith to the end. We thank You for teaching us that dark and difficult paths draw us home to Your heart, where comfort and joy await us.

May this now prompt me to follow pathways of faith like the mother of our Lord in the assurance that along desert roads You have prepared solace for me as well. Along meaningless paths, fraught with trials and temptations, You will graciously grant me a confirmation when Your time has come, and at the end of dark avenues of faith You will let the light of Your word shine into my life and let me taste joy in abundance. I will therefore trust You always, so that, like Mary, I shall experience the revelation of Your glory along difficult pathways and sing You many magnificats. You shall not wait in vain for me to raise such songs of praise in the night. I yearn to magnify the glory of Your name.

Amen.

Now over the Mountain

Now over the mountain there hastens a maiden;/

The ho-li-est treasure she bears in her womb,/

The Maker of all things, the Saviour of all men,/

The Son of the Highest—what grace here is shown!

She hides this her secret in love and in wonder.
Her spirit rejoices in God's holy will,
Rejoicing and weeping, for grace has united
Both bliss and foreboding in wondering love.

And yet this her secret, so high and so holy,
Is sensed by the valleys and hills that she treads;
The birds are all singing, the trees bend to greet Him,
The Saviour of all men, who now is so near.

The grasses are bowing, the treetops inclining
In honour to Mary, so blessèd by God.
In praise of the virgin, the mother of Jesus,
The Maker and Saviour of all the lost world.

We join in their praises, we call Mary blessèd,
The mother of Jesus, our Saviour and God.
Today we salute her, for out of all women,
God chose her as mother of Jesus, His Son.

Well-spring of Joy 137

THE CHURCH OF ST. JOHN THE BAPTIST

FROM THE HOLY BIBLE

In the days of Herod, king of Judea, there was a priest named Zechariah. He had a wife and her name was Elizabeth. And they were both righteous before God, walking in all the commandments and ordinances of the Lord blameless. But they had no child, because Elizabeth was barren, and both were advanced in years.

Now while he was serving as priest before God, it fell to him by lot to enter the temple of the Lord and burn incense. And there appeared to him an angel of the Lord, who said, "Your wife Elizabeth will bear you a son, and you shall call his name John. He will be great before the Lord, and he will be filled with the Holy Spirit, even from his mother's womb. And he will turn many of the sons of Israel to the Lord their God, and he will go before him in the spirit and power of Elijah, to make ready for the Lord a people prepared."

Now the time came for Elizabeth to be delivered, and she gave birth to a son. And her neighbors and kinsfolk heard that the Lord had shown great mercy to her, and they rejoiced with her. And on the eighth day they came to circumcise the child; and they would have named him Zechariah after his father, but his mother said, "Not so; he shall be called John." And they made signs to his father, inquiring what he would have him called. And he asked for a writing tablet, and wrote, "His name is John." And immediately his mouth was opened and his tongue loosed, and he spoke, blessing God. And fear came on all their neighbors. And all these things were talked about through all the hill country of Judea; and all who heard them laid them up in their hearts, saying, "What then will this child be?" And his father Zechariah was filled with the Holy Spirit, and prophesied, saying, "Blessed be the Lord God of Israel . . ."

And the child grew and became strong in spirit, and he was in the wilderness till the day of his manifestation to Israel.   cf. Luke 1

THE BENEDICTUS

"Blessed be the Lord God of Israel,
for he has visited and redeemed his people,
and has raised up a horn of salvation for us
in the house of his servant David,
as he spoke by the mouth of his holy prophets from of old,
that we should be saved from our enemies,
and from the hand of all who hate us;
to perform the mercy promised to our fathers,
and to remember his holy covenant,
the oath which he swore to our father Abraham, to grant us
that we, being delivered from the hand of our enemies,
might serve him without fear,
in holiness and righteousness before him all the days
    of our life.
And you, child, will be called the prophet of the Most High;
for you will go before the Lord to prepare his ways,
to give knowledge of salvation to his people
in the forgiveness of their sins,
through the tender mercy of our God,
when the day shall dawn upon us from on high
to give light to those who sit in darkness and in the shadow
    of death,
to guide our feet into the way of peace."

Luke 1 : 68-79

THE BIRTHPLACE OF JOHN THE BAPTIST –
A MESSAGE FOR US

Ein Kerem – the birthplace of John the Baptist. "What do you suppose this child will turn out to be?" the neighbours asked one another at his birth. And what did become of this child? Here in Ein Kerem a boy grew up whose whole life and greatness consisted in not seeking to be somebody in himself, but in being merely the messenger of Someone greater than he. Here God prepared a person who would later not work for his own satisfaction, proclaim his own message or seek glory for his own name, but rather be only a voice for Someone else. Here God must have been training him since childhood no longer to live for himself, but to live exclusively

241

for Him who had entirely captivated his soul – Jesus, the coming Messiah. And as he grew to manhood, a consuming desire grew in his heart to be the forerunner of this one Lord with all that he was and did.

Thus the greatest longing of John the Baptist was to fade into the background, to be a mere nothing before his Lord, who had come to earth from heaven. Under no circumstances did he wish to draw attention or win human love for himself, since these belonged by right to his Lord, the thong of whose sandals he was not worthy to untie. For this reason he rejoiced when his disciples grew fewer and Jesus' disciples became more numerous. Who can measure the fervour with which John the Baptist loved and revered Jesus? How great was his zeal! With his entire life, with all that he said and did, he spent himself in clearing the way of the Lord and removing every stone before He came! Jesus was to find a prepared people, in whose hearts the way had been paved by His precursor, so that they would fall prostrate before Him. It was this fiery love for Jesus that made John the Baptist a true forerunner.

But how did John the Baptist attain this selfless love that made him burn himself out in preparing the way for Jesus? What was it that later made him the mightiest preacher of repentance the world has ever known, a man whose dynamic words the people could not evade? Undoubtedly, the reason was that he permitted the Spirit of God to bring him to repentance – even before Jesus came to him at the River Jordan. The Spirit of God had shown him Jesus as the One who holds the winnowing fork in His hand to clear the threshing floor and who would gather the wheat into His granary and burn the chaff with unquenchable fire (Luke 3 : 17). This revelation compelled him to stand before Jesus in His authority as Lord and Judge.

John the Baptist was the first to allow his pride to be broken by Jesus. He was the first to let himself be brought to repentance. Hence the long years in the wilderness before his appearance as a preacher of repentance (Luke 1 : 80). He did not wear the garment of repentance as an external formality, that is, merely for appearances' sake, but he lived a life of daily repentance, since he was of the truth (Matthew 3 : 4). This was the source of his power as a herald who would prepare the way for Jesus. John had lived up to that which he now proclaimed to others in his call to repentance. Under the judgment of Jesus he had become small and humble and was thus prepared to be the herald of the coming Lord. Now he was truly nothing in himself, but only a "voice" – a voice, however, that had the power of authority and that brought thousands to repentance (John 1 : 6-8). Thus the words of the prophet were fulfilled, "The voice of him that crieth in the wilderness, Prepare ye the way of the Lord, make straight in the desert a highway for our God" (Isaiah 40 : 3 A.V.).

The life of John the Baptist, who prepared the first coming of Jesus, is a special challenge to us, now that the second coming of Jesus is imminent. Today, at the close of the age when Jesus' return is in the offing, He once again seeks people who will prepare the way for Him. Today He seeks souls like John the Baptist, who out of love for Him will work zealously, that the "stones of sin" may be removed from the hearts of both the Old and the New Testament people of God. Jesus is looking for those whose hearts are on fire that He may find many souls prepared and waiting for Him when He comes. Above all, Jesus seeks people who will prepare His way, people like John, who first let God judge them to the core. He longs for people who can preach repentance with the power of authority, because they lead a life of daily repentance, not striving for recognition, but desiring to be a mere nothing. These are His true messengers.

Indeed, God is seeking heralds like John, who will die to self and renounce their ego with all its demands, who are jealously on the guard that Jesus – and not they – shall receive love and honour. Today God is searching for people who will prepare the way for Jesus within the body of believers – people like John the Baptist, whose consuming love for Jesus will point to the returning King and Bridegroom. Then through their testimony many hearts will be kindled with the same love for Jesus.

The Body of Christ, the bride of the Lamb, needs such heralds, that she may be prepared for the coming of the Bridegroom and King. Today Jesus' return is imminent, but He cannot come until the way is paved for Him. Will He find people today to prepare the way for His coming? Do we who have come here to trace the footsteps of John the Baptist hear Jesus' call to us?

WHO CAN PREPARE THE WAY FOR JESUS?

A person who loves Jesus above all else and who therefore has but one ardent desire – to prepare many souls for His return.

A person who does not tolerate a single "stone of sin" in his own life, and who is therefore able to remove such stones from the lives of others, paving the way for Jesus' coming.

A person who no longer seeks glory and recognition for himself, but rather lets all that is exalted be brought low, so that Jesus will find the way smoothed when He comes.

A person who is willing to be placed in the background, so that the glory of God can shine forth.

PRAYER AT THE BIRTHPLACE
OF JOHN THE BAPTIST

Our Lord Jesus,
We thank You for Your humility in making Yourself dependent upon a human messenger at Your coming, who would clear the stones out of the way among Your people. Here at this site we give thanks that You were able to find this forerunner in John the Baptist.

Here let us also remember that You not only came long ago, but said that You will come again in glory when Your bride has prepared herself. Let us be alert and recognize the nearness of midnight, the hour of Your return. Let us not be deaf to Your summons in these last times when You are once more looking for those who will prepare the way for You.

Lord Jesus, I will heed Your summons and prepare the way for You. Help me to follow in the footsteps of John the Baptist, leading a life of daily contrition and repentance, so that I may have the power to bring others to repentance. Kindle my heart ever anew with the ardent love that John the Baptist had for You and that will constrain me to clear all the stones out of Your way.

I now dedicate myself to You for this holy commission. O Lord, I do not want to stand in Your way with my pride. Rather, like John the Baptist I want to be placed in the background. Break me, that I may be a mere nothing. I pray that Your image as the returning King and Bridegroom may shine forth from my life and testimony, so that Your own will hasten to prepare themselves in order to receive You.

Amen.

Let Me Prepare for You the Way

8. 8. 8.

Let me pre-pare for You the way,/

Let me re-move each stone I__ pray,/

That when You come the__ way__ is__ straight.

Let me prepare for You the way,
That soon will come the joyous day
When to Your people You will come.

First let me in repentance weep;
Bring many to contrition deep,
That You will then be hailed as King.

Let me prepare Your joyous day
By going with You on Your way,
Thus making straight Your path, O Lord.

EMMAUS

Now we are on the way to Emmaus. Today two places, El-Qubeibeh and Amwas, are considered to be the Biblical Emmaus. A third place, Abu Ghosh, is also connected with this tradition.

To reach **El-Qubeibeh,** which lies about 19 km. away from Jerusalem, we must set out from Jerusalem at the Damascus Gate and proceed northwards along the Nablus Road. Before coming to the last houses of the city outskirts, we find ourselves in the Judean hill country. Once more we appreciate what it is to be in the land of the Bible, where geography, history and religion are closely interwoven. On the left we see Nebi Samwil (Mountain of Joy), which is thought to be the site of Samuel's tomb. On the right, on a hill, are excavations confirming the site of Gibeah where Saul lived (1 Samuel 10 : 26). Three kilometres farther a road forks off to the right to the village of Er-Ram, the home of the prophet Samuel (1 Samuel 7 : 17; 19 : 18-23). The very next turning to the left is the road to El-Qubeibeh via Biddu.

As we pass by stony fields, mostly bordered by low stone walls, we have a view across the Judean hills. Before us we see vineyards with old towers (built with unhewn stones), such as Jesus mentioned in Matthew 21 : 33. Cultivated fields border the villages and for a few weeks in the year bright-coloured flowers carpet the otherwise barren land. The road makes a detour round a rocky knoll, El-Jib, commonly identified with Gibeon (Joshua 9), which still has a fortress-like appearance, and brings us to Biddu, a village lying on a hill, surrounded by orchards. Leaving Biddu, the road makes a sharp turn to the right and then proceeds to El-Qubeibeh. With its clusters of trees El-Qubeibeh resembles an oasis amongst the barren hills, and its high altitude provides us with a panoramic view of the hill country.

Upon entering the village, we first pass by the grounds of the Sisters of St. Charles Borromeo, and shortly afterwards on the right we arrive at the entrance to the Franciscan grounds. Surrounded by graceful conifers, the light-coloured, paved courtyard has an inviting appearance. Inside the church in the left nave we are shown the foundations of what is known as the house of Cleopas; behind the church are the extensive ruins of a wide Roman road. (The church is open all day.)

Amwas lies approximately 25—30 km. northwest of Jerusalem and to reach it we take the Nablus Road as far as El-Bireh, which is the Biblical Beeroth (Joshua 9:17). El-Bireh was the first resting place for pilgrims returning to Galilee from Jerusalem, and according to tradition it was here that Mary and Joseph first missed the twelve-year-old Jesus (Luke 2:44). Here a road forks off in a westerly direction, bringing us to Amwas, where we find only ruins — the remains of an ancient church and monastery. Nearby is the great Trappist Abbey of Latrun. Amwas can also be reached via the Jerusalem—Tel-Aviv Road.

West of Jerusalem, about 15 km. along the road to Tel-Aviv is **Abu Ghosh** with a beautiful Crusader church, which has an ancient spring in its crypt. On a hill not far from Abu Ghosh is the Biblical site of Kiriath-jearim (1 Samuel 7:1), now marked by a French convent and church.

THE HISTORICAL ASPECT

From Jerusalem to **El-Qubeibeh** it is approximately 12 km. as the crow flies. This would correspond to the 60 stadia in Luke's account of the two disciples' walk to Emmaus. Excavations have disclosed that the place was already inhabited in pre-Christian times. When the Crusaders attempted to identify Emmaus, El-Qubeibeh was ascribed greater importance than Amwas, since its distance from Jerusalem was more in keeping with Luke's report. And from the thirteenth century onwards the pilgrim way led from Akko to Jerusalem via Ramle and El-Qubeibeh.

In the twelfth century the Canons of the Holy Sepulchre built a monastery with a church and castle at El-Qubeibeh. The church is said to have been built on earlier foundations. During the following centuries this Crusader church was destroyed like most others. In 1861 the Franciscans received the land as a gift and in 1900 they erected the present church over the remains of the medieval one.

When the Crusader church was discovered, the ruins of a house were also found in the left nave. Today this is regarded as the house of Cleopas, which Jesus probably entered with His disciples, and it has been preserved as a memorial of the breaking of bread in Emmaus. North of the church a Roman road, dating from Jesus' day, and the notable ruins of houses belonging to an ancient settlement have been found. These remains indicate that this village must have been an important trading centre.

The other place regarded as Emmaus is **Amwas,** which retains the Biblical name in its Arabic form. However, from Jerusalem to Amwas it is about 23 km. as the crow flies and thus far more than 60 stadia. When Luke wrote his account, Amwas must have been only a village, which then rapidly developed into an important centre, conferred with the title Nicopolis.

The historian Eusebius (ca. 330) and the Church Father Jerome (ca. 400) refer to Nicopolis-Amwas as the home of Cleopas, the only place in Judea bearing the name of Emmaus. Consequently, until the Crusader period tradition on the whole regarded Amwas as the place where the risen Christ appeared to the two disciples. And this memory never quite vanished. The discrepancy in the distance from Jerusalem was explained by copyists' errors in later versions.

The fact that Amwas has an ancient tradition was verified by excavations in 1875 and 1924—30, revealing the remains of a large basilica with three apses. This basilica had been erected on the ruins of a late-Roman villa. However, it is not clear whether the basilica dates from the third or sixth century, nor whether the villa and later the basilica indicated the site of the house of Cleopas. The basilica was destroyed, and rebuilt, and in the seventh century it was converted into a mosque. The Crusaders built a small church on the same spot and this was also destroyed.

FROM THE HOLY BIBLE

That very day, the first day of the week, two of the disciples were going to a village named Emmaus, about sixty stadia from Jerusalem, and talking with each other about all these things that had happened. While they were talking and discussing together, Jesus himself drew near and went with them. But their eyes were kept from recognizing him. And he said to them, "What is this conversation which you are holding with each other as you walk?" And they stood still, looking sad. And they said to him, "Concerning Jesus of Nazareth, who was a prophet mighty in deed and word before God and all the people, and how our chief priests and rulers delivered him up to be condemned to death, and crucified him. But we had hoped that he was the one to redeem Israel.

And he said to them, "O foolish men, and slow of heart to believe all that the prophets have spoken! Was it not necessary that the Christ should suffer these things and enter into his glory?" And beginning with Moses and all the prophets, he interpreted to them in all the scriptures the things concerning himself.

When he was at table with them, he took the bread and blessed, and broke it, and gave it to them. And their eyes were opened and they recognized him; and said to each other, "Did not our hearts burn within us while he talked to us on the road, while he opened to us the scriptures?"

cf. Luke 24 : 13-32

EMMAUS – A MESSAGE FOR US

O Emmaus – what a joyful ring you have to your name! It speaks to us of Easter! You are not so well-known as the Mount of Olives, Gethsemane or Bethany, but you are familiar to all whose hearts have been warmed by Jesus just like the hearts of the two disciples long ago. For Emmaus speaks of joy after deep suffering. Emmaus tells us that people who had lost their Lord found Him again. He was dead and buried, and everything was over for them. They felt that they had been deceived by Him and His message. Yet Emmaus proclaims, "Joy – and not sorrow – is the final outcome", for the disciples found Jesus again as the risen Lord. Emmaus tells us of the fulfilment of Jesus' promises, "I will not leave you desolate; I will come to you" (John 14 : 18); and, "A little while, and you will see me . . . Your sorrow will turn into joy" (John 16 : 16, 20).

On the way to Emmaus from Jerusalem, the place of the Crucifixion, Jesus came to the downhearted disciples, who believed Him to be lying in the grave. Now they were permitted to walk this long distance at His side and in the end they even recognized Him. Thus Emmaus declares, "Jesus comes to those who have buried their hopes, who can no longer understand their God in the darkest hour of their lives. These are the ones that Jesus seeks out. He listens to the sighings of their hearts. He bears their sorrows with them. He hears their questions, as He did here on the road to Emmaus when the two disciples were discussing the matters that had burdened their hearts ever since the Crucifixion, "Why did the Son of God have to die? Why should He be the one to be taken away? Did He not proclaim the Kingdom of God with greater authority than anyone else? Did He not bring the kingdom of heaven close to man by performing signs and wonders? The sick were healed; demons were expelled; the dead were brought to life. Why then could He not establish His rule and finally introduce His kingdom of peace, righteousness and joy in this ailing world, ravaged by war and hatred, sickness, suffering and death? Why?"

Emmaus proclaims, "The One who has the answer to all your questions is present. He is standing beside you, seeking to lighten your darkness. Because He is Love, He shares your suffering, unable to watch you torment yourself with your thoughts." Jesus draws near to us today just as He did long ago to His disciples, who were so weighed down with their troubles. He has prepared an "Emmaus" for us too, a time of encounter, a time when He will answer our questions. This hour will come for us as it did for the disciples after they had experienced the darkest hour of their lives when Jesus was crucified.

During such "Emmaus encounters" Jesus says to His own, "Oh, don't be so foolish as to think that all is over whenever suffering strikes, whenever you are faced with seeming meaninglessness and can no longer understand God's dealings. If only you would believe that every end signifies a new beginning; death gives rise to new life; sorrow is turned into joy, and tears into laughter!" Is this not the message that Jesus proclaimed time and time again during His earthly life? And His words have eternal value. They are relevant today, for Jesus Himself is the proof that death yields life, that suffering and dying result in an overwhelming victory. By following such paths of suffering, Jesus became the Prince of Victory, who rose in triumph, and later, at His second coming, when He will have accomplished His work, everything will lie at His feet.

Emmaus – here the hearts of the two disciples began to burn. And whose heart would not burn – even today – when Jesus begins to speak, when He reveals Himself? Then we, like them, may perceive that in all that happens the eternal God is present. He has "plans for welfare and not for evil, to give you a future and a hope" (Jeremiah 29 : 11).

As Jesus once long ago broke bread with the two disciples in Emmaus, He does so today with us. It is a holy meal, in which He gives Himself as the most precious, blessed offering. In the Lord's Supper He grants us the deepest communion with Himself and lets us experience that He has the power to forgive sins, because He has "carried up our sins in his body to the tree" (1 Peter 2 : 24). He has the power to make us a new creation through the bread of life, which He gives us, for then He Himself enters us. He has the power to give us Holy Communion as a token of the New Covenant, in which we are united with Him, so that suffering can no longer separate us from Him and His love. And as we contemplate the ways of God, especially the paths of suffering in His life and ours, this love is revealed to us. Nothing can separate us from this love – neither fear nor affliction nor danger, nor even death, for we are united with Jesus eternally!

Just as we are privileged here on earth – wherever we may be – to have "Emmaus encounters" with Jesus when our hearts begin to burn, we shall see Him above for all eternity as He is and our hearts will be inflamed with a love that no human tongue can express. Thus the blessed fellowship in the breaking of bread that the Lord granted His disciples here in Emmaus, in the Holy Land, and which He continues to grant to His own throughout the world, will end in the eternal "Emmaus" in heaven, where we shall celebrate the Marriage Supper of the Lamb with Him in the heavenly banquet hall amid rejoicing and jubilation. Then we shall be able to see more than ever that all the ways of God lead to the supreme goal of glory – glory that far surpasses the suffering endured along these ways (Romans 8 : 18).

PRAYER IN EMMAUS

Dear Lord Jesus,

We thank You for showing us at this site that in Your love You are especially drawn to those who are filled with doubts and questions. I too come to You with my unanswered questions and inner conflicts when I cannot understand You, Your ways or dealings. Deepen my trust in You as I consider the love with which You came to the Emmaus disciples and answered their questions. I thank You that from the very outset I may have the assurance that You have the solution to my problems too. I humble myself in spirit before You, my Lord Jesus. Lovingly, but earnestly, You chided the Emmaus disciples for having such foolish questions. Lord,

I confess that You are right when You so often have to do the same to me.

Let me take Your helpful word to the disciples as the answer to my own questions. Help me to see that suffering brings glory if we willingly accept it and that this applies not only to Your life but to our lives also. How I thank You that with the consent and act of committal to suffering, all doubts and inner conflicts are silenced and You draw near with Your loving presence.

Amen.

EMMAUS QUESTIONS – EMMAUS ANSWERS

I see no way out – pitch-black is the night!
  O believe! Night has always brought forth the light.

My hopes lie shattered – I am undone!
  Wait but a while; fulfilment will come.

In vain I kept faith; I was deceived.
  O remember, remember, God never misleads!

I see only meaninglessness – nothing more.
  O believe, from such suffering glory is born.

My heart is engulfed in sorrow and grief.
  From tears will come laughter; from sorrow, relief.

My heart cannot fathom God's ways any more.
  Come, trust in the Father and help will be yours.

✝

Emmaus – the morning dawns.
Emmaus – all cares are banished.
Emmaus – our hearts burn within us.
Emmaus – our sorrows have vanished.
Emmaus – the Lord has come.
Jesus, Jesus is here
to break bread with us.

✝

"Whence comest Thou, Lord Jesus Christ,
Thou who art risen from the dead?
Where is Thy dwelling, dearest Lord?
Tell me, who giveth Thee Thy bread?"

"I need no lodging, money, food,
No one to find a room for Me.
No more doth Judas bear the purse.
Now angels minister to Me."

"Where art Thou going, dearest Lord,
Thou who art risen from the Tomb?
Doth not the Father wait and yearn
For Thee, His dear Son, to come home?"

"To you, My followers, I come,
Who caused Me such great agony.
And after sharing all with you,
I shall ascend in majesty.

Home to My dearest Father! Home!
Ended will be all pain and tears.
Then I shall be where I have yearned
To be for thirty-three long years."

O How Our Hearts Did Burn

6. 4. D.

O how our hearts did burn / As He drew near! / The pow'r of suff'ring fled, / for He was here.

Our darkness turned to light;
His words of grace
New meaning gave to life;
O blessèd place!

We did not understand
His grief and pain,
But He revealed to us
Its wondrous gain.

The meaning of all grief
And sadd'ning tears;
Yes, now the answer bright
Through Him appears.

Glad light to them He brings
Who grope in night,
For He through death and grave
Has won the fight.

O how our hearts did burn
When bread He broke.
And to our joy, our Lord
Of triumph spoke.

Well-spring of Joy 102
El-Qubeibeh
February 17, 1961

JACOB'S WELL

The first part of the Nablus Road, leading northwards from the Damascus Gate in Jerusalem, will already be familiar to us from our journey to Emmaus. But if we intend to visit Jacob's Well near Shechem, we must follow it even farther northwards to Samaria. Even though Jacob's Well is about 65 km. from Jerusalem, we shall not want to miss this site where Jesus led the Samaritan woman into the truth, thus setting her free. The journey is well worth it, for it takes us through a district rich in historical memories. Along the road or not far from it lie Anata (Anathoth, Jeremiah 1), Gabaa (Gibeah, 1 Samuel 10 : 26; 15 : 34), and a little farther on, Er-Ram (Ramah, 1 Samuel 1 : 19; 7 : 17; 15 : 34), Tell en-Nasbeh (Mount Mizpah, 1 Samuel 7 : 5 ff.; 10 : 17), El-Bireh (Beeroth, Joshua 9 : 17 and according to tradition, Luke 2 : 44), Beitin (Bethel, Genesis 12 : 8; 13 : 3; 28 : 19; Judges 1 : 22; 20 : 26; 2 Kings 2 : 2, 23) and Khirbet Seilun (Shiloh, 1 Samuel 1 : 3, 24; 4 : 4).

All these places are integrally bound up with events in the history of God's ways with His people. However, we know that we are following in the footsteps not only of Abraham, who passed here from north to south (Genesis 12 : 6-9), but also of our Lord Jesus as He journeyed from Galilee to Jerusalem and back again.

On our journey we pass through a landscape of contrasts. There are many ranges of hills, some of them rocky and bare, others clothed with olive trees. In the valleys between, especially near the villages, there are dark brown fields, which are a deep green in the spring. They grow more numerous as we approach the charming landscape of Samaria. The road, bordered by the typical low stone walls that enclose the fields, winds up and down the hills to the north.

We now approach the present-day village of Balata, not far from the ruins of Shechem. Jacob's Well lies on the eastern border of Shechem, south of the village of Askar, which is identified with Sychar. Here we are greeted by a lovely view — a fertile plain spreads out before us, wreathed by the hills of Samaria. Two mountains are outlined prominently against the western sky: the Gerizim and the Ebal. The former is densely covered with trees, whereas the latter is barren and stony. In the hollow between them lies Nablus. Soon we can make out Jacob's Well down in the valley, to the right, with the unfinished church surrounded by cypress trees. Shortly before Nablus we take the road that branches sharply off to the right and after 100 m. we arrive at the entrance to the grounds of Jacob's Well on the left. A Greek Orthodox monk leads us from the choir of the unfinished church down to the crypt where we stand by the same well at which Jesus once rested.

Times of opening: 8 a.m. till noon; 3 p.m. — 6 p.m.

THE HISTORICAL ASPECT

The authenticity of Jacob's Well by the ruins of ancient Shechem has never been disputed. It is the only draw-well in this historically significant area and its location at an important crossroad tallies with the description in John's Gospel, for when Jesus went through Samaria on His way from Judea to Galilee He must certainly have passed here. In the Gospel of John the additional information is given that the well lay near the field that Jacob had given his son Joseph. And this field too can still be found in the vicinity today. It is marked by the tomb of Joseph. Experts describe the masonry of the well as Canaanite workmanship of the eighteenth century B.C., i.e. dating from the time of Jacob, as the Samaritan woman told Jesus (John 4 : 12). Furthermore, the woman described the well as deep, and the well here is certainly deep — over 35 m. Presumably it has a ground-water supply; whether it is fed by a spring cannot be ascertained.

At this well since early times Christians have commemorated Jesus' conversation with the woman of Samaria. In about 333 the Pilgrim of Bordeaux mentions in his report that he found a baptistry here to which the water of the well was conducted. As early as 380 a church was known to have stood over the well and in ca. 400 reference is made to this church by the Church Father Jerome. The Samaritans destroyed this church during their insurrection of 529, but it was rebuilt later. By the time of the Crusaders it lay in ruins again. In the twelfth century they reconstructed the church over the well, but it fell into ruins after their departure. Only the crypt containing the well remained. During the latter half of the eighteenth century the Greek Orthodox Church acquired the grounds from the village of Balata and decided to rebuild the church. But the First World War stopped building operations, when only the crypt and some of the walls had been restored — and work has not been resumed.

FROM THE HOLY BIBLE

In reference to the mountains Gerizim and Ebal, between which lies Jacob's Well:

"Behold, I set before you this day a blessing and a curse: the blessing, if you obey the commandments of the Lord your God and the curse, if you do not obey the commandments. And when the Lord your God brings you into the land which you are entering to take possession of it, you shall set the blessing on Mount Gerizim and the curse on Mount Ebal."

cf. Deuteronomy 11 : 26-29

Jesus had to pass through Samaria. So he came to a city called Sychar, near the field that Jacob gave to his son Joseph. Jacob's well was there, and so Jesus, wearied as he was with his journey, sat down beside the well. There came a woman of Samaria to draw water. Jesus said to her, "Give me a drink." The Samaritan woman said to him, "How is it that you, a Jew, ask a drink of me, a woman of Samaria?" Jesus answered her, "If you knew the gift of God, and who it is that is saying to you, 'Give me a drink,' you would have asked him, and he would have given you living water." ... The woman said to him, "Sir, give me this water." Jesus said to her, "Go, call your husband, and come here." The woman answered him, "I have no husband." Jesus said to her, "You are right in saying, 'I have no husband'; for you have had five husbands, and he whom you now have is not your husband; this you said truly." ... So the woman left her water jar, and went away into the city, and said to the people, "Come, see a man who told me all that I ever did. Can this be the Christ?"

cf. John 4

JACOB'S WELL – A MESSAGE FOR US

When Jesus left Judea because of the Pharisee's plots, He "had to pass through Samaria" on His way back to Galilee, as recorded by the Gospel of John. Jesus may have had external reasons for travelling through Samaria, although there were routes that made it possible for Jews to by-pass this district. But He was probably also inwardly constrained to take this particular route. It was hardly coincidental that Jesus rested at Jacob's Well between the mountains Ebal and Gerizim where such solemn, momentous events in the history of His people had taken place long ago.

The patriarch Abraham had made his resting place at Shechem (Genesis 12 : 6 ff.). Here God met him and promised to give this land to his descendants, and in response Abraham built an altar to the Lord. And now Someone sat here – perhaps at the very same spot – who as the seed of Abraham was the fulfilment of all the promises made to Abraham along dark pathways of faith. Jesus, who now rested at this well, was the sure testimony that God is the Truth and that all His promises are yea and amen (2 Corinthians 1 : 20). Jacob also built the Lord an altar here – on a piece of land that he bought (Genesis 33 : 18 ff.) and later presented to Joseph. When the Israelites left Egypt, Joseph's bones were brought to Canaan and interred at Shechem by Joshua (Exodus 13 : 19; Joshua 24 : 32). Following God's promises to Abraham, Isaac and Jacob, the Israelites crossed the Jordan and once more moved into this land, which God had given to them as their possession. And at this site between Mount Gerizim and Mount Ebal, before the people entered the Promised Land, the Law was read again to them, and they heard the solemn oath of God that blessing or curse would follow depending on their obedience or disobedience. And God proved Himself to be the God of truth. Because of their constant disobedience throughout the centuries, Israel and Judah were led into the Babylonian captivity.

At this moment as Jesus was sitting here by the well, would not the entire history of His people – the plan of salvation which in the unity of the Father and the Holy Spirit He had conceived and carried out – have passed before His eyes? Gerizim and Ebal had a warning to proclaim. God is a holy God, a God that hates sin. He is a God of truth, who keeps His word, whether it be a promise of blessing or of curse. And Jesus had come to reveal and glorify this God among His people.

As Jesus sat at the well, contemplating all these things and resting a little after His strenuous walk in the heat of the Holy Land, a Samaritan woman came to draw water. Was it not inevitable that their conversation would be about the truth? The woman who came to Him was a sinner, and like all sinners, she will have been blind to her sin, and therefore living a lie, no longer thinking of the God of truth, who had decreed that sinning would be judged and punished. She probably no longer thought twice about her sinning; perhaps she excused herself by saying, "God has given us these instincts, so it's only natural to follow them." Consequently, she lived in complete self-deception, as we all do so often. She may have blamed the circumstances and her environment for her present way of life. In this way she hoped to excuse herself. And thus she became blind to her actions.

But now she finds herself face to face with Him who is the Truth. And it is impossible to meet Him without all sins being disclosed, for the light pierces the darkness and exposes all that is ugly, sick, dark and evil. A conversation with Jesus Christ at Jacob's Well! – it is inevitable that this well becomes the "well of truth". At first it seems to be only a matter of a drink of water, which Jesus humbly requests as He lovingly seeks to open the heart of the Samaritan woman. But in the end it is she who begs Him for water. And He fulfils her request. However, it is the water of life that He gives her – namely, the truth about herself, which sets her free. If we accept the truth, it will bring us from death to life. Falsehood covers up our sin and turns us into the living dead and leads us into the jaws of Satan, who will then make us suffer the torment of the second death in his kingdom. But the truth in our Lord Jesus sets us free. It lets us receive His forgiveness and leads us into a new life.

Jesus gives the Samaritan woman a drink from this well of truth. In the light of His truth He exposes her life in all its sin to her. And it becomes evident that this woman, blind though she is, is "of the truth" deep down in her heart, for she is willing to hear the truth about herself. Indeed, not only is she willing to hear the truth, but she has the courage to go into the village and to call the others to Jesus, who told her the truth about her life. And everyone knew what sort of life she was leading. With this act she makes a public confession of her sins and testifies to Jesus.

This woman has indeed drawn water from the well of truth and drunk of the water of life and truth. And behold, her eyes are opened – opened to see that which many of His own people never grasped, even though they followed Him in droves and daily heard Him speak. The woman of

Samaria recognizes Him as the Messiah, the Son of God, who reveals sins in order to forgive them and to make sinners into new beings. Indeed, whoever lets his eyes be washed in the water of truth and has the courage to acknowledge the truth and to confess his sins can see the Messiah as the Lord and Redeemer with a new clarity. He finds his way back home to the Saviour and, released from the stronghold of sin, he then becomes a true worshipper of Jesus, for the truth, which God tells us in His love, sets us free and leads us to love Him in return.

A CONVERSATION WITH JESUS
AT JACOB'S WELL TODAY

"Jesus, my Lord, I am blind – I cannot see myself as You do. Wash my eyes, that they may become clear-sighted. Let me see myself in Your light and recognize the truth about myself."

"I have come as the Light of the world to open the eyes of the blind. If you recognize your blindness and come to Me, there is no request that gives Me greater joy to fulfil than to give you sight."

"But my Lord Jesus, I fear that I shall scarcely be able to bear it if I have to gaze into the abyss of my sin."

"Take courage! When I give you sight, you will not only perceive your sin, but your eyes will be opened for God. By facing the truth, you will not only have a glimpse into the abyss of your sin, but you will also have a glimpse into the depths of the heart of God and perceive who He really is. With this glimpse your soul will be restored, for the heart of God is brimming over with love, mercy and forgiveness."

"O Lord, grant me this true perspective at all costs. Let me see the truth, that my soul may be healed and that I may know You, my Lord and my God, fathom the depths of Your being and learn to love You more than ever."

"He who asks shall receive. Go in peace. Let it be unto you according to your faith."

✝

Hearing the truth about ourselves makes us grieve over our sins – but it also makes us small and humble. Thus truth is the prerequisite for God's image to grow in us.

+

MIRROR OF TRUTH

Jesus is the mirror of truth. Gaze into this mirror, and you will see yourself as you are.

Jesus, though God, did nothing of Himself. In obedience and dependence on the Father, He did only what the Father desired. And you?

Jesus did not come to be lord, but to be the Servant of all, even of His disciples. And you?

Jesus did good to all men. And you?

Jesus had compassion on the people. He had mercy on all who were in distress. And you?

Jesus loved His own and loved them to the end, although they brought Him so much disappointment and grief. And you?

Jesus entered the house of His enemies, the Pharisees, and blessed them. And you?

Jesus bore in silence all the wrongs committed against Him during His Passion. And you?

Jesus did not return insult for insult. And you?

Jesus endured suffering without a complaint. And you?

Jesus bore His Cross, humbly stooping beneath its load. And you?

Jesus lived to glorify the Father. And you?

Give Me Your Light

11. 11. 4.

Give me Your light. The truth do let my eyes see,/Till J

can see my-self as You be-hold me./O give me light.

Give me Your light.
Without Your help I'm sightless.
Dear Lord, I'm blind –
My natural eyes are useless.
O let me see.

Give me Your light.
Lord, grant me this concession.
Heal all my blindness;
Show me my transgression.
O give me light.

Give me Your light.
'Twill bring my soul salvation.
Truth sets us free –
O hear my supplication,
And give me light.

Give me Your light.
And do not let it spare me.
Show me my sin
And true repentance grant me.
Then I'll be free.

Give me Your light.
Let it pervade my being
And shine forth through me,
Till this dark world's seeing
Your radiant light.

O Blessèd Fountain

10. 10. 11. 9.

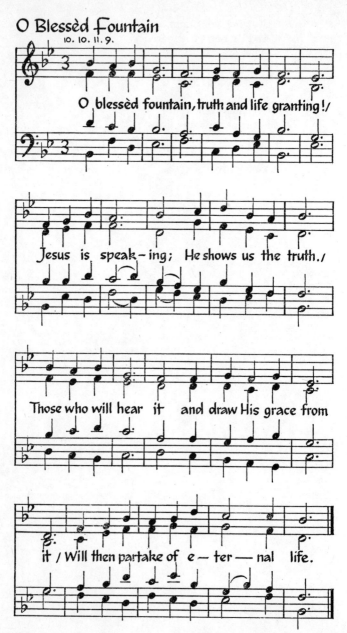

O blessèd fountain, truth and life granting! /
Jesus is speak-ing; He shows us the truth. /
Those who will hear it and draw His grace from
it / Will then partake of e-ter-nal life.

He who once came here seeks to draw near us;
Jesus still offers the water of life.
At Jacob's Well He now beckons the thirsty,
Showing the truth through His holy Word.

We may hear words that lighten our darkness;
Thoughts, words and deeds in His light are revealed.
Here is the water of life that can heal us
If we are willing to see the truth.

Mirror of truth, you show us our image;
We recognize now with shame what we're like.
Dearest Lord Jesus, O give us this mirror,
That we may ever behold the truth.

Blind from our birth, we come and beseech You.
O give us sight, Lord; the truth sets us free.
O let us humble ourselves 'neath Your verdict,
Seeing ourselves in Your holy light.

O well of truth, in you we find true life.
For this we're striving; 'tis better than gold.
Therefore, we thank You, O Lord, that You grant us
Here in this lifetime Your words of truth.

O blessèd fountain, truth and life granting!
Jesus is speaking; He shows us the truth.
We want to hear it, to draw His grace from it;
Then we shall have everlasting life.

Jacob's Well
February 17, 1961

NAZARETH

Leaving Jerusalem and Judea behind us, we now make our way to Galilee, to the other important area associated with the life and ministry of Jesus. Our journey takes us into the southern hills of Galilee, to Nazareth, Jesus' home town, where He spent most of His earthly life. As we approach it from the south via Afula and the Plain of Jezreel, we see the first hills rising in the distance and then the town itself spread out before us in a wide valley and climbing up the slopes of the neighbouring hills.

The present-day Nazareth (Hebrew *Natzrat*; Arabic *En-Nasra*) is a town of about 35,000 inhabitants, two-thirds of which are Arab Christians or members of various religious communities; the remainder are Moslems. There is also a recently established Jewish community in the modern township of Nazerat Illit, which overlooks the old town.

The old section of Nazareth with its narrow winding lanes, innumerable steps, tiny courtyards, flat roofs, open-air shops and noisy bazaar gives a typically oriental impression. Here, in the centre of the town, are the grounds of the Franciscan monastery, which is fairly conspicuous, because it lies on a hill. This is our destination, for here we find the newly built Basilica of the Annunciation and the Church of St. Joseph.

Near the centre of the town Casa Nova Road branches off to the left from the main road coming from Haifa or Afula. After following it uphill for 150 m., we arrive at the entrance to the Basilica of the Annunciation on the right. This is reputed to be the largest church in the Middle East. It was completed in 1969 after fourteen years of construction. The actual Grotto of the Annunciation is artistically embedded in the lower church, which also displays a mosaic from the second century and the remains of the Byzantine and Crusader churches. The vaulted ceiling of the grotto still reveals the original shape of the cave dwelling. Here we can sense a little of the mystery of that momentous event of the Annunciation.

Our next visit is to the Church of St. Joseph, which lies opposite, to the left of the monastery. It is built over a spacious cave, which is said to have been the dwelling of the Holy Family, and consists of an upper and lower church. In the latter the memory of Joseph's workshop is perpetuated.

Not long ago other cave dwellings of Jesus' time were found in the vicinity. We are directed to the school of the Dames de Nazareth opposite the Franciscan compound, on the other side of Casa Nova Road. A side street brings us to the school. The Sisters kindly lead us down to the extensive excavations beneath their building, where ancient tombs and cave dwellings dating from Jesus' day as well as the remains of a Byzantine church have been found. Although the archaeological study of the excavations has not yet been completed, it already confirms the location of Nazareth at the time of Jesus, as do the excavations near the Grotto of the Annunciation.

From Casa Nova Road we can see up the gently rising bazaar street, also known as *shuk*, and we have a view of the nearby towers of the Greek Catholic Parish Church. A modest room next to this church retains the memory of the synagogue in which Jesus taught. We shall also want to visit this place. To reach it we follow the bazaar street a short way and take the first turn to the left and then the first to the right. We pass through an iron door and walk across the narrow courtyard of the church in order to come to The Synagogue.

Our next quest is Mary's Well, which lies at a busy intersection on the road to Tiberias. Even from afar we can recognize it by the oval-shaped opening. Nearby is a grove of trees. A channel connects the well to the actual spring, which was probably used in Jesus' day and can now be found in a grotto beneath the Greek Orthodox Church of St. Gabriel, some 50 m. away. To the left of Mary's Well is the street that leads us to St. Gabriel's.

It is not only the special memorial sites in Nazareth that remind us of Jesus; everything speaks of Him, including the neighbouring hills, where He must have spent many hours in prayer. In springtime the surroundings are a delight to the eye — flower-strewn meadows dotted with boulders and shepherds' caves. Here we feel very near to the "hidden Jesus of Nazareth".

Times of opening:

The Basilica of the Annunciation & The Church of St. Joseph	open all day except from noon — 2 p.m.
The Synagogue	9 a.m. — 12.30 p.m. 2.30 p.m. — 6 p.m. closed on Sundays, and Wednesday and Saturday afternoons

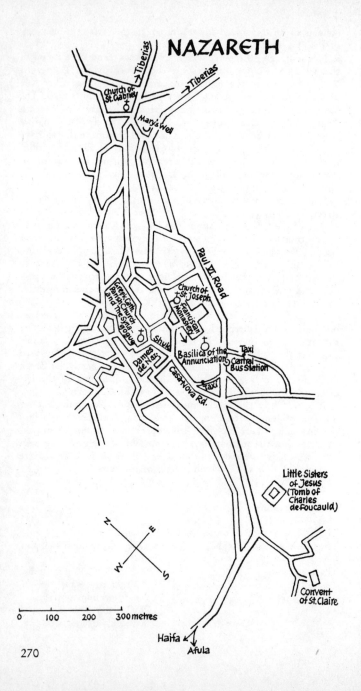

NAZARETH

Tiberias

Church of St. Gabriel

Tiberias

Mary's Well

Paul VI. Road

Church of St. Joseph

Greek Cath. Parish Church and the Synagogue

Franciscan Monastery

Shuk

Dames de Naz.

Basilica of the Annunciation

Taxi

Central Bus Station

Casa Nova Rd.

Taxi

Little Sisters of Jesus (Tomb of Charles de Foucauld)

Convent of St. Claire

N
E
W
S

0   100   200   300 metres

Haifa

Afula

Nazareth, the place chosen by God for the annunciation of the birth of His Son, and the town where He would grow to manhood, is unknown in the Old Testament. It is first mentioned in the Gospels. "The Nazarene" was the name Jesus' contemporaries conferred upon Him, and since then the name of Nazareth has accompanied Him all over the world. Although the exact date of the first settlement at Nazareth cannot be ascertained, it is evident from tomb finds that the place was inhabited at least 200 years before Jesus' day. The spring that still feeds the well on the Tiberias Road must have attracted the first inhabitants. Since ancient times it has supplied the town with water and the Mother Mary must also have come here often to draw water.

Nazareth was destined to remain unimportant because of its location. It did not lie on a main road, but somewhat off the beaten track in a geographical basin. The stony fields in this area meant poverty and hardship for the inhabitants. In Jesus' day Nazareth was apparently so poor and insignificant that the Jewish historian Josephus does not even mention it, although he shows great interest in the town of Sepphoris, only 5 km. away, which was the seat of Herod for a long time. We may even assume that Nazareth was not a town at all. Following the example of the Septuagint (the Greek translation of the Old Testament), the Gospels use the Greek word for town where originally an independent community was meant, regardless of its size.

Whereabouts in this insignificant town lay that highly significant place where Mary received the angel's wonderful tidings? Was it the Grotto of the Annunciation, over which a large basilica has now been built? Was this the Nazareth of old where the archangel Gabriel visited the Virgin Mary in her parental home? The excavations that began here in 1955 when the old Church of the Annunciation was demolished give strong evidence to support this view. A number of tombs came to light, but these were non-Jewish, since the Jewish law required graves to be located outside residential areas. They were the tombs of Crusaders, whose desire was to be buried at holy places. In addition, the foundations of many houses dating from Jesus' day were found, showing that the area round the Basilica of the Annunciation was inhabited then. These are the remains of dwellings, such as can still be seen in the Orient today, built in front of natural rock caves. The rear portion of the house would have been formed by the cool, dry rock cave and the front portion by additional walls. Mary may well have been in such a cave when the archangel Gabriel appeared and delivered the divine message to her. The Grotto of the Annunciation, as we can see it today, lies exactly in line with the other excavated houses of ancient Nazareth. Thus it can be assumed that the tradition considering this particular grotto as the site of the Annunciation is well-founded.

The excavations of recent years have attested the authenticity of the tradition concerning the Grotto of the Annunciation, but the previous history of the grotto was subject to many changes throughout the centuries. After the Roman occupation in A.D. 67 the Nazareth of the Gospels completely disappeared. The location of the place of the Annunciation could only be passed on by word of mouth. And this is probably what happened, for it is known that up till ca. A.D. 200 descendants of the female relatives of Mary lived at Nazareth.

When Nazareth was revived, many refugees from Jerusalem settled there, especially after the Emperor Hadrian expelled the Jews from the entire area of Judea. Thus in the third century Nazareth was again wholly Jewish and its Christian tradition was interrupted. But the Jews must have handed down the memory of the holy places here, for even negation has a good memory. However, a dark mystery seems to have lain over Nazareth in these early times, for the Christians avoided the place and did not search out the Biblical sites. Was it because this town had sought to stone Jesus, its greatest Son, and refused His teaching?

In about 359 it is recorded that the Emperor Constantine ordered the governor, Joseph of Tiberias, to build Christian churches in all the Jewish places of Galilee where none had yet been built. Nazareth is especially mentioned, because "no Greek, nor Samaritan, nor Christian dwelt there, for foreigners were strictly forbidden to settle there". However, it is not recorded whether or not the governor exerted his authority to have a church built at Nazareth.

Thus not until the fourth century was Jewish Nazareth gradually opened to Christians. In 386 St. Paula visited Nazareth, the first mention of a pilgrim's visit here. In 460 reference is made to a church in this town. And the pilgrim Anonymous of Piacenza, the first to mention the Church of the Annunciation, writes in ca. 570, "The house of Saint Mary is a basilica." In the following centuries Nazareth suffered the effects of many a war, especially during the Persian invasion of 614. When the Emperor Heraclius suppressed the Persians in 630, Jewish settlements like Nazareth, which had sympathized with the Persians, were entirely wiped out.

When the Byzantine Basilica of the Annunciation was destroyed is not known; however, its foundations have now been brought to light, and the original building is thought to date from the fifth century. On its site the Crusaders built a three-naved church, which was destroyed as early as 1263. The grotto, however, was preserved. The Franciscans, who have been living in Nazareth since 1620, erected a small church over the grotto in 1730. In 1955 they began to build a large, new basilica to replace it. The dedication took place in 1969.

The Grotto of the Annunciation has lost its original form through various alterations over the centuries and many different traditions have been attributed to it with the passing of time. For instance, it was also regarded as the house of Joseph and the home of the Holy Family. It was even considered to hold the tomb of Joseph and Mary. Later these suppositions were discarded. At the turn of the century the Gospel accounts and the earliest traditions were reconsidered and consequently the tradition that the grotto had also been the house of Joseph was abandoned. Now only the mystery of the Annunciation is commemorated at this site.

THE ANNUNCIATION

FROM THE HOLY BIBLE

In the sixth month the angel Gabriel was sent from God to a city of Galilee named Nazareth, to a virgin betrothed to a man whose name was Joseph, of the house of David; and the virgin's name was Mary.

And he came to her and said, "Hail, O favored one, the Lord is with you! Blessed are you among women!" But she was greatly troubled at the saying, and considered in her mind what sort of greeting this might be.

And the angel said to her, "Do not be afraid, Mary, for you have found favor with God. And behold, you will conceive in your womb and bear a son, and you shall call his name Jesus. He will be great, and will be called the Son of the Most High; and the Lord God will give to him the throne of his father David, and he will reign over the house of Jacob for ever; and of his kingdom there will be no end." And Mary said to the angel, "How can this be, since I have no husband?" And the angel said to her, "The Holy Spirit will come upon you, and the power of the Most High will overshadow you; therefore the child to be born of you will be called holy, the Son of God."

And Mary said, "Behold, I am the handmaid of the Lord; let it be to me according to your word."   cf. Luke 1 : 26-38

THE GROTTO OF THE ANNUNCIATION — A MESSAGE FOR US

Nazareth — a place that heard wonderful tidings when an angel descended to bring a unique message from heaven to a maiden called Mary!

Nazareth — a holy town where the Holy Spirit Himself overshadowed a virgin, so that she would bear the Son of God. Surely at such a place we must especially ponder on the mighty things God has done, humble ourselves and worship the God who manifests Himself.

Here in one of Nazareth's caves the messenger of God came to Mary, the pure maiden, and greeted her with the words, "Hail, O favoured one, blessed are you!" In awe and humility she asked herself what this greeting could mean. And in reverence she may have bowed low before this heavenly messenger. Her ears and heart now heard the incomprehensible tidings, the divine message of an election, which her human heart was scarcely able to grasp. "You have found favour with God. The Holy Spirit will come upon you, and the power of the Most High will overshadow you; therefore the child to be born of you will be called holy, the Son of God."

Mary, a chosen one of God – what does this mean? Election is the highest possible mark of favour; it is to be drawn into deep communion with God, to be tenderly looked upon by Him and used as His instrument. But election also entails suffering. A person chosen by God must be willing to be made worthy of his election in the furnace of affliction and to bear the burden of the grace received. He must now tread paths with the living God, paths of faith and not of sight. To be chosen by God is to follow the same paths as the Son of God. These are paths of deepest humiliation, disgrace and untold suffering. Only such paths can yield fruit for God, for a particular ministry and for the coming of His kingdom.

In every instance election is an offer from God that a person can either accept or reject. Election is God's question to His child. And He expects a response – our dedication, as in the case of Abraham, who, upon hearing God's call, surrendered himself unconditionally to God and obediently followed the path shown to him.

Thus the crucial question was how Mary would respond. And behold she replied with words, powerful in their simplicity, "Let it be to me according to Your word." This reply already contained the entire pathway for a soul chosen by God – the pathway Mary would then follow. This path, which she had freely chosen on that day with her consent to God, would be stamped by poverty, since she would call the poorest of all men that ever trod this earth her Child. It would be a path of untold suffering, since persecution, rejection, the flight to Egypt, indeed, the homelessness of the Son of man would now be her lot also.

The Grotto of the Annunciation – a holy chamber, where God called a virgin to consecrate herself to Him, so that the Holy Spirit could overshadow her and God could make His dwelling within her. O hallowed grotto that saw Mary filled with grace as a chosen one of God! O holy grotto that saw a holy person – holy, because God was able to take full possession of her! Mary gave herself unreservedly to God, placing her life completely at His disposal. She did not object, nor did she ask what would happen to her on this path. Her sole thought was, "Let it be to me according to Your will. I shall follow Your leading."

Will Mary find spiritual sons and daughters among the people who pray silently here in this grotto? Will she find people who walk in her footsteps and give God their unconditional surrender when He calls them to follow Him, and who will say, "Let it be to me according to Your will; whatever You say I will do, whatever You ask of me I will give You"?

PRAYER IN THE GROTTO
OF THE ANNUNCIATION

Our dear Father in heaven,

At this site we thank You for the wonderful event when the angel Gabriel announced to Mary that she would give birth to the only-begotten Son of God through the overshadowing of the Holy Spirit. We praise You for the mystery of Mary's election. In her You found a soul who responded to You with an unconditional consent, her will being utterly surrendered to Yours regardless of how much shame and hardship this leading might bring her. Let us join her in worshipping You for regarding the lowliness of Your handmaid and performing such wonderful things through her.

Accept my life and grant that I may humble myself as Mary did and with implicit trust in Your love take every path that You call me to follow. I pray that through the surrender of my will You will be able to do great things in me and through me, so that I too may bring Jesus to others.

Amen.

✝

"Behold, I am the handmaid of the Lord;
let it be to me according to your word."
How simple, yet how powerful are these words of Mary!
Saying "Yes" to the will of God, in faith in His love in spite
of all seeming impossibilities, makes people instruments of
God even today when they tread the path that Mary trod.

✠

O Mary, you were chosen,
Born to be God's handmaid!
To you an angel from on high came down.
In that holy hour
You heard blessèd tidings:
God Himself was to be born of you!

God's holy words were spoken . . .
The Virgin Mary answered,
Humbly submitting to His high decree.
She loved God with a pure love
And so her will she yielded,
Consenting to His holy claim on her.

Mary esteemed the will of God above her own understanding. At His word she consented to follow an inconceivable
path. God waits for souls who will have faith like Mary
when He makes an inconceivable request of them and who
will dispel the objections of their intellect by declaring,
"With God nothing is impossible!"

O Sacred Hour and Holy

7. 6. D.

O sacred hour and ho ——— ly

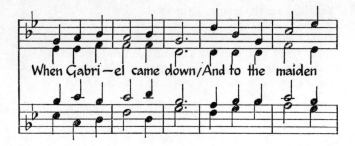

He came from highest heaven,
In glory bright arrayed,
Celestial splendour giving
The room of that poor maid.

His heav'nly salutation
To her whom God holds dear,
His holy, awesome tidings
First strike her heart with fear.

His gracious words amaze her.
"How can such things befall?"
The light and glory daze her,
She wonders at it all.

"O Mary, you are blessèd,
For God has chosen you
To bear His Son, the Saviour."
How can this e'er come true?

And Mary bows so humbly,
Awed at such wondrous grace.
Giving her life completely,
God's will she does embrace.

The maid, in simple rev'rence
Spoke words so hard to say,
"As You have willed, commanded,
So be it done, I pray."

The angel brought her answer
To God's most holy throne,
And through her willing, "Yes, Lord,"
The Son of God came down.

Can also be sung to the melody,
"Jesus, the Very Thought of Thee"

✝

Let us here humble ourselves before God as Mary did and
consent to His leading for us with the words:

I embrace Thy will and yearn
To still the longings of Thy heart;
My soul desireth nothing else.
May Thy heart now be comforted
By souls who only seek to know
What Thy will is, and Thy desire.

Take Thou my life into Thy hands;
Direct and fashion it each day
As Thou dost please. I give it Thee,
And troth my will anew to Thine.
O Lord, plan Thou my life and do with me
Whatever Thou dost wish.

THE CHURCH OF ST. JOSEPH

THE HISTORICAL ASPECT

Since Nazareth was Jesus' home town, we naturally wonder where the home of the Holy Family was located. Where did they live after their return from Egypt? Where did Jesus grow to manhood? But there is no definite tradition. Sometimes early tradition transferred the memory of the home to the Grotto of the Annunciation. At other times the dwelling of the Holy Family was thought to be where the Church of St. Gabriel now stands, near Mary's Well. According to the report of the pilgrim Arkulf in 670 a church stood here on the site of the house "in which our Saviour was nourished".

Today the home of the Holy Family is venerated in a cave dwelling dating from the time of Jesus, beneath the Church of St. Joseph. The Franciscans erected this church in 1914, after having previously, in 1754, built a chapel on this site over the ruins of a Crusader church. However, the tradition of this holy place is not mentioned until ca. 1600 when it was called Joseph's Home and Carpentry Shop, by which only Joseph's carpentry shop was meant. Not until later, in about 1900, did it venerate the home of the Holy Family as well.

Even though there are no definite traditions about the home of the Holy Family, we are grateful for a worthy site to perpetuate the memory of the place where Jesus spent most of His life. Is not the fact that the exact location of the home cannot be ascertained in keeping with the whole tenor of Jesus' life in Nazareth — the hidden years?

Another important site in Nazareth is the synagogue where Jesus taught. According to tradition a new synagogue was built on the same site after the destruction of the original one and in 1137 it was converted into a church. Today opinion varies as to where it actually stood. According to Kopp in *Stätten des Evangeliums* a portion of the Moslem cemetery is regarded as the site of the ancient synagogue. But the cemetery is not open to the public and there is no longer anything reminiscent of a synagogue to be found there. The commonly accepted tradition, however, considers the room next to the Greek Catholic Parish Church to be the authentic site.

There are also varying traditions concerning the location of the "brow of the hill" to which Jesus was led after His sermon in the synagogue (Luke 4 : 29). One tradition considers Jebel En Nabi Sain to be the hill on which ancient Nazareth lay. Although the round summit of this hill has no precipice, there are steep parts lower down with houses now clinging to them. Today there are also buildings on the hilltop, among them the Salesian church, school and monastery. Another tradition, dating from the ninth century, refers to Jebel Qafzeh as the "brow of the hill". But this tradition does not seem to be a very likely one. The hill lies beyond Nazareth with a sheer drop to the Plain of Jezreel.

FROM THE HOLY BIBLE

And being warned in a dream Joseph withdrew to the district of Galilee. And he went and dwelt in a city called Nazareth, that what was spoken by the prophets might be fulfilled, "He shall be called a Nazarene."

cf. Matthew 2 : 22 f.

And Jesus went down with his parents and came to Nazareth, and was obedient to them. And Jesus increased in wisdom and in years, and in favor with God and man.

cf. Luke 2 : 51 f.

Jesus, when he began his ministry, was about thirty years of age, being the son (as was supposed) of Joseph.

Luke 3 : 23

Philip found Nathanael, and said to him, "We have found him of whom Moses in the law and also the prophets wrote, Jesus of Nazareth, the son of Joseph." Nathanael said to him, "Can anything good come out of Nazareth?" Philip said to him, "Come and see."   John 1 : 45 f.

And Jesus came to Nazareth, where he had been brought up; and he went to the synagogue, as his custom was, on the sabbath day. And he stood up to read; and there was given to him the book of the prophet Isaiah. He opened the book and found the place where it was written, "The Spirit of the Lord is upon me, because he has anointed me to preach good news to the poor. He has sent me to proclaim release to the captives and recovering of sight to the blind, to set at liberty those who are oppressed, to proclaim the acceptable year of the Lord." And he began to say to them, "Today this scripture has been fulfilled in your hearing." And all wondered at the gracious words which proceeded out of his mouth; and they said, "Is not this Joseph's son, the carpenter? Is not his mother called Mary? And are not his brothers James and Joseph and Simon and Judas? And are not all his sisters with us? Where then did this man get all this?" And they took offense at him. And Jesus said to them, "A prophet is not without honor, except in his own country, and among his own kin, and in his own house." And he did not do many mighty works there, because of their unbelief. All in the synagogue were filled with wrath. And they rose up and put him out of the city, and led him to the brow of the hill on which their city was built, that they might throw him down headlong. But passing through the midst of them he went away.   cf. Luke 4 : 16-30; Mark 6 : 1-6; Matthew 13 : 53-58

NAZARETH – A MESSAGE FOR US

In the grotto beneath the Church of St. Joseph, which venerates the dwelling of the Holy Family, we are invited to think about Jesus' childhood in the prayerful stillness of this room. The boy Jesus grew up here in Nazareth in lowliness and obscurity, working for years as a carpenter, although He was the Son of God. This cave dwelling illustrates to us the extreme poverty Jesus knew as a Child. Nazareth was such a poor and insignificant place that no distinguished families of priests lived here as in the neighbouring town of Sepphoris – the pride of Galilee. The inhabitants of Nazareth were poor and apparently somewhat despised to judge by Nathanael's comment, "Can anything good come out of Nazareth?"

Perhaps Nazareth also had somewhat of a bad reputation. Its inhabitants seem to have had few ethical qualities. In any event there could not have been a good spirit prevailing among the people. That they were prone to hatred and anger, easily incited to murder, is shown by their later attitude towards Jesus. Although He was their fellow countryman, had grown up in their midst, was known to them since childhood, and was even related to many of them, they were infuriated after hearing His "gracious words" and attempted to throw Him down from a hill in order to kill Him.

We wonder why God chose to let His only-begotten Son, who was holy and pure, grow up in wretched, disreputable Nazareth. Here we can see the truth of Jesus' words when He said that He had come not to the righteous, to the respectable, but to sinners. His love, which was completely at one with the Father's choice, drew Him to the kind of place we naturally flee. We avoid those who are difficult and problematic, people who are evil. We seek other company. But the love of Jesus drew Him to the very place where the most arrows of antagonism would fly at Him, and where He would have the most opportunity to show merciful, forgiving love, even to His enemies.

How the little boy Jesus must have suffered among the other children in the streets of Nazareth, for was He not a Child of heaven, gracious in His bearing, reflecting the splendour of the Father's love? How the malice, the sins of His playmates must have wounded His divinely gentle and loving heart! Perhaps He even had to bear hostility and derision from the other children, since He was so different from them. Eternal Love had chosen suffering even before the foundation of the world out of love for us – His birth in a cave in Bethlehem with a cattle trough for a cradle, the flight through the desert to Egypt, and then His childhood in Nazareth, where He grew up in poverty among people who brought Him much trouble and heartache.

The love of Jesus, which constrained Him to serve, to enter lowliness and suffering for our sake, found many opportunities here in Nazareth. As the poor carpenter's son, He had to offer His services to others and perform menial tasks from morning till night. For years He fashioned ploughs and other farming implements for them. Here He humbled Himself daily, taking the lowest place. During these years He put into practice all that He would later preach to others.

In Nazareth the lamblike nature of Jesus grew to maturity; later He would become the Lamb of God, whose special attribute is patience. Here Jesus had to learn that which produces the fruit of patience. He had to learn to wait and wait again until the Father indicated that the moment had come for Him to step into the open, preach to the people, minister to them and reveal Himself as the Messiah and the Son of God. Yet even when this hour came, He experienced nowhere so keenly as in Nazareth, His home town, the truth of the words, "He came unto his own, and his own received him not."

Indeed, here in Nazareth Jesus was not appreciated. His townsfolk failed to recognize Him as the Son of God; they did not even recognize Him as a prophet when as a grown man He proclaimed the "acceptable year of the Lord" in their synagogue. Here Jesus learnt obedience through the hostility and misunderstanding He suffered from His fellow men – obedience to His Father in heaven and to His parents (Hebrews 5 : 8; Luke 2 : 51). Here Jesus was prepared by His heavenly Father for His Passion. And during these preliminary years He must have voluntarily dedicated Himself time and time again to follow His path of bitter sorrow out of love for us.

Thus we can only walk through the streets of Nazareth today in worship and adoration to the Lord Jesus for choosing such a small, wretched town when He came to dwell among us wicked sons of men, for singling out Nazareth of all places, for choosing that which was "low and despised in the world" (1 Corinthians 1 : 28).

Here in Nazareth Jesus bids us, "Come, follow Me. Do not seek places and company where life is pleasant for you, where your love is returned and you are honoured. Rather go to those who are difficult and who humiliate you. Invite them, serve them and do good to them, even if you know that your kindness will only be repaid with evil (Matthew 5 : 44 ff.; Luke 14 : 12 ff.). Commit yourselves to this path, for it is the way of love – love that humbles itself and serves others, love that desires to help and release them, the love of the Son of God."

Jesus yearns to live on in the members of His Body. Love Himself, who chose the hidden pathway of humility, longs to walk across the earth in His own, so that the world will see Him today.

✢

Jesus made himself of no reputation, and took upon him the form of a servant, and was made in the likeness of men.

Philippians 2 : 7 A.V.

No one on earth, with respect to his background and abilities, has ever been so misunderstood, unappreciated and degraded as Jesus, the Son of God, when He lived as a boy and carpenter in Nazareth. Whoever loves Jesus chooses His pathway.

Nazareth, a Treasure You Hold

8. 8. 7. 5. 8.

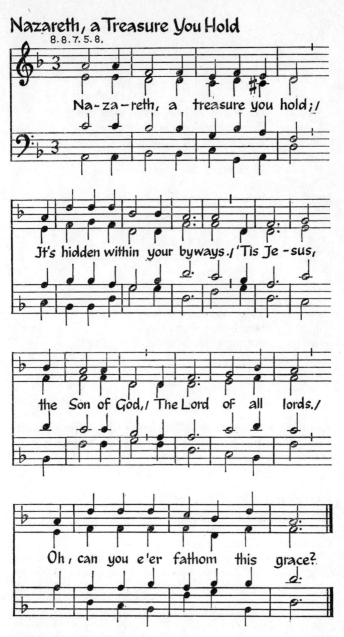

Na-za-reth, a treasure you hold;/ It's hidden within your byways./ 'Tis Je-sus, the Son of God,/ The Lord of all lords./ Oh, can you e'er fathom this grace?

Nazareth, the Lord dwells in you,
Though in your streets none can hear Him.
His greatness is here concealed,
Completely veiled,
In lowliness beyond compare.

Nazareth, the Lord walks your streets.
The One who made all creation
Now goes ways of lowliness –
A carpenter's son –
Until He is thirty years old!

Nazareth, great fruit ripens here
In suffering, veiled and hidden.
The Lord stoops beneath the Cross,
Goes bravely to die;
He suffers and loves without end.

Nazareth, you ne'er cease to call
The pilgrims who walk your byways
To go ways of lowliness,
Humility,
For these are the paths of our Lord!

+

Jesus' life in Nazareth is an illustration that every powerful ministry must be preceded by a time of obscurity and preparation in lowliness and obedience.

PRAYER IN THE GROTTO
OF THE HOLY FAMILY

Our heavenly Father,

We humble ourselves before You, because Your beloved Son, who played here as a child in the streets of Nazareth, was neither recognized nor treated as Your beloved Son by us men. We think of His many childhood sufferings when He was such a stranger among the children of Nazareth, homesick for His Father and His heavenly home, since He was completely different – a divine Child.

Dearest Jesus, gracious Child, we yearn to love You for all those in Nazareth who did not love You. We want to show You our love by accompanying You along the paths You trod as a child and a carpenter's son, the hidden paths of serving and self-abasement. Therefore, we want to choose the most insignificant place among men voluntarily and love especially those who are difficult for us to bear.

Send us Your Holy Spirit, who will constrain us to do so.

Amen.

CANA

Cana of Galilee is familiar to us all, because here at the wedding feast Jesus wrought His first miracle. And now that we are in Galilee, we shall surely want to visit Cana. But we are told that two places commemorate this event.

The most-visited site is **Kfar Cana** (Arabic *Kefer Kenna*), which lies on the road from Haifa to Tiberias. From Nazareth it is only 9 km. to the village, which lies in a delightful landscape, surrounded by olive and pomegranite groves. Its houses extend eastwards up the slope of a hill.

When we enter the village, we find a Greek Catholic church on the right. A little farther on, a lane branches off to the right, leading to the Roman Catholic parish church, which is served by Franciscans. It commemorates the miracle performed by Jesus at the wedding feast of Cana. Even from afar we can recognize it easily by its two towers and shining red dome. Beside it to the left is a Greek Orthodox church. Both properties are enclosed by high walls. A narrow paved path between them leads us to the courtyard of the Franciscan church, which commemorates the wedding feast. In the stillness of the church, but especially down in the crypt, we contemplate that which began in the life of our Lord Jesus with the wedding feast at Cana and which John bore witness to when he wrote, "We have beheld his glory."

Chirbet Cana, *(Kh. Qana),* the other place commemorating the miracle at the wedding feast, is 9 km. from Kfar Cana as the crow flies, and 14 km. north of Nazareth. Owing to the poor road conditions it is difficult to reach.

THE HISTORICAL ASPECT

According to the Gospel of John Cana of Galilee, where Jesus worked His first miracle, lay in the hill country to the west of the Sea of Galilee, for we are told that Jesus "went *down* to Capernaum" (John 2 : 12). When Jesus was at Cana on a later occasion, an official whose son was ill bade Him, "Come *down* before my child dies" (John 4 : 47, 49). The third time that Cana is mentioned in the Gospels it is as the home of Nathanael, who is thought to be the later Apostle Bartholomew (John 21 : 2).

The Franciscan church in **Kfar Cana,** commemorating the wedding feast, was built in 1880 and stands on the ruins of ancient buildings dating from the fourth or sixth century. An ancient inscription was discovered here, bearing the name of Joseph. This has led some to believe that the ruins are the remains of an early shrine erected here as at many other holy places by Joseph of Tiberias, the favourite of the Emperor Constantine. Others consider the finds to be the remains of a synagogue dating from the same period.

Later a mosque stood here and in the sixteenth century this was regarded as the site where the miracle took place. Consequently, in 1566 the Greek Orthodox built a church opposite the mosque. The Franciscans from nearby Nazareth acquired a neighbouring house in 1641. For 200 years they struggled to gain possession of the mosque. Finally in 1879 they were able to buy the dilapidated building and erect their church. In the crypt, which according to ancient pilgrim reports was sometimes regarded as the room where the feast was held and sometimes as the place where the water jars stood, now stands a replica of a Jewish water jar of Jesus' day.

Chirbet Cana, the other site commemorating the miracle at the wedding feast, now consists only of ruins on a hilltop and an ancient cistern. Finds at this site show that it was an inhabited settlement as early as 1200 B.C. and a place of considerable size in Jesus' day. The name Chirbet Cana seems to be evidence that an ancient tradition sought to identify it as the Cana of Galilee. Later the commemoration of the wedding feast and the miracle was transferred from Chirbet Cana proper to a cave at the foot of the hill. It was thought that the water that was miraculously changed into wine was drawn from the cistern still visible upon the hilltop.

Down through the centuries traditions have varied and many pilgrim reports do not clearly indicate which of the sites they regarded to be Cana. Until after the time of the Crusaders many reports refer to Chirbet Cana, but then it fell into utter ruin and today, as already mentioned, it is nothing but a few remains in a desolate place. Ever since the late sixteenth century Kefer Kenna or Kfar Cana has been preferred as the authentic Cana of Galilee, especially after the Greek Orthodox church was built and later the Franciscan shrine.

+

FROM THE HOLY BIBLE

On the third day there was a marriage at Cana in Galilee, and the mother of Jesus was there; Jesus also was invited to the marriage, with his disciples. When the wine failed, the mother of Jesus said to him, "They have no wine." And Jesus said to her, "O woman, what have you to do with me? My hour has not yet come." His mother said to the servants, "Do whatever he tells you."

Jesus said to them, "Fill the jars with water ... Now draw some out, and take it to the steward of the feast." When the steward of the feast tasted the water now become wine, and did not know where it came from, the steward of the feast called the bridegroom and said to him, "Every man serves the good wine first; and when men have drunk freely, then the poor wine; but you have kept the good wine until now."

This, the first of his signs, Jesus did at Cana in Galilee, and manifested his glory; and his disciples believed in him.

cf. John 2 : 1-11

✝

Jesus of Nazareth, a man attested to you by God with mighty works and wonders and signs which God did through him in your midst.   Acts 2 : 22

Cana proclaims that Jesus is the Lord Almighty, who turns water into wine and who can still today, by one word, transform anything: sorrow into joy, and mountains of difficulties into straight paths. But do we bring our needs to Him?

✝

CANA – A MESSAGE FOR US

The name Cana calls to mind the great miracle wrought by Jesus at the wedding feast when He manifested His glory. This miracle at Cana stands out from all His other miracles, which demonstrated His omnipotence, since it was Jesus' first miracle, the first revelation of His glory as the Son of God, as Scripture tells us.

For thirty years the Son of God lived a hidden life, unnoticed in the small, insignificant town of Nazareth. Throughout those years He who possesses all power in heaven and on earth daily chose lowliness and humiliation, offering His services to His fellow countrymen as a simple carpenter and fashioning farming implements for them. Year after year passed by. It was an exceedingly long waiting period. But in those years before beginning His actual ministry, Jesus learnt to endure that which He would later have to suffer in full. "He was despised, and we esteemed him not." Indeed, through that which He suffered He learnt obedience and complete humility – humility, which then emanated from Him as He trod the path of the Cross, wearing the crown of thorns; humilit , which contained all power and authority.

During those long years of waiting and suffering, of lowliness and obedience, all the divine power in Jesus came to maturity. And when He was about thirty years of age, the time ha at last come for Him to reveal His glory and might, which stemmed from is liness and obedience. Here in Cana He manifested to the world for the first time who He really was and demonstrated the divine power and authority that dwelt in Him, previously unknown to those about Him.

In the same attitude of obedience and humility Jesus now performs the miracle at the wedding feast. When His mother draws His attention to the lack of wine, He replies, "My hour has not yet come." In humble dependence upon the Father Jesus waits until He receives permission to perform a new and mighty deed that would reveal His divine ministry. Jesus can do nothing but what the Father bids Him to do. And His mother senses that the secret of His actions and nature is His humility and dependence upon the Father and that these are also the source of His power of authority, which would be revealed in His time. Thus she bids the servants, "Do whatever he tells you." She knows that when He does act, He will prove His power and do something wonderful. And behold, He utters a word, which they obey – and a miracle takes place.

The wedding feast at Cana shows us Jesus as the humble Lord, who is endowed with authority because of His humility. He can transform every situation. He can solve all man's difficulties when He deals with them. Water, which could not be offered to the guests, is changed into wine; the need is supplied. Indeed, Jesus transforms water, used for ceremonial cleansing, to provide the wine of gladness as a sign that He was sent to prepare the eternal feast of joy, the final preparations of which would be completed when the hour came for Him to die on the Cross for our salvation.

Overwhelmed by His deed, the disciples realize that this humble son of a carpenter is truly the Son of God. All power and might are His. Nothing is impossible for this Lord, because He is the very Son of God, who came down to our earth to perform signs and wonders in the power of God.

When confronted with difficulties, we are often like the people of long ago and think that Jesus' power is as limited as ours. Thus Cana has a message for us today. It declares that Jesus is not a mere human being as we are, but the Son of God. All power and might in heaven and on earth has been given to Him, especially since He is the most humble of all. Cana tells us that we have a Lord who can do all things, for whom nothing is impossible. In Him we have a God who performs miracles, who helps us in wonderful ways when people can no longer help us. Impossibilities need no longer exist for us, since we may bring them to this almighty Lord and ask Him for help. And behold, today as long ago, He says but a word, and impossible situations are transformed. Just as the water was subject to Jesus and turned into wine, all things are subject to Him and must obey His will today, for as the Son of God, He was found obedient and subject to the Father at all times and is now seated at the right hand of God, waiting to reveal Himself majestically in our lives too.

However, Jesus does not merely desire to transform the impossible situations in which we find ourselves. He also wants to make us vessels of His glory who, as members of His Body imbued with His divine authority, will display

His power here on earth. But this will only be possible if we tread the path Jesus trod before us. The most humble will be granted the greatest authority and those who abase themselves the most will be given the greatest power. Those who patiently endure long periods of waiting, gladly performing the most humble tasks in obscurity, will receive ministries from God at the end of these paths, ministries in the Kingdom of God, which will bring forth fruit a hundred-fold and manifest His glory.

O How Great Is the Lord
6. 7. 8. 8. 7.

O how great is the Lord! / Honour, praise to Him accord! / All His thoughts and plans are wondrous— / All the things He does to help us! / Je-sus, no one is like You!

O how great is the Lord –
Joyfully by us adored!
Naught can match His pow'r so boundless
And His proofs of loving-kindness,
Which He shows to us today.

PRAYER IN THE CHURCH AT CANA

Our dear Lord Jesus,

We thank You that You are a mighty Lord, who turned water into wine, who indeed can transform everything. You need to say but one word and sorrow is turned into joy, mountains of obstacles are levelled into smooth paths.

Lord, here we want to claim Your power, praise Your might, and honour You with a great faith. In all our difficulties and impossibilities we want to trust You, the living Lord, and believe that You are the same yesterday and today. You see our needs and still perform miracles today, sending us aid when we call upon You and trust You. We thank You for this.

Amen.

✝

Our difficulties and hardships are Jesus' opportunity to display His power, which turns water into wine, multiplies loaves and fishes, and performs many different miracles. Our need moves Him to help us and exert His power on our behalf.

✝

Cana miracles still occur today whenever God finds people who believe in His power and await His miracles as Jesus' mother did.

NAIN

The name Nain, which comes from the Hebrew word *na'im*
meaning "pleasant", has   warm sound to it, for here our Lord
Jesus once raised a you   man from the dead, the only son of a
widow, and restored h   to his mother. Today Nain is a poor,
small Moslem village, · lecting little of the charm of the Gospel
narrative. It lies south of Mount Tabor, on a low ridge of Givat
Hamoreh, which is also called Jebel Dahi or Little Hermon.
Coming from Afula, we can see Nain lying on the right-hand
side of the motor road to Tiberias. A narrow road forks off the
main road and after 2 km. we arrive at the village from the
north. A crowd of noisy children surrounds us as we approach the
church and the Arab family who are the guardians of the church
open it for us upon request.

THE HISTORICAL ASPECT

According to the details supplied by the historian Eusebius in
ca. A.D. 300 and the Church Father Jerome in ca. 400, the ancient
village of Nain, where Jesus raised the widow's son from the dead,
was situated on the site of the present village. Ancient rock tombs
have been found in the southeastern part of the village. Probably
the funeral procession was heading in this direction (Luke 7 : 12).
In the area traditionally associated with the miracle a church was
built in its commemoration. This church is first mentioned by
pilgrims in about 900, but when it was erected is not known.

After the departure of the Crusaders there were reports of a
church that had been destroyed. The ruins of this and of another
church in the vicinity were later rebuilt as mosques by the
Moslems, but these too fell into ruin. In 1880 the Franciscans
purchased the ruins of the first church after long, drawn-out
negotiations with the local authorities and built a chapel on the
foundations of the ancient sanctuary. In this way the site has been
preserved.

FROM THE HOLY BIBLE

Soon afterward Jesus went to a city called Nain, and his disciples and a great crowd went with him. As he drew near to the gate of the city, behold, a man who had died was being carried out, the only son of his mother, and she was a widow; and a large crowd from the city was with her. And when the Lord saw her, he had compassion on her and said to her, "Do not weep." And he came and touched the bier, and the bearers stood still. And he said, "Young man, I say to you, arise." And the dead man sat up, and began to speak. And he gave him to his mother.   cf. Luke 7 : 11-15

NAIN – A MESSAGE FOR US

The Gospels tell us how Jesus journeyed throughout the country, preaching the message of the kingdom of heaven everywhere He went. And perhaps one day Jesus decided to visit Nain, which lay somewhat off the caravan route to Jerusalem, in order to bring the people the good news that "the kingdom of heaven is at hand". Followed by His disciples and a large crowd, Jesus makes His way across the beautiful Plain of Jezreel with Mount Tabor lying in the distance. As He is about to enter the village of Nain, He is met by a crowd of people mourning and lamenting. They are carrying the bier of the young son of a widow. A dead person is being taken to his final resting place – an event that occurs a thousand times a day.

But for Jesus this is not an unalterable fact. He does not grow accustomed to seeing a funeral procession, as we do. Jesus, as it is written, has compassion on this woman in her distress. Jesus bears in His heart all the sorrows and troubles of His children. His heart is stirred by such distress. He is moved to tears and weeps with us just as He wept at the death of Lazarus (John 11 : 35).

To this day Nain is for us the place where Jesus reveals His loving, compassionate, tender heart, which warmly embraces us in our suffering. Here we are shown that Jesus cannot "pass by on the other side" when He sees someone in distress. When He meets this procession of mourners, He is unable to continue His way. He stops and exerts the power at His disposal, raising the young man from the dead.

God did not send Jesus to raise the many thousands of dead people of His day. The time had not yet come for that. Death, the last enemy, will not be overcome and abolished until the end of time when all powers lie at Jesus' feet. But even now Jesus gives a sign that He is the One who destroys the power of Death and that, therefore, all who believe in Him need not fear a second death after their physical death. As a sign that the dominion of Death will be completely abolished one day, Jesus, in His overwhelming love and compassion for this widow, says to her son, "Arise!" He commands Death to yield and the youth is restored to life. Here at Nain Death met the One who is stronger than he – Jesus, the Vanquisher of Death. Here Death was forced to show his true position before all the world – he is subject to Jesus and must obey His commands. Consequently, this deed of Jesus at Nain is a sign and a guarantee that Death will be forced to retreat more and more through Jesus' victory. First Death had to yield from Jesus Himself. Later he will yield from the first fruits, who will either rise from the dead at the first resurrection or be raptured, not tasting death at all. Finally Death will lose his power over all mankind (1 Corinthians 15 : 23 ff.). Thus Nain encourages us as we await Jesus' return. On that day Death will be swallowed up in victory and have no hold on those who belong to Jesus.

And Nain also brings us comfort in the present age when Death still holds sway and we must bear the grief caused by him. As we tarry in the church at Nain and think about Jesus calling the widow's son back to life and returning him to his mother, we cannot fail to see Jesus' abounding love and compassion for all who are in sorrow. Here at Nain He wants to demonstrate the power of His love, which is constrained to help us in all our suffering and which is able to transform every sorrow. And even though the time has not yet come for Him to raise our loved ones from the dead, He will show us the love that He showed to this widow, for the great love in His heart is unchanging. Every time we come to Him full of trust with our sorrows, He will speak a word of command and a miracle will happen – the power of sorrow will be broken and our hearts will be immersed in comfort instead. Jesus is the Son of God, who still performs miracles today. And is it not a great miracle when He fills despairing hearts with peace, comfort and heavenly joy even in the face of death? For then life, divine life, is victorious.

✛

Nain proclaims how great God is.
Nain bids us to trust and honour Him,
For Jesus is the mightiest Lord,
Who conquers all the world.
Even Death lies at His feet,
For he too has been vanquished by God.

PRAYER IN THE CHURCH AT NAIN

Dear Lord Jesus,

I praise Your love, which could not bear to see the distress of the widow and mother of Nain without helping her. I thank You that her plight so moved Your heart that You returned her only son to her. And I thank You that when we are in need and sorrow, You do not pass us by, but come to us out of compassion and transform our distressing situation.

May Your power and merciful love be deeply impressed upon my heart, so that in all my troubles I shall trust Your might and love implicitly. I know that You are the same yesterday and today and that You always have a way to help me too. You can even call back to life those who are on the verge of death. But if You do not return our loved ones, You will comfort us like a mother, so that our hearts are soothed by Your love and immersed in comfort and ever-lasting joy. You come to us, longing to help us in our sorrows, for You are almighty and love us with an inexpressible love.

And thus here in Nain I praise and worship the victorious power of Your love. Filled with expectancy, I wait for the hour of Your return when You will vanquish Death, the last foe.

Amen.

Jesus, You're the Mighty Victor

8. 6. 7. 6. 8.

Jesus, You're the mighty Victor. / You
help us in our plight, / from Death's dread hold men
snatching, / Because You won the fight. / Hallelujah! Halle-lu — — — — — — — jah!

Jesus, You are my Redeemer;
I trust in Your great might.
Jesus, You are the Victor;
For me You won the fight.
Hallelujah! Hallelujah!

Jesus, You indeed are Saviour;
By You all wounds are healed.
Jesus, You are the Sovereign;
Your people's mighty shield.
Hallelujah! Hallelujah!

Jesus, Breaker of all fetters,
The Lion of Judah's line.
Earth is filled with Your glory;
We praise You, Lamb divine.
Hallelujah! Hallelujah!

Jesus, Ruler without equal,
Triumphant Lord and King,
All pow'rs must pay You homage,
To You all honour bring.
Hallelujah! Hallelujah!

MOUNT TABOR

Approximately 580 m. in height, Mount Tabor is located in the northeast of the Plain of Jezreel, or Esdraelon (Hebrew *Emek Jezreel* or simply *Ha'emek*). As the most conspicuous mountain in southern Galilee, rising in isolation without foothills or neighbouring heights, the bell-shaped Tabor is visible at a great distance from all directions. But its external appearance, which is truly majestic, is not its only remarkable feature. Mount Tabor is a special place for us, since it holds the memory of the Transfiguration of our Lord Jesus. As we now journey to the mountain, our thoughts are turned to the three disciples who were privileged to accompany our Lord to the summit.

The motor road from Afula to Tiberias runs in a northeasterly direction, skirting the foot of Mount Tabor. Just before the village Kfar Tavor we take the road that branches off to the left to Daburiya. This Arab village lies on the west side of the mountain, which is covered with bushes, trees and boulders. From here the road climbs up the northwest slope in hairpin bends, leading to the summit.

Each bend reveals a more extensive view. First we see the fertile plain with its straight, well-cultivated fields. It is the Biblical Plain of Megiddo, named after the ancient city of Megiddo, now a mound lying to the southwest. There excavations have been made, disclosing the ruins of ancient cities and fortresses, among them remains from the time of Solomon (1 Kings 9 : 15). We are reminded of the many battles that this Plain of Megiddo (Armageddon in the New Testament) has seen (Judges 5 : 19; 2 Kings 9 : 27; 23 : 29; 2 Chronicles 35 : 22). We also think of the significance of this place for the future (Revelation 16 : 16). To the west we can see the hills surrounding Nazareth and the Carmel range in the far distance.

Now we have reached the summit of Mount Tabor, a wide platform where we find two churches, the Franciscan Basilica of the Transfiguration and a Greek Orthodox church also commemorating this event. A little-used road branches off to the left, leading to the Orthodox church. The main road continues to the right, passing through the rebuilt Wind Gate in the remains of an ancient fortress wall, and bringing us to the Franciscan Basilica of the Transfiguration. We walk the last stretch of the way to the basilica past the ruins of the ancient Benedictine abbey. From the terraces beside the church we have a panoramic view. Eastwards we look across the Sea of Galilee to the Golan Heights. On a clear day we can even see Mount Hermon in the northeast blanketed with snow. The view of Galilee, the chief scene of our Lord's earthly ministry, and the quiet moments spent in the church help us to ponder on the unforgettable hour when Jesus embarked upon His path of suffering.

The Franciscan Basilica of the Transfiguration is open from 8 a.m. till noon and 3 p.m. till sunset.

THE HISTORICAL ASPECT

Mount Tabor is connected with many Biblical and historical events. The village of Daburiya at its foot is most likely named in honour of Deborah the prophetess, who at Mount Tabor spurred Israel on to victory (Judges 4). Perhaps it was also near this village that Jesus drove the dumb spirit out of a boy after His disciples had attempted to do so in vain (Mark 9 : 14 ff.). In pre-Christian times and later, the level summit served as a place of refuge during wars as it did for the Jews in the battle against the Romans in A.D. 70. Traces of a fortified wall built at that time as well as the remains of the Crusader wall can still be seen.

But Mount Tabor's chief significance is that since early times tradition regards its summit to be the site of the Transfiguration. A modern view, however, considers Mount Hermon to be the Mount of Transfiguration, for before the Transfiguration, according to Matthew 16 : 13 ff., Jesus spoke to the disciples about His divine Sonship at Caesarea Philippi, which is close to Mount Hermon. But an entire week lay between that momentous conversation and the Transfiguration (Matthew 17 : 1) and this would have allowed for a journey to Mount Tabor. Moreover, when Jesus came down from the mountain, He found His disciples engaged in a conversation with scribes. This too speaks more in favour of a site in a Jewish district than a location in the diaspora near Caesarea Philippi.

Since the Gospels give no exact indications about the location of the Mount of Transfiguration, tradition had to be consulted. As early as the mid second century an account of Jesus' life, not included in the Bible, makes a reference which suggests that Christians commemorated the Transfiguration on Mount Tabor. For a short while it was erroneously supposed that the Transfiguration took place on the Mount of Olives, but in 348 St. Cyril, then Bishop of Jerusalem, confirmed the fact that Mount Tabor was the site of the Transfiguration. This was reaffirmed shortly afterwards by Epiphanius, who was born in Judea in 315 and later became the Bishop of Salamis. In the following centuries many pilgrims refer to Mount Tabor as a place of pilgrimage, where monasteries and churches were also situated. In 518 a synod in Jerusalem even speaks of a "Bishop of the holy Mount Tabor". In about 570 the pilgrim Anonymous of Piacenza reports that three basilicas stood on the summit in accordance with the words of Peter, "Let us make three tabernacles". Even after the conquest of Palestine by the Arabs in the seventh century, there is mention of a bishop and monks living on Mount Tabor as well as churches built in honour of Jesus, Moses and Elijah respectively.

In ca. 1100, during the Crusader period, the Benedictines founded a monastery there. They erected their abbey next to a rebuilt Church of the Transfiguration, which probably embraced the three original buildings. A fortified wall was built round the whole complex. In the twelfth century there is also reference to a Church of St. Elijah and a monastery belonging to the Greek Orthodox on Mount Tabor.

After the defeat of the Crusaders in 1187 the mountain was seized by the Saracens, who built a fortress on it. In 1263 Sultan Bibars razed all the Christian buildings on Mount Tabor. Not until 1631 did the Franciscans regain permission from a Turkish prince to settle on Mount Tabor. At the end of the nineteenth century the Greek Orthodox began rebuilding their Church of St. Elijah and the Franciscans undertook extensive excavations. Between 1921 and 1924 the Franciscans erected their new basilica, drawing their inspiration from ancient Roman-Syrian architecture. The two entrance towers, which stand on the sites of the previous sanctuaries dedicated to Moses and Elijah, still contain commemorative chapels for them.

Hence the Franciscan property occupies the area, which since the sixth century has been confirmed as the site commemorating the Transfiguration by the churches that have been built here. On the western side of the Franciscan grounds, beside the path leading down the mountain, stands a small chapel called "Descendentibus" (for those descending), which is now closed. It reminds us of Jesus' command to His disciples after the Transfiguration to tell no one what they had seen until He was raised from the dead.

FROM THE HOLY BIBLE

Tabor and Hermon joyously praise thy name.

Psalm 89 : 12

And after six days Jesus took with him Peter and James and John, and went up on the mountain to pray. And he was transfigured before them, and his garments became glistening, intensely white, as no fuller on earth could bleach them. And behold, two men talked with him, Moses and Elijah, who appeared in glory and spoke of his departure, which he was to accomplish at Jerusalem.

And Peter said to Jesus, "Lord, it is well that we are here; if you wish, I will make three booths here, one for you and one for Moses and one for Elijah." He was still speaking, when lo, a bright cloud overshadowed them, and a voice from the cloud said, "This is my beloved Son; listen to him." And suddenly looking around they no longer saw anyone with them but Jesus only.

And as they were coming down the mountain, he charged them to tell no one what they had seen, until the Son of man should have risen from the dead.

cf. Luke 9 : 28-36; Mark 9 : 2-9; Matthew 17 : 1-8

MOUNT TABOR – A MESSAGE FOR US

In Psalm 89 King David writes that Tabor and Hermon joyously praise the name of the Lord. Since ancient times Mount Tabor must have been a holy mountain for Israel, a symbol and a testimony to the glory of God, also in memory of Deborah's song of victory, which she sang at its foot. This special mountain must certainly have been a holy place for our Lord Jesus as well. Mount Tabor lay in the neighbourhood of Nazareth, and Jesus may well have often gazed at it or even climbed it as a child or a youth. Would He not have felt especially drawn to this mountain? It was here, we can assume, that Jesus experienced the holy event of Transfiguration towards the end of His earthly life.

We do not know whether Jesus knew beforehand what tremendous grace awaited Him on Mount Tabor. Yet we can sense that it must have been a day of supreme joy for God the Father to display the Son in the glory of the Transfiguration. It was a source of deep grief to the Father that He almost always had to conceal the glory of His Son during His earthly life. Jesus was His beloved Son. To display Him before all mankind in His divine glory and heavenly beauty – was that not the Father's deepest longing all those years? But time and time again the Father had to refrain from glorifying the Son, since it was necessary for the redemption of sinful man that Jesus' divine glory be veiled.

When Jesus ascended Mount Tabor with His disciples, He had already suffered much at the hands of the scribes and Pharisees, who had misunderstood Him and harassed Him as He walked among His people. But now the time had drawn near when He would be covered with shame and tortured to death like a criminal. Because of our sin the Father had to let His Son drink the cup of disgrace, contempt and humiliation to the dregs during His earthly life. Therefore, the Father's heart probably could not do otherwise but strengthen His Son through the Transfiguration and reveal Him in His glory to His three closest disciples in the solitude of this mountaintop. Before the Son had to endure the deepest humiliation and the rejection of mankind, God wished to reveal the true identity of Jesus. He is the Son of God, whose countenance shines like the sun. One day He will illumine the City of God and the whole universe with the radiance of His love. He is the Son of God, clothed with splendour and power, whose garments are truly whiter than the snow, which He created in its dazzling whiteness.

The hour of Transfiguration reveals the tremendous glory God creates through suffering, for the Transfiguration on Mount Tabor occurs in the face of suffering, as Jesus sets out to follow the bitter path of sorrows that will lead to the Cross. Indeed, Elijah and Moses speak with Him about the end His life would take at Calvary.

Mount Tabor, the Mount of Transfiguration, tells us that the Father not only transfigured His only-begotten Son long ago, but desires to grant the grace of transfiguration to all who are redeemed by Him. Therefore, does not the very name "Mount Tabor" awaken in every heart a deep longing to be transfigured, to be remoulded into the image of God? We men were created in His image, and Jesus redeemed us, that we may reflect God's image once more. Indeed, as transfigured souls, "the righteous will shine like the sun in the kingdom of their Father" (Matthew 13 : 43).

However, Jesus' Transfiguration demonstrates that there is only one way to victory and transformation into the image of God – and this is through suffering. Scripture tells us that even Jesus, who was without sin, was made perfect through suffering (Hebrews 2 : 10). Along paths of chastening and suffering God purges us sinners of the evil that is in us, so that our souls will be more and more pervaded by Jesus' light and His nature until we are completely transformed. Then His virtues will be seen in us: love, humility, meekness, mercy, forgiveness. Indeed, love will shine forth from the transfigured with such clarity, power and glory that, as with Jesus, even their bodies will be pervaded with light. This will be evident to its fullest extent when, as it is written, we are "raised in glory" (1 Corinthians 15 : 43).

Only with hearts full of adoration can we ascend Mount Tabor, the Mount of Transfiguration. To shine like the sun and to wear the robe of transfiguration were Jesus' due. But how incomprehensible that we sinful men, who by nature are engulfed in darkness and are under the dominion of Satan, should be counted worthy to experience transfiguration and reflect the divine attributes of God again! We cannot but worship God for such amazing grace.

At the same time Mount Tabor asks us whether we are willing to pay the price for this. Are we, like Jesus, willing to descend the mountain and enter the vale of humiliation? Are we willing to follow the way of the cross, humbly stooping beneath its burden as Jesus did? There is no other way to transfiguration. And only those who are transfigured will inherit the glory of God for ever and ever. How vital, therefore, is the message of Mount Tabor for us today!

✝

God desires to imprint the beauty of His image once more upon us, His sinful children. What could be more wonderful? The Transfiguration of the Son of man is the guarantee, for He has come to transform us into His likeness through His redemption.

PRAYER ON MOUNT TABOR

Lord Jesus Christ,

We thank You that here we may inwardly behold You in Your Transfiguration when You were resplendent with beauty. And we thank You that one day we shall behold You in even greater glory. O Jesus, we worship You in Your beauty of Transfiguration.

We also thank You that Your Transfiguration shows us that we are to be changed from glory to glory, since You paid the price for us to become like unto You. Lord, Your radiance is like the sun. How we praise You for redeeming us, that we too may shine like the sun in Your kingdom! We worship You for giving Your sinful children such a high calling.

Lord Jesus, I want to be remoulded into Your radiant image of love at any cost. Purify me, therefore, as a goldsmith purifies gold, in Your fiery furnace of chastening, so that the image of God will shine forth from me and I shall inherit eternal glory one day. I here commit myself to such paths of chastening.

Amen.

✝

The hour of Transfiguration came for Jesus when He was about to enter the night of suffering and death. As members of His Body, we can only receive the grace of transfiguration, which He has won for us, by following the same path – the path of humiliation and purification.

Jesus, Transfigured upon Tabor's Height

10. 10. 10. 9.

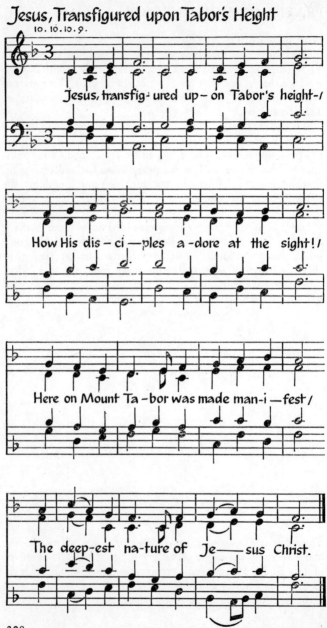

Jesus, transfig-ured up-on Tabor's height-

How His dis-ci—ples a-dore at the sight!

Here on Mount Ta-bor was made man-i—fest

The deep-est na-ture of Je——sus Christ.

Noble and beauteous, what glory He owns!
His garment shines forth like radiant suns.
Love gave His nature such glory and light.
'Twas love, the source of His hidden might.

Mount Tabor! Listen, bells ringing proclaim
That we today can experience the same.
Jesus transfigured is our guarantee
That we by grace may transfigured be.

Just as the night brings the bright morning sun,
Transfiguration through judgment will come
To those who see all their sins in the light
Of Jesus' glory and radiance bright.

God will transfigure us gloriously,
That we may shine forth in His radiancy.
Thus He refines us through sorrow and pain
And so prepares us with Him to reign.

And we shall shine like the sun pure and bright
As did our Saviour upon Tabor's height.
Worshipping we shall behold Him above –
His image shining with tender love.

✦

And we all, with unveiled face, beholding the glory of the
Lord, are being changed into his likeness from one degree of
glory to another.   2 Corinthians 3 : 18

Jesus, Radiating Beauty

8.7.8.7. D.

Jesus, ra—di—at——ing beauty, / Light—en—
Jesus, throned and high ex—alted / O——ver

circled ma—jes—ty! / every sovreign—ty! / Beau—ty marks now all Thy

bearing, / Decked with God's no—bil—i—ty, / Love now shines

from all Thy features, / Which the angels joy to see.

Thousands throng adoring round Thee
There majestic on Thy throne.
All earth's monarchs bow before Thee
And Thy right to homage own.
Saints and angels, full of wonder,
Worship Thee unceasingly,
In the sunshine of Thy splendour
Shout Hosannas now to Thee.

       All the heavens throb and quiver,
       Praising God in ecstasy;
       Cherubs, seraphs, wings a-shimmer,
       Sweep through heav'n exultantly.
       For amid the jubilation,
       All the triumph round the throne,
       God holds out for adoration
       In His arms His only Son.

Holy rev'rence, awe-struck silence
Reign while heaven's hosts bow down,
Worshipping the Sole-begotten
Seated now upon the throne.
Still He bears those scars so sacred,
Signs of endless love divine,
Love that triumphed over suff'ring;
They with deathless glory shine.

       Father, Son and Holy Spirit,
       Joined in deepest love Thou art,
       Bring together saints and angels
       Home to God the Father's heart.
       O the depths of God's compassion!
       O the glory of His love,
       Which embraces every creature,
       Draws them to their home above!

Silence, deep as time eternal,
Broods around the throne divine,
Where in loving, blissful union,
Father, Son and Spirit shine.
Then the heav'nly Sanctus thunders,
As Thy prostrate hosts adore,
Cast their crowns before Thine altar,
Praising Thee for evermore.

Well-spring of Joy 250
Can also be sung to the melody, "Love Divine, All Loves Excelling"

BY THE SEA OF GALILEE

We now approach the Sea of Galilee, the king of lakes, for it has borne Jesus, the King of kings, upon its waves, and its shores have beheld His mighty works. It is also called Kinneret, derived from the Hebrew word *kinnor* (harp) because of the lake's harp-like shape. The lake, 21 km. long and up to 13 km. wide, is about 50 m. deep at the centre and lies approximately 200 m. below sea level. As in Jesus' day it has an enchanting loveliness about it. The warm climate favours a rich vegetation along its shores, which are beginning to flourish again where the land is cultivated. The landscape, especially in springtime, is of exquisite beauty.

We feel especially drawn to the region north and west of the lake because of the sites associated with Jesus. Starting out from Jerusalem, Tel-Aviv or Haifa, we can reach this district via Afula or Nazareth. Or else we can drive from Jerusalem through the Jordan Valley. The two motor roads coming from the south and west respectively run into Tiberias, the largest city by the lake, which lies about halfway along the western coast. We continue north along the shore road in the direction of Safad, passing by the places where Jesus ministered. The first stretch of the road makes gentle curves as it follows the coast-line. Hills with rocky summits rise up on the left and the lake lies on the right. In its changing moods the waters are a different colour each hour and season, a sight of unique beauty. Looking across the lake, we see the Golan Heights beyond the eastern shore, and behind the slopes of the northwestern shore loom the mountains of Upper Galilee with Safad, the "city set on a hill".

About 3 km. farther along the western shore we come to a spot familiar to us from the New Testament — the warm springs of Dalmanutha (Mark 8 : 10). Today there is only a small Russian Orthodox monastery here with a new chapel. Next to it lies the Y.M.C.A. hostel with a small chapel. Two kilometres later we see the ruins of Magdala on our right. The remains of the houses date from more recent times, but the New Testament Magdala must also have lain here. Although these ruins seem so forgotten, we cannot forget that this was once the home of Mary Magdalene *(see chapter on Magdala).*

The steep hills on the left recede from the shore to make way for the fertile Plain of Gennesaret (Genesar, Ginossar), which extends for about 6 km. On a hill to the left is the village of Migdal, which perpetuates the heritage of Magdala in its name. Soon after the ruins of Magdala on the way to Migdal, a road branches off to the left, which also leads to Safad. After about 1 km. a side road branches off into Wadi el-Hamam, the Valley of the Pigeons, a wild pass closed in between two perpendicular rocky walls. In Jesus' day this was the only way to reach Nazareth from the lake.

Continuing northwards along the shore road, which leads to Safad, we cross the Plain of Gennesaret with its many banana plantations, vineyards and fields of vegetables. At the northern border of the plain is a rocky hill, Tell el-Oreimeh, which slopes down to the lake. Making a sweeping bend, the main road ascends the western spur of the hill. At this point we see before us the small, picturesque Plain of Tabgha. According to historical accounts there used to be seven springs here, whence the area was called Seven Springs, in Greek *Heptapegon*. The Arabs dropped the first syllable of the name and pronounced it Tabgha. Looking down to the right, we have a view of the monastery and church of Tabgha on the shore and immediately above them the Church of the Beatitudes. Soon after we have crossed Tell el-Oreimeh, a road forks off in a southeasterly direction. This road leads to the lake, to Tabgha, Simon Peter's Landing Place and Capernaum, a distance of altogether 3 km.

First let us visit the Mount of Beatitudes in remembrance of the mighty proclamation of the kingdom of heaven, which Jesus probably uttered on one of these lakeside hills *(see chapter on the Mount of Beatitudes)*. To reach the Mount of Beatitudes, we stay on the main road to Safad, which leads away from the lake climbing gradually uphill. Three kilometres later we take a right-hand turn onto a lane that leads directly to the Mount of Beatitudes. A hospice run by Italian nuns has been built here. Nearby is an octagonal church surrounded by shrubs, palms and other trees, with a pillared porch. We can easily picture the multitude sitting and listening to the Sermon on the Mount on these slopes.

Here we enjoy the lavish beauty that God bestowed on this land. In spring the flower-strewn meadows and hillsides are a blaze of colour, reminding us of Jesus' words in the Sermon on the Mount when He said that the "lilies of the field" are more beautifully arrayed than "Solomon in all his glory". The panorama here is exquisite with an expansive view across the lake in the south, the hills in the east and the bay in the northwest with the Plain of Gennesaret, the Valley of the Pigeons and the Horns of Hattin in the background. The latter are a reminder of the crushing defeat suffered by the Crusaders here in 1187.

Across the fields we can see Capernaum below, which is easily identified by the deep green foliage of its dense groves. A narrow footpath leads down to the motor road connecting Tabgha and Capernaum. The fertile, green fields with boulders and rocks, which have been laboriously moved to the sides, give the place an atmosphere of hope. After 2,000 years of desolation the promises of God are beginning to be fulfilled and remind us that the King is coming soon.

But we are not content with merely viewing the lakeside places from a distance. If we prefer to drive there, we must first return to the Safad-Tiberias Road and follow it to Tabgha. A few hundred metres east of the crossroads is the entrance to the property of the Benedictines, who care for the site where the multiplication of the loaves and fishes is commemorated. A spacious church built over fifth-century mosaics reminds us of this event *(see chapter on Tabgha)*. We continue along the main road. Fifty metres later on a slope to our left are fenced-in grounds containing ruins. These are the excavations of the Franciscan Chapel of the Beatitudes. Another 50 m. farther on the right lies the entrance to the Franciscan church. It was built in memory of the event when the risen Lord appeared to the disciples and commissioned Peter to feed His flock. Situated on a rocky protrusion on the lake shore, it is surrounded by eucalyptus trees and palms. Here at Simon Peter's Landing Place we feel very near to Jesus, who lived and ministered with His disciples by the lake *(see chapter on Simon Peter's Landing Place)*.

And now we shall want to seek out Capernaum *(see chapter on Capernaum)*, the place where our Lord once "found faith" in the centurion whose servant He healed. After about 2 km. along the lakeside road from Tabgha we come to the wall of the Franciscan grounds of Capernaum (Kfar Nahum). A road lined with trees leads to the monastery, behind which lie the ruins of Capernaum near the edge of the lake. We follow the paths through the site of the excavations and soon stand before the ancient steps of the partly restored synagogue. Recent excavations have also disclosed the site of the House of St. Peter. As we stand among the ruins of the ancient synagogue, we yearn that our Lord, who comes alive for us here as at the other places by the lake, may find faith and love in our hearts — not just once, but ever anew.

Times of opening:

Magdala, Y.M.C.A. grounds	8 a.m. — 7 p.m.
The Church of the Beatitudes	all day except from 2 p.m. — 3 p.m.
The Church of the Multiplication of the Loaves and Fishes, Tabgha	7 a.m. — 6 p.m.
Simon Peter's Landing Place (Mensa Christi)	8:30 a.m. — 4:30 p.m.
The Franciscan grounds of Capernaum	8:30 a.m. — 4:30 p.m.

THE SEA OF GALILEE

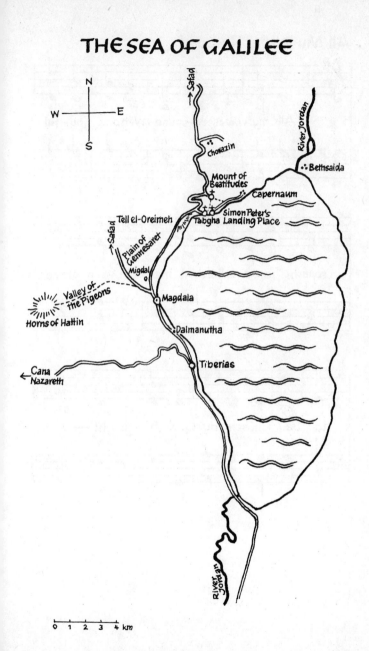

All My Waves Resound

5.5.5.5.7.

All my waves re-sound /With one joy-ful sound,/ "Jesus walked on me."/ Oh, what grace to be/ Chosen by God Al-might—y!

Here I saw one night
God show forth His might,
Speaking but a word.
Wind and water heard;
All became calm and quiet.

Oh, what gracious words
At this place I heard!
All my waves rejoiced
As His loving voice
Announced the heav'nly kingdom.

I saw many men –
Sick, made well again,
Full of happiness
At the news of bliss,
"Here is the Great Physician!"

Seeing Him, my waves
Beat a song of praise
For my Lord and King,
Who made everything.
I was allowed to see Him!

Oh, what joy is mine!
I am counted Thine.
May I always be
But a harp for Thee,
Bringing Thee praise and honour.

Sea of Galilee
November 23, 1959

MAGDALA

THE HISTORICAL ASPECT

According to the Gospels Magdala, also called Magadan, lay on
the western shore of the Sea of Galilee (Matthew 15 : 39) in the
district of Dalmanutha (Mark 8 : 10). The name is derived from
the Hebrew word *migdal* meaning "tower" or "fortress". According to the Talmud, the Biblical Magdala was a lakeside town of
considerable importance with wool merchants and dyers and a
fishing fleet. Situated at the edge of the fertile Plain of Gennesaret,
it was probably the most important of the lakeside towns until
competition arose with Tiberias. According to Jewish/tradition
Magdala was later destroyed by Jews from neighbouring towns
because of the moral corruption of its inhabitants.

In the Gospels Magdala is mentioned as the place where the
Pharisees demanded a sign from Jesus, who answered that they
would receive only the sign of Jonah (Matthew 15 : 39; 16 : 1, 4).
But most of all Magdala is known as the home of Mary Magdalene,
from whom Jesus cast out seven demons. However, we are not
told whether this deliverance took place in her home town. Of
all the women who followed and served Jesus during His Galilean
journeys, Mary Magdalene is the first to be mentioned by the
Evangelists. And in the Passion narrative she is named among the
women who stood beneath the Cross and who discovered the
Tomb empty on Easter morn. Often she is regarded as being the
unknown penitent, who anointed the feet of Jesus in the house
of Simon the Pharisee, probably in Capernaum (Luke 7).

Several ancient pilgrim reports mention the location of the
Biblical Magdala. The pilgrim Theodosius writes in ca. 530, "From
Tiberias to Magdalum, whence came Mary Magdalene, it is two
miles." The English pilgrim Willibald visited the "village of
Magdalene" north of Tiberias in 725. About the year 800 the
monk Epiphanius of Jerusalem writes that there was a church in
the place where the Magdalene was cured. In 940 there is also
record of such a church being in "Magdala near Tiberias". During
the Crusader period, ca. 1106, the Russian Abbot Daniel mentions
only a "house of the Magdalene". And in about 1300 a pilgrim
states that the church there was turned into a stable.

According to later reports Magdala was deserted for a long
period, although there has never been any question about its
location. In the nineteenth century a settlement sprang up here,
but was later destroyed. Only the ruins of its houses can be seen
now. The name Magdala lives on in the village of Migdal about
1 km. north of the old town above the lake.

FROM THE HOLY BIBLE

Soon afterward he went on through cities and villages, preaching and bringing the good news of the kingdom of God. And the twelve were with him, and also some women who had been healed of evil spirits and infirmities: Mary, called Magdalene, from whom seven demons had gone out.
Luke 8 : 1 f.

But standing by the cross of Jesus were his mother, and his mother's sister, Mary the wife of Clopas, and Mary Magdalene.
John 19 : 25

Now when Jesus rose early on the first day of the week, he appeared first to Mary Magdalene, from whom he had cast out seven demons. She went and told those who had been with him, as they mourned and wept.
cf. Mark 16 : 9 f.

✝

The life of Mary Magdalene tells us that Jesus is able to use our hardest chains of sin to demonstrate the power of His redemption to His glory.

The life of Mary Magdalene tells us that contrition and repentance are most precious and desirable gifts, since they set our hearts aflame with a deep love for Jesus.

MAGDALA – A MESSAGE FOR US

What is it that made Magdala so famous that its name is still well-known throughout the Christian world? Not its former prosperity, but one of its inhabitants – Mary Magdalene. What kind of woman was she? A sinner. But how could she have won such renown for Magdala? A citizen of a rich, flourishing, commercial town, no doubt a worldly woman abandoned to self-indulgence and lust, and possessed by seven demons – these were hardly qualities to bring fame to a place. Such women must have lived in other parts of the country too. However, the special thing about Mary Magdalene was that her sins and demons were confronted by Jesus.

Mighty, extraordinary things now happened. Jesus transformed this woman. The seven demons departed from her and the sinner became the great penitent. Few ever repented as she did. But more than that. She became a soul that loved Jesus and was a witness of His Resurrection. She was the first to whom the risen Lord appeared in the glory of that blessed Easter morn and it was she whom He chose as His messenger to others. This is why she could bring such fame to her town. And to this day its name has a familiar sound, because people everywhere know of Mary Magdalene and the transformation she underwent.

The terrible fact that Mary Magdalene was possessed by seven demons now became a testimony to the glory of Jesus. Her sin led her to a deep repentance and dedication and her example has inspired people down through the ages to walk in repentance and love for Jesus. Mary Magdalene! Who has wept so much over sin as she did? Who has had such an experience of Him who forgives weeping sinners as she did? Yes, who has loved Jesus so much, who has loved Him so extravagantly as she did? And who has thus found such bliss and happiness?

The life of Mary Magdalene testifies that "where sin increased, grace abounded all the more." Chains of sin and demon possession are broken if they are brought to Jesus and placed under the power of His redemption. And God causes a wonderful stream to flow from broken and contrite hearts – a stream of gratitude and love for Jesus and one's fellow men. Mary Magdalene shows us what tremendous power lies in contrition and repentance. It is the source of true love for Jesus. A penitent sinner loves Him with a humble, sacrificial spirit and wholehearted dedication.

It is this humble love that made Mary Magdalene not fear the condemnation and scorn of others. She had but one desire – to be with the One who had forgiven her so much and whom she now loved with all her heart. Thus Mary Magdalene was one of the very few, who, like the Lord's mother and John, followed Jesus to the Cross and knelt at its foot when He died like a criminal.

And after His death Mary, in her ardent love for Jesus, did not cease to wait for Him until He revealed Himself. She remained by the Tomb after all the others had departed, for true love perseveres and continues to wait, unable to believe that all is lost. Love hopes against hope. In spite of everything, Mary hoped to see Jesus, to find Him whom her soul loved, and her love was not disappointed.

Mary Magdalene, from whom Jesus had cast out seven demons, is an example of His power and glory, of the greatness of His forgiveness, of the rich gain that comes from repented sin. Likewise, the unknown penitent in Luke 7, whether it was Mary Magdalene or another woman, is praised by Jesus and given as an example to the Pharisee, a man who strictly observed the Law, for in her grief and contrition over her sin she had done what she could – she loved Jesus as few have ever loved Him. Over such a sinner, who wept tears at His feet, He pronounced the most precious words of all, "She loved much."

Thus to this day Magdala proclaims the joyful message that sinners who repent of their sins are blessed, that they are the ones who love Jesus with all their hearts and become His messengers and witnesses. Magdala, once the home town of Mary Magdalene, shows us that tears of repentance are a priceless treasure. May Magdala kindle in our hearts the ardent prayer for contrition and repentance, and the fervent plea to love Jesus, so that at the end of our lives Jesus will be able to pronounce the most beautiful words of all upon us also, "You have loved much."

One Single Name We Love to Hear

8.8.7.7.

One sin-gle name we love to hear–

'Tis   Je — sus Christ, God's Son__ most dear, /

Who brings such joy__ to sin ——— ners, /

Who brings such joy__ to sin ——— ners.

One single name we love to hear –
'Tis Jesus Christ, God's Son most dear,
Who is our soul's true Saviour. (Rep.)

One single name we love to hear –
'Tis Jesus Christ, God's Son most dear,
Whose love for us is boundless. (Rep.)

One single name we love to hear –
'Tis Jesus Christ, God's Son most dear,
Who kindles us to love Him. (Rep.)

Well-spring of Joy 218

Like Mary Magdalene Lamenting

9.9.8.

Like Mary Magdalene lamenting,/
for all my grievous sins re — pent — ing,/
Lord, let me show my pen — i — tence.

Like Mary Magdalene to love You
As much as once I used to grieve You,
Always to please You is my prayer.

Like Mary, give me deep contrition,
That I admit my great transgression
And kneel before all those I wronged.

Like Mary, too, Lord, let me ever
Come quickly to You, leave You never;
This is the sinner's sole desire.

Well-spring of Joy 171

PRAYER IN MAGDALA

Dear Lord Jesus,

Hear my prayer at this site where we think of Mary Magdalene and the tears she once shed in contrition. I confess that my heart is not broken and contrite and that You have been waiting in vain for my tears of contrition.

I humbly confess that I have often been indignant at the sins and faults of others, but failed to deplore my own sins. Forgive me for being so blind, self-confident and self-righteous. Forgive me for so easily condemning others but not myself. I entreat You, Lord, grant me the Spirit of truth, that I may see myself in Your light and be given a shock. Grant me the spirit of contrition, so that I can truly grieve and weep over my sins as Mary Magdalene did.

Please do not let me be a self-righteous Pharisee any longer. Rather let me take my stand with the sinners who beat their own breast, for such souls are pleasing to You.

My Lord Jesus, I humble myself before You, for I have not loved You above all things, although You alone are worthy to be loved. I have not loved You with a spendthrift love that would have gladdened and consoled You. I entreat You to give me tears of contrition, which will wash my eyes, that I may truly come to know You and love You with ardour and devotion out of gratitude for Your forgiveness.

Amen.

THE MOUNT OF BEATITUDES

THE HISTORICAL ASPECT

From early times attempts have been made to determine the site of the Sermon on the Mount. There is no exact tradition, but there is good reason to suppose that it was near Tabgha in the region of Seven Springs. The centre of Jesus' public ministry by the Sea of Galilee was Capernaum and according to the Gospels the Sermon on the Mount was held near "his city". It is further stated that after the sermon Jesus "came down from the mountain" and "entered Capernaum", with great crowds following Him (Matthew 8 : 1). Such multitudes can be envisioned on the way from Seven Springs to Capernaum, perhaps better than anywhere else. On the gentle slopes, however, there are many spots that could have provided space for a large crowd to settle down. And Jesus may well have addressed such crowds on several occasions in this area. Thus it was difficult for a tradition concerning this particular sermon to be preserved at any one place in this extensive and lonely countryside.

As early as 385, however, the pilgrim nun Etheria mentions a spot that one tradition associated with the Sermon on the Mount. In her description she says that Matthew's customs office lay on the way from the Church of the Multiplication of the Loaves to Capernaum and "nearby is the mount on whose slopes the Redeemer uttered the Beatitudes". During the time of the Crusaders, in about 1150, the site of the sermon was said to be two miles from Capernaum and one mile from the place commemorating the multiplication of the loaves.

From subsequent reports of the twelfth century it appears that tradition decided that the scene of the sermon was on the heights between Capernaum and Seven Springs. Thus the opinion prevailed that in this area was "the mountain that inspires us to deep contemplation", as a fourteenth-century pilgrim expressed it. Only in the sixteenth and seventeenth centuries when this lakeside district was difficult to reach, did other suppositions arise.

But even if it is not possible to determine the exact location to this day, the Church of the Beatitudes on a hill above Seven Springs near Tabgha and Simon Peter's Landing Place serves to commemorate the event. In 1938 Italians built this church and the nearby hospice, which is run by Italian nuns.

+

FROM THE HOLY BIBLE

Seeing the crowds, he went up on the mountain, and when he sat down his disciples came to him. And he opened his mouth and taught them, saying:

"Blessed are you poor, for yours is the kingdom of God.

"Blessed are those who mourn, for they shall be comforted.

"Blessed are the meek, for they shall inherit the earth.

"Blessed are those who hunger and thirst for righteousness, for they shall be satisfied.

"Blessed are the merciful, for they shall obtain mercy.

"Blessed are the pure in heart, for they shall see God.

"Blessed are the peacemakers, for they shall be called sons of God.

"Blessed are you when men hate you, and when they exclude you and revile you, and cast out your name as evil, on account of the Son of man!

Rejoice in that day, and leap for joy, for behold, your reward is great in heaven.

And when Jesus finished these sayings, the crowds were astonished at his teaching, for he taught them as one who had authority, and not as their scribes.

cf. Matthew 5 : 1-12; 7 : 28 f. & Luke 6 : 20-23

THE MOUNT OF BEATITUDES –
A MESSAGE FOR US

O Mount of Beatitudes, mount of enchanting loveliness overlooking the Sea of Galilee and bearing the name of the Beatitudes, how privileged you are! What gracious words you were permitted to hear – words spoken by the Lord and Saviour of mankind and all creation! We cannot but rejoice to find ourselves on your slopes!

But what is it that thrills our hearts here? Not the charming view of the Sea of Galilee surrounded by hills and mountains, which would be enough to inspire us, as would the beauty of any other lake, to burst out in song. No, it is He who far surpasses the loveliness of this lake, who contains all the beauty of heaven and earth, who is called the Saviour. It is Jesus, who is the source of all blessedness. He, more than anyone or anything else, draws strains of joy and gladness from our hearts.

And here on the mountainside we remember the Beatitudes once uttered by Jesus in His desire to make His children happy. In the Sermon on the Mount He has shown us the way to true happiness. Is that not reason to worship and rejoice at this site and to make this path our own?

Before our eyes we can almost see the people whom our Lord Jesus called blessed here: the merciful, the poor, the meek and the peacemakers, those who hunger and thirst for righteousness, the pure in heart, those who mourn and those who are persecuted for His name's sake. A strange group of people to be called blessed. Are they really happy? Can they really be called blessed? Yet this is what Jesus declared here on this mountain and the experiences of life prove the truth of His words.

The merciful, instead of condemning others in their sins, look upon them with mercy. They can forgive and their love covers a multitude of sins. Their hearts are moved with compassion at the misery that others suffer in body, soul and spirit. They are truly happy people, for their hearts are filled with love. And nothing can make us so happy as loving and being able to lavish our love on others; whereas nothing makes us so unhappy as a hard, bitter and unforgiving heart.

Here on the Mount of Beatitudes Jesus shows us those who are truly blessed. Let us think of the peacemakers and the meek. They do not quarrel or lose their temper, nor do they create discord wherever they go or let themselves be drawn into disputes. Truly, they may be called blessed; whereas those who are at odds with others, who wear themselves out with quarrelling, envying and hatred are considered unhappy. But to make peace in humble love is to experience a foreshadowing of the kingdom of heaven in our lives.

Then there are the poor and those who hunger and thirst for righteousness. We can also envision them in this throng of those whom Jesus calls blessed. And they are truly happy. The sun of grace shines upon them. Because they are filled with hunger and thirst, they are richly endowed with unmerited favours. As Love eternal, God grants His gifts to such souls. In prayer they cling to God like poor, little children dependent upon their heavenly Father. How can He not give them all they need for body and soul? The Father is merciful to the poor and needy. He imparts divine life to those who thirst for Him and seek to obey His will and commandments. This brings true happiness just as God declared in the Old Testament when He said that he who keeps His commandments will have divine life and therefore deep joy and the fullness of His blessing (Deuteronomy 5 : 29).

Likewise God reveals Himself in His love to those who are pure in heart, because their hearts are set on Him alone.

But are the suffering and the persecuted also numbered among those whom Jesus calls blessed? Indeed, they are. They can boast of something special. They have received comfort from the living God; they are surrounded by the Father's love – a privilege that is granted only to those in suffering. Those who are persecuted for His name's sake even rejoice and leap for joy, for the Spirit of God, who is a Spirit of glory, rests upon them (1 Peter 4 : 14). And a great reward awaits them in heaven.

On the Mount of Beatitudes Jesus could not have given us a more challenging illustration of truly happy souls. We can almost hear Him calling and entreating us to walk the path outlined in the Sermon on the Mount – the path of love, which alone can bring us happiness. He bids us to walk the path of the peacemakers, the poor, the merciful, the meek and the pure in heart, the persecuted and those who mourn. Take this path; the sun of grace shines upon it. Your heart will be immersed in peace and love, consoled in every situation and every kind of suffering. And the glory of God will rest upon you.

And one day these people whom Jesus called blessed on the Mount of Beatitudes will enter eternal glory in the heavenly kingdom. There, for all eternity, they will experience the fullness of the joy that they have tasted here below in their struggles and sufferings. Who would, therefore, not choose to go this way? Jesus, the Bringer of joy, is inviting us to follow it!

+

BEATITUDE PRAYERS

Lord Jesus,

Make me willing to be poor for Your sake – poor in gifts for body, soul and spirit and in material possessions. I know that You will then let me experience true wealth for body, soul and spirit in this lifetime, for You shower blessed gifts upon the poor. And I thank You that this will give me a foretaste of heaven on earth.

Lord Jesus,

Make me willing to bear my cross. In every hardship let me say, "Give me the cross. I will bear it gladly." Let me bear my burden in the assurance that as our loving Lord You come to those who have a cross to bear and find themselves in suffering. You bring them divine comfort and strengthen them with Your love and presence, so that even in the midst of severe affliction heaven will come down.

Lord Jesus,

Give me the courage and complete willingness to choose Your path and follow Your example of meekness and lowliness. When unjustly accused, I want to remain silent, trusting that You will defend me and contend for me. When I am insulted and threatened, help me to follow in Your footsteps and not to retort in anger or vehemence. Help me to bear everything in love.

Lord Jesus,

Deliver me from all complacency and satiation in my spiritual life, for they lead to spiritual death and You have condemned them. Let me hunger for Your righteousness. Make me yearn to reflect Your image as a truly redeemed soul. Grant me the power of Your Spirit in my battles against my sins and weaknesses. I want to proclaim Your victory over my sin daily in the assurance that those who hunger and thirst for righteousness shall be satisfied.

Lord Jesus,

You know my hard, unmerciful heart, which is so quick to find fault with others, especially those who are hard for me to bear or those who have wronged me. I pray that You will set me free from my hardheartedness and grant me a merciful heart that does not condemn, but forgives the sins of others. Help me to show mercy even to my enemies. May the loving-kindness and forgiveness that You show me day by day make me see my obligation to forgive others. I believe You have redeemed me to reflect the image of merciful love.

Lord Jesus,

Grant me a pure and sincere heart that loves You alone. O grant me a heart that loves You above all people and things. Set my heart aflame with a spendthrift love that will bring You many gifts and sacrifices, a love that will gladden and comfort You. Grant me such a love, that I may ever think of You, come to You in prayer and be wholly devoted to You. Lord, help me to love You so much here on earth that I may one day behold You face to face. Grant me this most precious gift of all.

Lord Jesus,

Make me a peacemaker. When there is contention, let me say as Abraham did, "If you take the right hand, then I will go to the left" and thus give up my rights for the sake of peace. Grant that I may bring You joy by creating peace wherever I can. I am ready to pay the price out of gratitude to You, O Prince of Peace, for You have won us peace by relinquishing all Your rights.

Lord Jesus,

Bind me so tightly to You that I may follow You uncompromisingly, even if this arouses hatred, scorn and persecution as Your life did. Give me the courage to share Your path of disgrace out of love for You. You have made tremendous promises for those who follow such paths, and when I suffer slander and persecution for righteousness' sake and the sake of Your name, help me to rejoice in You because of these wonderful promises of Yours.

✝

No one can make us as happy as Jesus can. But only he who seeks his happiness in Jesus and follows the path shown in the Sermon on the Mount will find true happiness and be able to make others happy too.

Who Makes As Happy, Jesus, As You

9. 9. 7.

Who makes as hap—py, Jesus, as You?/
Therefore, my heart re—joices in You,/
Je—sus, O Joy— E—ter———nal.

Jesus, my well-spring of joy ever new,
Heaven's great joy to us comes through You,
Jesus, O Joy Eternal.

Jesus, my joy-spring, flow into my heart;
Bringing me joy, make sorrow depart,
Jesus, O Joy Eternal.

331

You create joy when hearts let You in,
For You cleanse guilt and blot out all sin,
Jesus, O Joy Eternal.

Kingdom of heaven shall truly begin
Where sinners are repenting of sin.
Jesus, O Joy Eternal.

Jesus, my Lord, my God and my King,
You fill my heart with praises to sing –
Jesus, O Joy Eternal.

Jesus, my joy-spring so deep and so broad,
Joy on this earth You've richly outpoured,
But O the joy when we see You!

Well-spring of Joy 221
Mount of Beatitudes
November 26, 1959

RULES FOR HAPPINESS

Do you wish to find true happiness?
Begin to love,
For he who loves
Is always truly happy.

Do you wish to find true happiness?
Choose to be poor
And God will bless
You with His richest blessings.

Do you wish to find true happiness?
Humble yourself
Beneath your cross
And then you will taste heaven.

Do you wish to find true happiness?
Let go of all
That brings you grief:
Your anger, strife and quarrels.

Do you wish to find true happiness?
Then do not seek
Contentedness –
The "hungry" fight faith-battles.

Do you wish to find true happiness?
Let mercy come
Into your heart –
Also for those who hate you.

Do you wish to find true happiness?
Love God alone
And then one day
In glory you shall see Him.

Do you wish to find true happiness?
Renounce your claims
And then you can
Always bring peace to others.

Do you wish to find true happiness?
Then choose to walk
His path of shame –
The reviled are crowned with glory.

TABGHA

THE HISTORICAL ASPECT

The name Tabgha is derived from the Greek word *Heptapegon* meaning seven springs. The district of Tabgha was well known from ancient times because of its warm springs. This fertile plain by the Sea of Galilee with its small bay of Simon Peter's Landing Place is rich in Biblical tradition and it is here that the multiplication of the loaves and fishes — the feeding of the five thousand and the four thousand — is commemorated.

Since early times these miracles have been commemorated at this site, although according to the Gospels they most likely occurred on the northeastern shore and not here. In John 6 : 1 it reads, "Jesus went to the other side of the Sea of Galilee." And after the feeding of the five thousand, the disciples were hit by a storm on the lake as they returned to the western shore (Mark 6 : 53). It is especially clear that the second miracle took place on the eastern shore, for immediately before this account it is said that Jesus "went through Sidon to the Sea of Galilee, through the region of the Decapolis" (Mark 7 : 31), which lay on the eastern side of the lake.

However, it is not possible to define the exact location of the miracle. Scripture only indicates that the site was on some hills offshore, not far from Capernaum, from where the multitudes came. It may have been a mountain pasture on the northeast shore, where the people could gather in a hollow. Jesus was higher up on the mountain, where He could see the crowds coming to Him (John 6 : 3, 5). However, no place in this area is associated with a tradition concerning this event.

The memory of the site commemorating the miracle on the eastern shore seems to have vanished in Early Christian times, probably because the district was so remote. At an early date the site of commemoration was transferred to the western shore of the lake near Seven Springs, close to an ancient travelling route and therefore more easily accessible to pilgrims. Their way would have taken them in any event to Biblical places such as the site of the Sermon on the Mount, Simon Peter's Landing Place, Magdala and Capernaum, all of which lay in this district.

In ca. 385 the pilgrim nun Etheria speaks of a Church of the Multiplication of the Loaves where the Benedictine church of Tabgha now stands. She mentions a sacred stone on which Jesus was said to have placed the loaves and fishes; this stone can still be seen beneath the main altar. Excavations in 1932 revealed that a small church must have been built here about the year 350 and that its successor was a magnificent fifth-century basilica. Floor mosaics of this period, depicting a bread basket, fish and other symbols, are still well preserved. This basilica was probably destroyed some time during the sixth or seventh century, perhaps in 614 by the Persians, for pilgrim reports dating from that time make no reference to a church, although they mention the site of the multiplication of the loaves at Seven Springs. Later the basilica seems to have been partly rebuilt together with a monastery at Seven Springs, which in 808 is specifically mentioned as the site of the feeding of the five thousand.

That the feeding of the four thousand was also commemorated here by the lake is attested by the Church Father Jerome about the year 400. Since Byzantine times a small church, dedicated to the second miracle, stood near the basilica. At one point it was also known as the Church of the Twelve Thrones in memory of Jesus' promise to the disciples (Matthew 19 : 28).

✛

Jesus, Love incarnate, is constrained to help wherever He sees His children in want and distress. But He waits for empty hands outstretched to Him, wherein He may lay His gifts.

FROM THE HOLY BIBLE

FEEDING THE FIVE THOUSAND

After this Jesus went to the other side of the Sea of Galilee, which is the Sea of Tiberias. And a multitude followed him. Jesus went up into the hills, and there sat down with his disciples.

Lifting up his eyes, then, and seeing that a multitude was coming to him, Jesus said to Philip, "How are we to buy bread, so that these people may eat?" This he said to test him, for he himself knew what he would do. Philip answered him, "Two hundred denarii would not buy enough bread for each of them to get a little." Andrew said to him, "There is a lad here who has five barley loaves and two fish; but what are they among so many?"

Jesus said, "Make the people sit down." Now there was much grass in the place; so the men sat down, in number about five thousand. Jesus then took the loaves; and when he had given thanks, he distributed them to those who were seated; so also the fish, as much as they wanted. And when they had eaten their fill, he told his disciples, "Gather up the fragments left over, that nothing may be lost." So they gathered them up and filled twelve baskets with fragments from the five barley loaves, left by those who had eaten.

cf. John 6 : 1-13

FEEDING THE FOUR THOUSAND

And Jesus went on from there and passed along the Sea of Galilee. And he went up into the hills, and sat down there. And great crowds came to him, bringing with them the lame, the maimed, the blind, the dumb, and many others, and they put them at his feet, and he healed them.

Then Jesus called his disciples to him and said, "I have compassion on the crowd, because they have been with me now three days, and have nothing to eat; and I am unwilling to send them away hungry, lest they faint on the way." And the disciples said to him, "Where are we to get bread enough in the desert to feed so great a crowd?" And Jesus said to them, "How many loaves have you?" They said, "Seven, and a few small fish."

And commanding the crowd to sit down on the ground, he took the seven loaves and the fish, and having given thanks he broke them and gave them to the disciples, and the disciples gave them to the crowds. And they all ate and were satisfied; and they took up seven baskets full of the broken pieces left over. Those who ate were four thousand men, besides women and children.   cf. Matthew 15 : 29-38

TABGHA,
THE SITE OF THE MULTIPLICATION
OF THE LOAVES – A MESSAGE FOR US

At the feeding of the five thousand and the four thousand Jesus revealed Himself as the almighty Lord, the Son of God, who works miracles. He took a few loaves into His hands, prayed to the Father and behold – the five loaves were multiplied, and thousands ate and were satisfied. Likewise He took a few fish, blessed them and gave thanks to the Father and behold, they were multiplied, so that everyone could partake of them and be satisfied.

Had the Lord called together this great multitude in order to perform a miracle and display His omnipotence? Not so! Jesus had come to preach the Good News to the crowds that flocked after Him. Only because His heart was suddenly moved with compassion for the hungry crowds, did He perform the miracle of the multiplication of the loaves and fishes. Calling His disciples to Him, He said, "I have compassion on the crowd, because they have been with me now three days, and have nothing to eat; and I am unwilling to send them away hungry, lest they faint on the way." His words are expressive of His divine compassion for His children, whom He does not want to send away hungry. Indeed, He cannot bring Himself to do this, for they could faint on the way. Jesus says this in His great love as the Good Shepherd, who cares for His sheep, for a good shepherd tends his sheep when they are sick, weak and hungry, with nowhere to graze.

From the miracle of the loaves and fishes we can see that the power of Jesus and the miracles of God will be experienced by those who are faint and languishing, for His heart is touched by their distress. Because He is Love, it is impossible for Him not to help in some way. "God showers His gifts upon the poor" – this would be a fitting title for the story. Love gives so generously that our needs are more than supplied. Twelve baskets full were left over. This would never have happened if the disciples had bought bread. With this event God revealed His merciful heart to the faint and hungry people, the vast, helpless crowd, who knew little about Him.

But of His disciples Jesus expects something else in such a situation. He called Philip to Him in order to test his faith. "How are we to buy bread, so that these people may eat?" Jesus asked him. But Philip failed the test like all the other disciples. Disciples of Jesus should know where to turn in such difficulties. Jesus did not expect His disciples to say to Him, "Where shall we go und buy food? Where can we turn?" Nor did He expect them to rely on human, earthly resources. All He wished was that they would bring Him the little they had and lay it in His hands. But since they did not do so of their own accord, Jesus was obliged to bid them, "Bring them to Me. Bring Me the five loaves and two fish!"

Likewise Jesus bids us to bring Him what little we have, for even the smallest things that we place in His hands will be multiplied there. Then we shall receive from His hands as much as we need physically and spiritually, for the next few hours, for the next day. However, when we are detached from Him, we are at the mercy of every distress, hunger and want. Our human calculations, endeavours and efforts to ease the plight are often in vain. But He always helps as His wisdom deems best.

Jesus waits for us to come with our earthly problems and bids us, "Bring them to Me. Place your needs in My hands in full confidence and I shall take care of them for you." But He also has another, far more important request, which He mentioned after the feeding of the multitudes. In the Gospel of John we read that Jesus disappeared and crossed the lake, because He realized that the people wanted to make Him king (John 6 : 22 ff.). And when many followed Him to Capernaum, He told them sorrowfully, "You seek me, not because you saw signs, but because you ate your fill of the loaves. Do not labour for the food which perishes, but for the food which endures to eternal life, which the Son of man will give to you; for on him has God the Father set his seal." The account of the miraculous feeding of the multitudes ends with Jesus' heartfelt plea not to be so concerned about our daily bread, but rather to seek Him, Life eternal, for that is the all-important matter.

Likewise Jesus addresses us, for in many earthly needs we too may have experienced miracles similar to that of the feeding of the multitudes. "Seek Me for what I am, that you may behold an even greater miracle. I shall give you imperishable food – My own flesh, the bread that was broken for you, and My blood that was shed for you. Receive Me in Holy Communion and you will no longer suffer want." Whoever partakes of the body and blood of the Son in faith has divine life. Indeed he has the life of God within him – peace, love and joy and union with God.

This is what Jesus yearns to grant us when we come to Him, open our hearts wide and seek Him, above all in His Word and in the Lord's Supper. When Jesus sees us not only in physical need, but lying before Him in the misery of our sins, temptations and spiritual needs, how much more will He say, "I have compassion on your soul. I cannot send you away like this lest you faint on the way." He will let us partake of His divine riches, so that we too may go forth in praise and thanksgiving, all our needs having been truly satisfied in Him who gave Himself for us.

But who does come to Jesus when He invites us and offers us the bread of life? In those days when He spoke of this, even some of His disciples departed from Him, although they had been full of enthusiasm when they saw the signs and wonders He performed, such as the feeding of the multitudes (John 6 : 66). The love of Jesus seeks souls who will abide with Him instead of departing when He wants to give Himself to them. He looks for souls who, in their desire to receive Him, long to partake of the Lord's Supper.

Tabgha has a twofold message for us. "Come to Jesus with all your needs and troubles, and expect His wonderful intervention." But more important than this is the challenge, "Seek Jesus for Himself. Seek Him alone. Whenever He intervenes in wonderful ways, He longs to have an encounter with you, to open His heart to you. Only in Jesus will all your needs be satisfied. However, if you seek only His gifts, aid and miracles, it could be that you will lose Him one day, as many of His disciples did long ago."

PRAYER IN THE CHURCH
OF THE MULTIPLICATION OF THE LOAVES
AND FISHES

Dear Lord Jesus,

I thank You that Your loving heart is so full of compassion for those in need and that You took pity on the hungry multitudes. I thank You for demonstrating that You are the Creator and Sustainer of body and soul and that You care for both with Your divine power, which performs miracles and can even multiply a little so greatly that everyone's needs are satisfied.

But most of all I thank You that You are the same today and that You bid me too to bring my needs to You when I am in distress or when I am suffering some lack. I thank You for taking what little I have in Your hands and increasing it. And when I lack something altogether, You pronounce Your mighty words, "Let there be."

Lord Jesus, strengthen my faith, so that I truly expect great things from You in the way of assistance in whatever hardship I find myself. From now on I shall not seek help from people or earthly resources. I shall come to You, for I know You are waiting for me. You always have advice and know a way out. When I am in need, I shall come to You in prayer – not only for Your help and gifts, but for Yourself, since communion with You is the most precious gift and the sweetest consolation. O Jesus, I know You are waiting for me. I will come to You and be united with You in the Lord's Supper in thanksgiving that You have become the Bread of Life for me.

Amen.

Faith Penetrates to Heaven's Throne

8.7. 8.7. 8.8.7.

Faith penetrates to heaven's throne / And moves Christ's arm to help us. / He ends the troubles of His own; / His power makes them vanish. / If we are lacking any-thing, / With joyful courage we can sing, / "We trust in God Al-might——y!"

It makes no difference what we need,
Be problems few or plenteous.
Our Saviour, Christ, is rich indeed
And He has power to help us.
He always chooses what is best,
His gracious love to manifest,
All wants and needs supplying.

O gift of grace so wonderful
To trust a Lord so mighty!
His power comforts heart and soul.
What then could e'er depress me?
He sees my bitter poverty
And in His tender love for me
He even stills all hunger.

How wondrous is God's word so sure,
His promise failing never.
It is a rock, firm and secure,
On which to stand for ever.
This world of ours will pass away,
But all God's words remain for aye.
They never will mislead me.

Oh, clearly shines His sacred name,
"Amen" and all-affirming.
Each promise we can safely claim;
They need no more confirming.
We praise in heartfelt gratefulness
His steadfast truth and faithfulness;
To God be all the glory!

✝

Jesus bids us, "Come to Me;
I will help you in your need.
Come, trust My ability
To transform your poverty
Into rich abundance!"

Jesus bids us, "Trust in Me!
You shall see what you believe.
He who is your Saviour, Lord,
Will His wondrous help accord
In your every trial."

Jesus says, "To you I give
Everything I am and have.
I shall be your very own
As your highest jewel and crown,
Your most precious treasure."

Jesus bids us, "Come to Me.
Ready is the blessèd feast,
Where all hunger shall be stilled.
With Myself you shall be filled.
I am the Bread of Life."

✝

If we bring what little we have to Jesus, believing in His
omnipotence, it will be increased in His hands.

✝

Whoever obeys Jesus' words, "Bring it to Me!" when he
suffers want, will find help, and the little he has will be
increased, now as long ago. Jesus is the same yesterday and
today in His love and His almighty deeds.

343

SIMON PETER'S LANDING PLACE
(also known as Mensa Christi)

THE HISTORICAL ASPECT

In the Gospels the Sea of Galilee is also called the Lake of Gennesaret and the Sea of Tiberias. It was along the densely populated shores of this lake that Jesus began to preach about the Kingdom of God. Why did Jesus choose this particular region and not Jerusalem, Nazareth or the banks of the Jordan? When John the Baptist was imprisoned (Matthew 4 : 12; Mark 1 : 14), Jesus withdrew into Galilee, for after John's arrest the Jordan Valley became unpropitious and even unsafe for Jesus. He would not have been able to perform His ministry effectively there. Nazareth, His home town, would not receive Him as a prophet, as it soon proved. Moreover, the lakeside district was comparatively safe from Herod and the zealots of the Sanhedrin.

Thus the area northwest of the lake became the centre of Jesus' activity at the beginning of His public ministry. These shores hold the most precious memories of those days. Here He called His disciples and taught them as He began to prepare them for their great mission (Matthew 4 : 18-22; 9 : 9). Many of His miracles were performed here. At Jesus' command the waves of the lake were stilled (Mark 4 : 39). On another occasion Jesus walked upon the waves (John 6 : 19) and Peter began to sink when he saw the strong wind (Matthew 14 : 30). Even the fish served Him, and one of them bore the tribute money for the Lord in its mouth (Matthew 17 : 27). Thus the Sea of Galilee and its shores where Capernaum, Bethsaida, Chorazin and Magdala once flourished all speak of Jesus.

But one spot on the shore is especially connected with the life and ministry of Jesus, and that is Simon Peter's Landing Place. A small, sheltered bay near Seven Springs, it lies just below the Mount of Beatitudes. The springs that used to flow into the bay here have made the area round the rocky protrusion a pleasant grove of shady trees. The landscape is probably much the same as it was in Jesus' day. Not only did the warm springs irrigate the land, but when they emptied into the lake, they attracted shoals of fish. Since time immemorial this small bay was the best fishing place on the western shore. Now the course of the springs has been redirected.

Fishermen were attracted to the bay and we can assume that Peter, Andrew, James and John frequented this spot. On these shores they would have moored their boats. Here they would have spent many an hour with Jesus. The trees would have provided welcome shade from the hot sun when Jesus preached to the people. On these shores the multitudes might have gathered when Jesus asked for the boat to be rowed away from the beach, that He might preach to them. And it was here that Simon Peter spoke the words, "Depart from me, for I am a sinful man!" Since this was a place familiar to Jesus and His disciples, the latter may have sought it out again after His death. Therefore, it was most likely here that the risen Lord appeared to them and said, "Children, have you any fish?" And perhaps it was here that He asked Simon Peter, "Do you love Me?" These shores must have been the scene of the feast of love that He prepared for His disciples. Thus we are treading on truly Biblical ground when we visit Simon Peter's Landing Place.

The Franciscan chapel here has an ancient tradition. As early as 385 the pilgrim nun Etheria describes rock-hewn steps leading down to the water as they do now. On these steps the risen Lord is said to have stood (John 21 : 4). Etheria does not mention a church, but in Byzantine times there is mention of a church at this site. During the Crusader era it was destroyed and rebuilt twice. Its final destruction took place in 1236. Not until 1933 was the present church built by the Franciscans, who care for the site.

FROM THE HOLY BIBLE

While the people pressed upon Jesus to hear the word of God, he was standing by the lake of Gennesaret. And he saw two boats by the lake; but the fishermen had gone out of them and were washing their nets. Getting into one of the boats, which was Simon's, he asked him to put out a little from the land. And he sat down and taught the people from the boat.

And when he had ceased speaking, he said to Simon, "Put out into the deep and let down your nets for a catch." And Simon answered, "Master, we toiled all night and took nothing! But at your word I will let down the nets." And when they had done this, they caught so many fish that their nets began to break.

When Simon Peter saw it, he fell down at Jesus' knees, saying, "Depart from me, for I am a sinful man."

cf. Luke 5 : 1-8

After this Jesus revealed himself again to the disciples by the Sea of Tiberias. Just as day was breaking, Jesus stood on the beach and said to them, "Children, have you any fish?

Cast the net on the right side of the boat, and you will find some." So they cast it, and they were not able to haul it in, for the quantity of fish.

That disciple whom Jesus loved said, "It is the Lord!" When Simon Peter heard that, he sprang into the sea.

When they got out on land, they saw a charcoal fire there, with fish lying on it, and bread.

When they had finished breakfast, Jesus said to Simon Peter, "Simon, son of John, do you love me more than these?" He said to him, "Yes, Lord; you know that I love you." He said to him, "Tend my sheep."   cf. John 21 : 1-17

SIMON PETER'S LANDING PLACE –
A MESSAGE FOR US

Simon Peter's Landing Place! Who would not feel drawn to this especially delightful spot, which speaks so much of Jesus? Unlike most commemorative sites it is not built up, and with its rocky shores it is probably much the same as it was when Jesus walked here. The same landscape greets our eyes; the lapping of the waves sounds as it did of old.

Here, perhaps more than anywhere else, we can envisage the earthly life of Jesus, His preaching and His deeds. Watching the fishermen at work by the shore, we can almost see Peter, James and John before us. These fishermen are rough folk as they must have been in those days. And among them lived Jesus, not merely a rabbi or teacher, but the Messiah and Son of God. He was not ashamed to take these rough, uneducated men into His closest fellowship. Indeed, He came to men who were so proud and arrogant like Simon Peter and yet so wretched that they would later deny their Master. These were the sort of men He appointed as His apostles, who were to fill the world one day with His name. Jesus was so humble that He kept company with these fishermen. His great love drew Him to the poor and lowly, to those who were of no account in the world. He made Himself at home with them. He preached the Good News first and foremost to them, and it was to them He opened His heart. The waves still whisper and sing of this humble, loving Jesus as they lap against the stone steps.

But suddenly they grow louder as they break against the rocks and begin to tell of the mighty deeds of this humble Jesus of Nazareth. At His command the fish gathered in such numbers that the nets almost broke. And to this day the lake does not seem to have lost its sense of awe at the mighty events it was privileged to experience. On these shores once stood Someone whom not only living creatures, but the lake and its raging waves obeyed. And not only mute creation but a proud and arrogant man like Simon Peter was subject to Jesus. Peter, overwhelmed by the power of Jesus' holiness, cast himself down at His feet and exclaimed, "Depart from me, for I am a sinful man."

Simon Peter's Landing Place proclaims the glory and greatness of Jesus. It tells us that whoever believes and obeys the words of Jesus, as Peter did here, will see the manifestation of His glory. At what seemed to be a senseless command of Jesus, Peter rowed out into the middle of the lake in broad daylight to let down his nets at the very place where fish did not aggregate. The order went completely against the common sense of a fisherman. But in obedience Simon Peter replied, "At Your word, I will let down the nets." Peter had high expectations of what Jesus would do, because he believed that Jesus could make the impossible possible and that miracles would occur at His word.

Here, at Simon Peter's Landing Place, will the disciple Peter find people today who will follow his example, daring to act upon Jesus' words in obedience, even when they appear to be incomprehensible? They, like Peter, will then recognize who Jesus truly is – the almighty Lord. All creation, all the powers in heaven and on earth, the wind and the waves are subject to Him. Will Peter find followers at this site, who, overwhelmed by the glory and majesty of Jesus as he was, will cast themselves down at Jesus' feet in spirit, saying, "Depart from me, for I am a sinful man"?

Jesus was able to entrust a great commission in His kingdom to the man who made this humble confession. Will He find such people today? Surely, here at Simon Peter's Landing Place Jesus, the risen Lord, is seeking an encounter with many to ask them, as He did Peter, that all-important question, "Do you love Me?" Who will give Him the response of love here?

Jesus is not only the Lord of yesterday; He is the Lord

of today. As the living Lord He waits at this spot for people to come to Him with unlimited faith, ready to act in blind obedience in the face of meaninglessness, with the humble confession that they are sinners and with the response of their love. The Apostle Peter has set an example for us. Let us heed the words of Scripture, "Remember your leaders ... consider the outcome of their life, and imitate their faith" (Hebrews 13 : 7).

PRAYER AT
SIMON PETER'S LANDING PLACE

O Lord Jesus,

King of kings and Lord of lords, who descended from heaven, we thank You for choosing wretched fishermen to be Your disciples. We thank You for the humble love with which You prepared them before sending them out. You taught them to trust Your word and to act upon seemingly meaningless commands in obedience as Peter did when he let down his nets in the middle of the lake in broad daylight and then experienced Your power and glory.

Dear Lord Jesus, I also long to taste Your power and glory in my life. Therefore, at this site I dedicate myself to You with the words once uttered here by Your disciple Peter. At Your word I will do as You bid, even if it actually seems too difficult or impossible to carry out. I trust You and thank You in advance for responding to such faith today too with the revelation of Your power and glory and with Your aid and miracles.

But I pray that You will also hear my second request, for I know that You rejoice when much is asked of You. In beholding Your glory and majesty, let me, like Peter, recognize what I am like in Your sight – an abyss of sin. Grant me a deep repentance, that I may love You with a great and fervent love. As a gift of Your grace grant me here at Simon Peter's Landing Place my share of faith, obedience, repentance and love just as You bestowed them upon Peter.

Amen.

The Waves Whisper

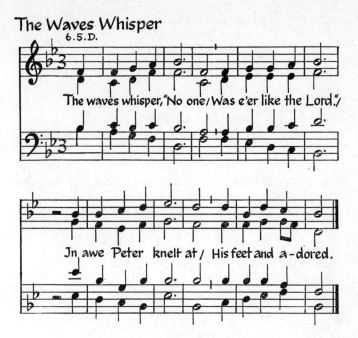

6.5.D.

The waves whisper, "No one / Was e'er like the Lord."/

In awe Peter knelt at / His feet and a-dored.

The very banks praised Him
When He trod their shore;
The waters upheld Him,
His holy feet bore.

The fishes came swimming
In shoal upon shoal
At their Master's bidding;
The nets soon were full.

Here thousands came flocking
To see Christ the Lord,
Stayed days by the lakeside
To hear His true word.

To me you are holy,
O Galilee Sea.
Here Jesus' great glory
In spirit I see.

O Jesus, my Saviour,
I worship Your name.
The marvels You did here
I'll always proclaim.

Today You draw near me
And wonders I'll see
If I trust Your word and
Obey faithfully.

✝

The deeds and miracles of Jesus are not actions of the past.
Jesus is waiting for those who are still prepared to take risks
at His word, because they trust His power utterly.

✝

Here at the Lord's word let us say like Peter:

Gladly for You, dear Lord,
I'll follow where You will.
Whate'er You ask I'll do
And never rest until
Your work is all completed.

Gladly for You, dear Lord!
What would I rather do
Than at Your word obey,
Giving my life to You?
Your love has overwhelmed me.

Gladly for You, dear Lord,
And for Your honour's sake,
All that You ask I'll do;
Your greater glory make
The aim of all my living.

Gladly for You, dear Lord –
Whate'er the cost may be –
My heart and will I give,
For You are all to me.
I give You all I treasure.

CAPERNAUM

THE HISTORICAL ASPECT

Capernaum (Hebrew *Kfar Nahum*) was one of the chief scenes of
Jesus' ministry. It was "his city". According to the Gospels, it lay
"by the sea, in the territory of Zebulun and Naphtali" (Matthew
4 : 13). The prophecy of Jesus about the destruction of the city
(Matthew 11 : 23) was fulfilled. For a long time its location could
not even be ascertained. But modern excavations and research into
ancient sources have proved almost beyond doubt that the expanse
of ruins by the seashore just over 2 km. to the northeast of Seven
Springs are those of Capernaum. The Arabs have named these
ruins Tell Hum.

Jewish sources state that the city Capernaum was still in existence in the second century at this site. And the Early Christian
witnesses all agree that the city stood here. At the beginning of
the fourth century the historian Eusebius writes, "Capernaum, on
the shore of the Lake of Genesar, is still today a village in Galilee,
in the district of Zebulun and Naphtali." The report of the
pilgrim nun Etheria in 385 is particularly informative. She describes her visit to the synagogue "in which the Lord healed the
demoniac; we reach it by climbing up many steps." When the
synagogue at Kfar Nahum was excavated, steps leading to the
terrace in front of the synagogue were brought to light, a feature
not known in other synagogues. Thus it is confirmed that Etheria
found Capernaum on the site of the present Kfar Nahum — and
that at a time when Jewish and Christian tradition was still fresh.

Excavations after 1920, however, showed that this synagogue
was not built until the second or third century after Christ,
though it was probably erected on the ruins of its predecessor,
built in Jesus' day by the believing Roman centurion for the Jews
(Luke 7 : 5). Later pilgrim accounts do not mention the synagogue,
and the date of its destruction is unknown.

In the time of Etheria a Christian sanctuary was already in
existence at Capernaum on the site of Simon Peter's house. She
writes, "The house of the Prince of the Apostles has become a
church; the walls of the house are still preserved. There our Lord
healed the paralytic." The indications given in the Gospels seem
to support the early tradition that during His ministry Jesus lived
at Simon Peter's house where Peter's mother-in-law and his
brother Andrew also lived (Mark 1 : 29). Therefore, this house,
the scene of so many miracles, became a church dedicated to the
Apostle Peter. Recent excavations have completely exposed the
site of St. Peter's House. Portions of an octagonal floor mosaic

belonging to a fifth-century church built over the venerated house are found immediately before the ruins of the synagogue.

Later pilgrim reports also proving that the present-day Kfar Nahum is the old Capernaum indicate that the place became more and more desolate. Even the Crusaders, who built churches at almost all the holy places, did not do so at Capernaum. In the thirteenth century it was reported that there were only seven poor fishermen's cottages standing and the whole district was of ill-repute. In the fifteenth century the place was in complete ruins and uninhabited "because of the wicked people in this area."

Even today Capernaum is not a town. All we find here are ruins in the midst of palms and eucalyptus trees by the lakeside behind the Franciscan monastery. The most remarkable traces of the ancient city are the broken columns, the basalt flour mills and oil-presses as well as the huge stone blocks of the synagogue. Since 1894 the ruins have been in the possession of the Franciscans, who in 1925 partly reconstructed the site with the excavated stones. Beyond the Franciscan compound lies a Greek Orthodox monastery.

FROM THE HOLY BIBLE

Now when Jesus heard that John had been arrested, he withdrew into Galilee; and leaving Nazareth he went and dwelt in Capernaum by the sea.   cf. Matthew 4 : 12 f.

And Jesus went into Capernaum; and immediately on the sabbath he entered the synagogue and taught. And they were astonished at his teaching, for he taught them as one who had authority, and not as the scribes.

And immediately he left the synagogue, and entered the house of Simon. Now Simon's mother-in-law lay sick with a fever. And he came and took her by the hand and lifted her up, and the fever left her.

That evening, at sundown, they brought to him all who were sick or possessed with demons. And the whole city was gathered together about the door. And he healed many who were sick with various diseases, and cast out many demons.
cf. Mark 1 : 21 f., 29-34

After Jesus had ended all his sayings in the hearing of the people he entered Capernaum. Now a centurion had a slave who was dear to him, who was sick and at the point of death. When he heard of Jesus, he sent to him elders of the Jews, asking him to come and heal his slave. And when they came to Jesus, they besought him earnestly, saying, "He is worthy to have you do this for him, for he loves our nation, and he built us our synagogue."

And Jesus went with them. When he was not far from the house, the centurion sent friends to him, saying to him, "Lord, do not trouble yourself, for I am not worthy to have you come under my roof; therefore I did not presume to come to you. But say the word, and let my servant be healed."

When Jesus heard this he marveled at him, and turned and said to the multitude that followed him, "I tell you, not even in Israel have I found such faith."
cf. Luke 7 : 1-10

And getting into a boat Jesus crossed over and came to his own city [Capernaum]. And behold, they brought to him a paralytic. When Jesus saw their faith he said to the paralytic, "Take heart, my son; your sins are forgiven." And behold, some of the scribes said to themselves, "This man is blaspheming."

But Jesus, knowing their thoughts, said, "That you may know that the Son of man has authority on earth to forgive sins" – he then said to the paralytic – "Rise, take up your bed and go home." And he rose and went home.
cf. Matthew 9 : 1-8

And thou, Capernaum, which art exalted unto heaven, shalt be brought down to hell: for if the mighty works, which have been done in thee, had been done in Sodom, it would have remained until this day. But I say unto you, That it shall be more tolerable for the land of Sodom in the day of judgment than for thee.
Matthew 11 : 23 f. A.V.

CAPERNAUM – A MESSAGE FOR US

Capernaum, the city that Jesus said was exalted unto heaven! It was "His city", the place the Son of God chose to reside when He began His public ministry on earth. Why did His choice fall upon this place? Here He could reach large numbers of people. Capernaum was the border town between Galilee and the land beyond the River Jordan, with a customs office where Matthew was probably sitting when he received his calling. In addition, it was an important and rich trading centre on the caravan route from Damascus to the Mediterranean, and its location by the lakeside drew fishermen to the town. Thus it was densely populated and people of all classes settled here.

That is why Jesus liked to be in Capernaum. Here He could gather hundreds and thousands to hear His message, which He preached with authority and not like the scribes (Matthew 7 : 29). Here He healed large numbers of the sick and the people pressed so close to Him that sometimes He could not even leave the house. On some occasions He did not even have time to eat (Mark 3 : 20), since all day long and even at night He was surrounded by crowds of people seeking His help (Mark 1 : 32 f.). Here He opened the eyes of the blind and delivered the possessed by driving out evil spirits. It was here that the dramatic healing of the paralytic took place and the centurion's servant was healed as a result of his master's faith. It was here that Peter's mother-in-law was cured of her fever. Capernaum witnessed all these healings and even saw Jairus' little daughter raised from the dead (Mark 5 : 22-43). Who has sufficient words to describe the tremendous events that occurred in this city and the mighty way in which the Lord and Saviour Jesus Christ revealed Himself here to His people?

Capernaum tells us of the love of God, which came down to His children. The Son of God became man and dwelt among us – here in Capernaum. This town speaks of the love of Jesus, who had compassion on those about Him, healing the sick, delivering the demon-possessed and preaching salvation to thousands. Capernaum shows us that Jesus is the Good Shepherd, who cares for His sheep, leading them into the very best pastures.

But Capernaum also heard other words from the Lord, which have come true. "And thou, Capernaum, which art exalted unto heaven, shalt be brought down to hell: for if the mighty works, which have been done in thee, had been done in Sodom, it would have remained until this day" (Matthew 11 : 23 A.V.). Capernaum has been set as an example that just as judgment will be turned into grace if men repent and turn from their sin, grace will be turned into judgment if men do not respond to God's words and actions. Capernaum bears testimony to this truth today – ruins are the only remains of the flourishing city that saw so many wondrous deeds of God. The Capernaum of Jesus' day with the many who were healed or delivered from demons was a powerful testimony. She proclaimed the greatness of Jesus, who performed such mighty deeds in her streets. Equally so the ruins of Capernaum today are a mute but eloquent testimony to who Jesus Christ is – the Lord God, whose name is Yea and Amen, and who fulfils His promises, whether they be promises of blessing or of curse.

To whom much is given, much is required. These words of Jesus are true. The more we are exalted – and Capernaum was "exalted unto heaven" because of the miracles of God she experienced – the more we must humble ourselves and fall down at Jesus' feet as Simon Peter did when he witnessed the miraculous drought of fish. His sole reaction was to humble himself and say, "Depart from me, for I am a sinful man." But although Capernaum witnessed the mighty actions of God, she did not humble herself. She accepted Jesus' help but only boasted about the wonders He performed in her streets. She remained arrogant, self-confident and proud. She did not repent of her sins with a broken and contrite heart. Thus the word of God came true. He who exalts himself will be brought low. He who is exalted unto heaven and does not respond to such grace and goodness of God with thanksgiving and dedication, which entails turning from our old way of life, will be cast into the depths of hell. To this day we can see the visible fulfilment of these words of Jesus here. Capernaum, which according to ancient Jewish reports became utterly demoralized, has almost vanished from the face of the earth – whether as the result of an earthquake or a war is not known.

Today Capernaum preaches through its ruins. Privilege entails responsibility! Revelations and unmerited favours of God place us under an obligation. The miracles of God, His aid and the goodness that we have experienced should make us fall down and humble ourselves in the dust before God. Indeed, His goodness towards us must constrain us to lead a life of thanksgiving and to turn from all that grieves Him. Capernaum seeks to impress upon our hearts the words of the Magnificat, "He has put down the mighty from their thrones, and exalted those of low degree."

On the other hand, the fact that the columns of the synagogue have remained testifies how precious a humble faith – like that of the centurion – is to Jesus, how highly He values such a faith and what joy it brings to Him. Indeed, Capernaum demonstrates to us today the reality of both the blessing and curse of God. She entreats all of us who seek out her ruins to take the words of Jesus as absolutely binding and obey them, so that the blessing of God may be poured out on our lives. And this we shall experience if we act upon His word and respond to the loving-kindness of God in our lives with humility, thanksgiving and implicit trust.

✝

O city of Capernaum,
Upon you fell God's blessèd choice;
God dwelt within your streets.
Yet you would not believe in Him.
You saw the miracles Christ did,
But did not heed His teaching.
And so the Lord waits here today
For us to honour Him with faith,
To act according to His word.

PRAYER IN CAPERNAUM

Our Lord Jesus Christ,
We thank You for the mighty deeds and miracles You performed here and for proving Yourself indeed as the almighty Lord. But we humbly confess that we are no different from the people of Capernaum. Although You have often displayed Your power in our lives too, we usually neglect to thank You. We remain unbroken, arrogant and proud. And consequently, You have no choice but to turn grace into judgment, to humble and break us till we lie in the dust as Capernaum now does.

Dear Lord Jesus, I want to thank You today for each time You demonstrated Your power in my life and showed me Your goodness. Keep me from becoming self-confident, self-satisfied and proud. Help me to humble myself when You are gracious to me; help me to give You the glory. Grant me a humble spirit. May Your goodness always bring me to repentance and constrain me to put Your word into practice in my life. Grant that I may no longer grieve You, but bring joy to You by leading a life of discipleship and faith, which You can bless and use to glorify Your name.

Amen.

O Make Me Thine
II. 11. 4.

O make me Thine, my Saviour, Lord most ho-ly, / That J may on—ly live to give Thee glo—ry. / O make me Thine.

O make me Thine; Thou art my life and treasure.
In Thee alone my heart finds joy and pleasure.
O make me Thine!

O make me Thine, for Thou to me hast given
Thyself, and so my heart leaps up to heaven,
Loves Thee alone.

O make me Thine, who for my sake didst suffer.
Let me in gratitude Thee solace offer
By hating sin.

O make me Thine; take all I love and treasure,
My life, my honour, if that brings Thee pleasure
And shows my love.
Yes, make them Thine!*

* Repeat last line of music.   Well-spring of Joy 227

✛

Capernaum challenges us to be bold in faith, for the power
of God and His readiness to perform miracles far exceed the
boldest expectations of our faith.

BIBLIOGRAPHY

The following works have been consulted for historical details:

Kopp, Dr. Clemens. *Die heiligen Stätten der Evangelien*. Regensburg, Verlag Friedrich Pustet, 1959.
Stenner/Wilmes. *Pilgerführer durchs Heilige Land*. Jerusalem, Franciscan Printing Press, 1961.
Wilkens, Karl Erich. *Biblisches Erleben im Heiligen Land*. Lahr-Dinglingen, Verlag St. Johannisdruckerei, 1956.

Other works consulted are:

Kaiser, Franz. *Hier ist Heiliges Land*. Stuttgart, Schwabenverlag.
Meistermann, P. S. *Durchs Heilige Land*. Trier, Mosella-Verlag.
Weiser, Franz. *In der Heimat des Herrn*. Regensburg, Verlag Joseph Habbel.

We wish to express our gratitude here for all the assistance received.

The sources for determining the authenticity of the holy places are chiefly the accounts of early Christian writers and pilgrims. Since a number of names appear frequently, a list of them is appended.

Origen made Palestine his permanent residence in 232 and founded a famous school of theology in Caesarea.
Eusebius (265—340), "The Father of Church History", born in Palestine and the most reliable authority for the country during the reign of Constantine.
The Pilgrim of Bordeaux (333) gave a short report about the holy places. As the earliest pilgrim account, it is of high value.
Epiphanius, born in 315 in Judea, founded a monastery there, and in 367 became the Bishop of Salamis in Cyprus.
Etheria, a nun from northern Spain or southern France, made a pilgrimage to the Christian sites of the Orient from 385 to 388 and wrote a very clear report.

Jerome lived from 385 to his death in 420 by the Church of the Nativity in Bethlehem. He led and described the pilgrimages made by St. Paula.

Theodosius (530) left a short and faithful account of places of pilgrimage in the Orient.

The pilgrim Anonymous of Piacenza (570) described the sanctuaries at the zenith of their development in Byzantine times.

Arkulf, a bishop of Gaul, travelled through the Orient in 670 and gave valuable reports.

Willibald, an Anglo-Saxon, undertook an extensive pilgrimage in 724—726. A relative, who was a nun in Heidenheim, wrote down his narratives.

Epiphanius (ca. 750/800), a Greek monk and priest in Jerusalem, compiled a description of Palestine from ancient sources.

Saewulf (1102), an English monk, was the first to describe the Holy Land after the conquest of the Crusaders.

Daniel, a Russian abbot, travelled through the Holy Land in 1106—1107.

Theoderich (1172), a German pilgrim, reported during the time of the Crusaders.

LIST OF HYMNS

LIST OF SKETCH-MAPS

Books by M. Basilea Schlink, supplementing some of the topics in
THE HOLY LAND TODAY

BEHOLD HIS LOVE 144 pp.
Nothing can bring us closer to Jesus than meditating upon His
Passion, for in doing so we search the depths of His heart. This
book will help us to find a warm, vital relationship with our Saviour
when we behold His amazing love which compelled Him to choose
suffering and death for our sakes.

MY ALL FOR HIM 160 pp.
"Here is described first-hand, vital, all-demanding discipleship, but
not as an ideal possible only to the few — for it depends not upon
our abilities but upon our Lord's love burning in our hearts."
(translated into 14 languages)

REPENTANCE — THE JOY-FILLED LIFE 64 pp.
"When the reality of this book is truly grasped, it marks the end of
spiritual stagnation and the beginning of a most blessed life with
Christ."
(translated into 22 languages)

PATMOS — WHEN THE HEAVENS OPENED
128 pp.
Vividly and arrestingly Basilea Schlink takes us into the events of the
mighty revelation once given on the island of Patmos. Today they
are beginning to be fulfilled before our very eyes. This timely book
helps us to see the age we are living in and will be a source of encouragement to us in these dark days. It gives our generation a completely new perspective to the future and creates in us a tremendous hope.
(translated into 24 languages)

MORE PRECIOUS THAN GOLD 224 pp.
Daily Readings
God, who is Love eternal, has opened His heart and revealed to us
something very precious and beautiful, imbued with everlasting life,
glory and splendour — His commandments of love. This book of daily
readings is designed to help us to re-discover the blessings contained in God's commandments — not only in the Ten Commandments but also in the many commandments that can be found throughout the Old and New Testaments — and to see their significance for
our times.
(translated into 5 languages)

A FORETASTE OF HEAVEN (Autobiography) 418 pp.
(Illustrated)
(American edition: I FOUND THE KEY TO THE HEART OF
GOD)
A reader says,
"In Mother Basilea's personal story we are given an insight into the
ways of the heavenly Father as He prepares His child for a ministry
that is to be unique in the annals of the Christian Church. We turn
the pages as we would the score of some great symphony and whether
the music is light or whether it is the deep chords that are struck, our
hearts cannot fail to respond. The response will be an inner searching
of our own hearts and lives followed by love and adoration for our
Lord Jesus. The reader seeking a greater fulfilment in his Christian life
and service will discover in these pages the key to the very heart of
God. In a day when the dark clouds of God's judgment are beginning
to gather and the forces of evil are threatening the human race as
never before — this book comes as a clarion call and a tremendous
source of encouragement to the Christian."
(translated into 16 languages)

FATHER OF COMFORT (Daily readings) 128 pp.
God so often seems to be far away and in times of sadness and
misery it is difficult to realize that He wants to reveal His fatherly
love to us . . . These readings help us to develop that close contact,
a personal relationship of love and childlike trust in the Father, which
we need in order to nurture our faith in Him.
(translated into 15 languages)

YOU WILL NEVER BE THE SAME 192 pp.
Prescriptions of "spiritual medicine" for 45 different sins. This intri-
guing book not only brings to light the sins which mar the Christian's
life, but it also helps us to recognize them in our own personal lives
and points out the remedy.
(translated into 16 languages)

Songbooks:

O NONE CAN BE LOVED LIKE JESUS
37 Songs of Love for Jesus

I WANT TO CONSOLE YOU
36 Songs of Love and Comfort for Our Lord
in His Suffering Today

THE KING DRAWS NEAR
37 Songs about Jesus' Second Coming and the Heavenly Glory

MY FATHER, I TRUST YOU
38 Songs of Trust and Dedication

SONGS AND PRAYERS OF VICTORY 62 pp.